North American Indian
ORNAMENTAL &
CEREMONIAL ARTIFACTS

ISBN 0-89689-081-3

Front Cover:
COPENA CELTS – *These two ceremonial celts were found together as a cache. Possibly made from the same stone. Considered by many collectors to be the best ever found. Winners of 42 first place awards at past relic shows. They measure 20½'' and 15½'', are highly polished.*
Hardin County, Tennessee
Museum quality
T. Hendrix

Back Cover (clockwise from top right)
TUBULAR PIPE – *Used in healing and ceremonial affairs. Length 10½''. Made from Lauderdale County pink limestone. Largest found in Tennessee Valley.*
Lauderdale County, Alabama
Museum quality
T. Hendrix

CEREMONIAL SPATULA – *Made of white limestone. This type is found primarily in ceremonial complexes. 8'' long and 6'' wide.*
Lauderdale County, Alabama
Museum quality
T. Hendrix

QUARTZITE BANNERSTONE – *Roseate quartzite, highly polished. Length 4''.*
Hardin County, Tennessee
Museum quality
T. Hendrix

ACKNOWLEDGEMENTS

The below persons are gratefully thanked for the many fine photographs that appear thoughout this book. Without their kind assistance the book in present form would not have been possible.

Zell Adams	CA	Larry Carter	IN
Charles Allen	AL	Darrell Thompson	TX
Dennis Bushey	AL	Willie Fields	TX
Gerald Bernacchi	IN	Michael Darland	KY
Lee Fisher	PA	Gary Fogelman	PA
Cliff Markley	AL	Doug Pilcher	TX
William F. Garis, Sr.	PA	John Baldwin	MI
Steven R. Dowell	KY	Larry G. Merriam	OK
James M. Dethrow	AR	Larry Shaver	OK
Robert C. Calvert	CAN	Howard Bell	OH
Bud Burke	VA	Jon & Bonnie Mau	WI
Lee Hallman	PA	Sam & Nancy Johnson	AR
Private collection	AR	The Guy Brothers	IL
Harold Brubenhoff	WA	James E. Maus	NC
Chris Callaway	LA	Marguerite & Stewart Kernaghan	CO
Wilfred Dick	MS	Dr. Gary Meek	AR
Lawson Corley	AL	David Austin	OK
Mike George	MO	Private collection	OH
Blake Gahagan	TN	Len & Janie Weidner	OH
Larry Gahagan	TN		

TABLE OF CONTENTS

INTRODUCTION

A dictionary precisely defines ornaments. They decorate or adorn. They are an embellishment, a special added touch. Decorate, in turn, means to furnish with fashionable or beautiful things.

The desire or need to ornament or decorate may be innate in humankind. Even our lives today are so full of ornaments – jewelry, expensive cars, decorations in the home, medals, wall plaques, trophies, desk sets – that a list would be nearly endless. So, too, were ornaments a very important, even crucial, aspect in the lives of those who inhabited North America countless centuries before most of us ever arrived on these shores. This was long before contact with outsiders, long before others were aware of the gigantic landmass between the Atlantic and Pacific oceans.

Here, ornamental objects made by humans, artifacts, developed in a general American Indian cultural atmosphere. But each region and even time period developed variations and unique creations, and the range of ornamental objects is truly astounding. Even then, most of the Indian artifacts that are around today survived because they were made of highly durable materials such as flint or stone. One wonders what wonderful other objects the centuries slowly nibbled into dust that was blown away by the winds.

The outstanding thing about much Amerind ornamental art is that it is precious without being made of precious materials. The Arctic had ivory and jade, Central America had jade and gold, South America had gold and silver. Except for some pearls and turquoise, North American artifacts were largely made from non-precious materials and so are valued mainly for design and workstyle and finish.

This is a genuine compliment to the ancient makers. Very few people today could pick up a stone or a piece of wood and make something, anything, that would be highly treasured and admired thousands of years from now.

American Indians did just that, millions of times, with their ornamental objects. And this was not just as an occasional test of skill or random inspiration, but as a whole and routine way of life. What a wonderful legacy was left for those who came after.

Chapter 1
INDIAN ORNAMENTS

No one knows what the first Amerind ornaments really were in North America. Even the times when humans first peopled this continent are open to dispute, though ages beyond 50,000 years ago are now no longer unthinkable. Such pre-Paleolithic lifeways almost certainly had ornamental artifacts made of animal teeth or claws or shell, but time has taken such organic materials away.

It is known that several types of ornaments were used in the 15,000-8000 BC Paleo period. Again, very likely beads of organic materials may have been used as necklaces or bracelets, but little sign of them remains. It is, however, a certainty that various types of pendants were made late in Paleo times.

At the Lindenmeier Site of the Folsom people, several dozen miles north of Fort Collins, Colorado, a hematite (iron ore) bead was found that had a carved design. Also found was a smaller broken bead made of lignite, a low-grade brownish-black coal. Lindenmeier also produced small bone discs with incised tally-marked edges, which may have been ornaments or even gaming tokens or markers.

A number of true ornaments were found at the Paelo period Reagan Site in Vermont. These consisted of ornaments made of talc, a fine-grained green, grey or white mineral. Of various shapes and sizes, most were drilled with a suspension hole at the smaller end. Some of the holes had cord-wear marks. Several of the pendants had abraded grooves as if to add to the decorative effect.

Zone I of Modoc Rock Shelter, Illinois, dated probably in excess of 8000 BC, contained a perforated stone pebble which may have been a pendant.

Other Paleolithic ornamental artifacts have been found at other North American sites, but they are few indeed. There are several possibilities why this is so. As mentioned, some objects may have been made of material that cannot withstand weathering and bacteria, and simply ceased to exist.

Very possibly, Paleo peoples were concerned primarily with survival and secondarily with ornamentation. The few extant examples suggest that when durable material was used, it tended to be rather unusual for the area. And with a few exceptions, the work was not extremely well executed. Most of the artistic work of these early times seems to have gone into the design and making of highly serviceable tools and weapons, artworks in themselves.

The Archaic period (8000 - 1000 BC) was quite different in some ways, and considerably more complex than the Paleo. The lifeway changed from basically hunting large herd animals to hunting other game and gathering of various wild foods. There are traces of ceremonialism, villages became established, and hardstone tools (grooved axes, adzes) were made.

Ornamental artifacts became common by Middle Archaic times. *Atl-atl* weights or balance and decorative stones in dozens of forms were made, and a number of pendant types developed. All across North America, new ways of working stone (pecking, grinding and polishing) allowed the creation of new objects. The makers were no longer restricted mainly to chipping cryptocrystalline materials.

The Archaic period, 7000 years of adaptation and development, saw the rise of innovative artifacts such as charmstones, plummets, lizard effigies (both in flint and glacial slate), birdstones, bannerstones, and more. Shell and antler and bone were worked into beads, effigies and whistles. Many of the finest objects seem to have been used in daily life, and some of the artifacts eventually became burial offerings or grave goods.

The Woodland period (1000 BC - AD 1000) was at least as different a lifeway from Archaic times as Archaic was from Paleo times. Pottery (probably of minor importance) and agriculture (of major importance) were developed and large year-round villages came into being. In many parts of the country mounds were raised and ceremonies and rituals reached a high level of practice. Whole new classes of pendants were made, and the gorget-type weight or ornament was widely used. Ornaments of copper and mica were made by the Hopewell and Adena Indians, and some very ornate and rare objects (some never made before or after) were turned out.

Pipe-making reached a high degree of achievement and some of the Middle Woodland effigy forms were never equalled anywhere other than in the Midwest. Some knife and point forms were made extra-large and were probably ceremonial or status in purpose, for they were never used as tools. Refined art objects were made. While the Archaic had animal-tooth necklaces and pendants, the Hopewell Indians sometimes set grizzly bear teeth with pearls.

The Mississippian period, 900 - 1650 AD, had widespread use of the bow and arrow. These people also were mound-builders and constructed large groups of earthworks, some of the huge, flat-topped "temple" type. They carved beautiful pendants from shell and carried fine celtiform axes in dances. Their pottery was excellent, and was made in dozens of fine forms. The Mississippians also built North America's most ambitious earthworks site, the four-thousand-acre Cahokia, in Illinois. This was a massive complex of mounds, villages and fields.

In general, ornamental artifacts made in prehistoric times were, with few exceptions, based on natural substances. The raw material was modified and shaped until it had achieved the final form, whether decorative or ornamental or both. Relatively simple working techniques resulted in some highly sophisticated artifacts that are extremely attractive to those who collect early Native American art.

Prehistoric times changed to historic times in North America at a hard-to-define point when Europeans met and traded with Native Americans. Such dates range widely, but begin around 1492 with Columbus' first landing. However, there is some evidence Vikings traded goods around the year 1000. Some encounter-dates took place as late as the 1800's, but one commonly accepted and average date for the beginning of historic times is AD 1650.

Then, whether by direct or indirect exchanges (via other Indian groups), more goods became available to Amerindians. And, not only did the new trade goods supplement existing ornamental objects (and were sometimes intermixed), but they often replaced them. This was due to the novelty of "imported" objects (though many came to be made in North America, especially trade silver), enhanced usefulness and attractive appearance.

Novelty explains itself, for often the new is seen as better or at least more appealing. But in fact a steel fish-hook was better than one made of deer-leg bone, and a brass or copper kettle was better than a fragile pottery vessel. So, too, in ornaments, which were made from silver, brass, copper, pewter and German silver, an alloy of copper, zinc and nickel. Glass was another material totally unknown in North America, and became instantly successful as a trade item. These offered a new prestige, and were obtained ready-made, bright and shining.

Glass came in the form of "looking glass" or medium-sized mirrors, and in small mirrors used as decorations. Beads were made in three major types. The large and the medium-sized were used for bodily adornment, while the medium and smaller sizes were used for sewing on clothing and accoutrements, often in intricate and pleasing designs. The popularity of such very small "seed" beads was so great that in the Eastern Woodlands design-making with dyed moose-hair and porcupine quills almost faded away.

The new trade goods, especially all of the metals, quickly became sought-after treasures. Even pieces of broken brass and copper kettles were reworked to become pendants, rolled-cylinder beads and cone-shaped "tinklers" for necklaces and clothing. Small scraps of metal were carefully saved for some possible future use.

The influx of trade goods nearly eradicated the traditional ways of working natural materials. Still, the ornamental objects made for trade with the Indians are considered Indian artifacts today. Even if it cannot be proven that the artifacts were actually used by Indians, they at least were made for such use.

PAINT PALETTE, polished grey stone (possibly steatite) and very heavy. It is from Blount County, Alabama, and probably Mississippian in time period. Size, 7½ inches in diameter. $1200-1800
Courtesy Marguerite L. Kernaghan collection; photographers Marguerite L. & Stewart W. Kernaghan

PEBBLE PENDANT, unknown period but possibly quite early. Material is an attractive reddish tan slate with dark brown banding. It is ⅞x1⅝ inches, and from Coshocton County, Ohio. Private collection. $20

CRYSTAL PENDANT, from an Archaic site, unusual piece made of clear rock crystal. Ground and polished, the first drill-hole wore through and a second was made on the opposite end. Size, ¾ inches in diameter. Specimen is from the Buckeye Lake region, south-central Ohio. Private collection. $25.

CHARMSTONE, artifact made of quartzite, probably for ceremonial use. It is 1x1½ inches, Anasazi, ca. AD 900-1200. From Catron County, New Mexico. $15
Courtesy Lee Fisher collection, Pennsylvania; Anthony Lang, photographer

Chapter 2
FLINT, CHERT AND OBSIDIAN

Important as were the easily chippable cryptocrystalline materials – flint, chert and obsidian – in making tools and weapons, they may not have been the first. There is some evidence, not yet overwhelming but present nonetheless, that pre-Paleo groups used bone and ivory for much of their hunting gear. If so, they probably used the same materials for any decorative objects.

For most of the solidly documented prehistoric period, some ornamental objects were indeed chipped into form. There are five classes that can be explained. It should be mentioned that in some cases, such as Shaman's, the materials are present even though the original purpose is unknown and can only be explored with inspired guesswork. All this, however, is part of the attraction and satisfaction of studying ancient artifacts, for most collectors appreciate a mystery.

Ceremonial

This is one of the more over-used words in regard to prehistoric objects. It usually means an artifact that is extremely well made, shows no evidence of actual use, and may be made in an atypical form or of a scarce material. Sometimes the word is also applied to extremely large specimens that seem designed more for show than use. It might be said that such objects served as tribal or community ornaments.

Chipped examples would include many of the large Hopewell (Middle Woodland) blades from mounds in the Eastern Midwest. These are rare in the extreme, for a large number were ceremonially ''killed'' by fire or purposeful breakage. Another good example would be the Mississippian-era maces or scepters from various mound complexes in the Southeast.

Ornamental chipped ceremonial objects are not restricted to the Eastern parts of the country. Extra-large obsidian double-pointed knives were used in dances on the West Coast, and were items both of prestige and commercial value. They were sometimes wrapped with deer-hide at the center for a non-slip handhold, and further secured with a thong as a safety line in case they were dropped.

Some of the extra-long blades from the Etowah Mounds, Bartow County, Georgia, almost defy belief. One example of a bipointed blade was 26¼ inches long. Another – from the famous Duck River, Tennessee, 46-item cache – was a bit longer. This category seems to contain many items that obviously are too large for ordinary utility use.

Drills

Drills are long and narrow, 3- or 4-sided, and with hundreds of different basal configurations. These have long been somewhat of a puzzle. While many examples, especially shorter specimens, evidence wear on the side or tip, many fine examples do not.

In fact, a fairly accurate rule-of-thumb is that the larger and better-made the piece, the less likely it is to show use-wear signs. It is thought that many examples were in fact hairpins, or were used to secure other objects to the hair. Thus, many would be ornamental artifacts.

Eccentrics

Eccentrics are to chipped objects what problematicals (a very old term) are to the fields of stone and slate artifacts. It is only known that they are highly unusual forms, and the real purpose or use remains a problem.

Chipped eccentrics have a further problem of their own. While old and authentic examples exist, there is a tendency to classify all eccentrics as fakes. This is because of the huge proliferation of fanciful forms, effigy-like or not, that once flooded the market. Most collectors of today simply stay away from the spectacular chipped thunderbirds and fish-hooks and buffalos and snakes, and this has carryover in a suspicion of anything out of the ordinary.

Other, more difficult-to-detect chipped objects may have non-standard shapes, as if the knapper idly passed time by random and haphazard chipping, perhaps a form of prehistoric whittling.

Genuine eccentric chipped artifacts do exist, and can be found in the three major types of material. Flint is usually glossy and sometimes bright in color. Chert is dull in appearance, and usually chips less well than flint. Obsidian, from the Western U.S. and Mexico, is volcanic glass in many different shades.

Genuine eccentrics are usually fairly small and often unspectacular in material and workstyle. A very common form, and actually possibly a tool rather than ornament, is the notched or stemmed blade-like form with very large sawtooth or serrated edges.

While serrated-edge blades are rather common, eccentric-class serrations have edge protrusions that are often larger and deeper than usual. And, due to this, there are fewer serrations per edge. Some of these examples have the edge wear expected for tool use, while others may have served as pendants.

Some eccentrics appear to have been purpose-made as-is. Others were made from broken and damaged points and blades, and still retain the original basal hafting area. No matter the type, eccentrics sometimes exhibit wear-polish on the faces instead of use polish on the edges. This indicates they were probably ornaments of some kind.

Effigies

These are chipped objects that seem to represent something else, and are of two classes. Realistic effigies may depict an animal, including humans, and the most common is probably a profile of the human face. These are still extremely rare, and again there are many modern examples or fake pieces. Until recently, the Eskimos chipped miniature bears and fish in chert, and these may have been hunting or fishing charms.

Four flint human head profiles were found near Waverly, Tennessee, in 1902. They depict the neck, chin, lips, nose, forehead, skull and a protusion at the back which may be a roll of hair. A small profile (with a high forehead, and about 2 inches high) in black flint from Ohio and in the Author's collection has a thin neck that expands to form a small knob. Likely, this was for a suspension thong, and the profile was hung upside-down as a pendant or necklace element.

Stylized chipped ornamental objects also exist. A good example is the so-called lizard effigy. From the Midwest, most are chipped from a light-colored chert and then very highly polished. These forms are long and narrow, and seem to have a head and tail end, with four short limb-like protrusions that extend from the body region. They are probably decorative *Atl-atl* charms, for lance-throwing sticks.

Some large and extremely rare chipped animal-like stylized forms have been found, generally in a late prehistoric context. These may represent turtles, flying squirrels or the like, and some have been associated with underground deposits of ceremonial-grade artifacts.

Shaman Pieces

This is a catch-all category, and may explain some of the chipped forms that otherwise defy explanation. Such objects are neither tools nor effigies nor eccentrics. Most are small, may be of colorful or unusual material, and many of them are highly polished. They in fact do look as if they might have been carried in a leather pouch for many years. It is known that the contents of historic ''medicine'' bundles or pouches may include many curious objects, and these may be in that category.

While some Shaman pieces may simply be lumps of natural material, others may evidence random or ordered flaking. None, however, is ever in the form of a known tool or weapon tip. Some examples appear to have been abraded and/or polished in whole or in part, and the reason is unknown. So, such objects may have been used for purposes that range from the common (family keepsakes) to esoteric (magic or ritual).

CEREMONIAL-GRADE HOPEWELL POINT OR BLADE, a 1979 find from Jackson County, Florida. Size 3/16 in. thick, 2½ x 6½ in. long. An amber translucent flint not of local origin, the piece is large, very well chipped and without use-wear. One of a cache of four taken from a river bottom. Pieces of this high grade can sell for thousands of dollars. Photo courtesy CTA Collection.   Museum quality

CEREMONIAL-GRADE HOPEWELL POINT OR BLADE, a 1979 find from Jackson County, Florida. Size is 3/16 in. thick, 3x5¾ in. long. Material is an amber translucent flint not of local origin. It is one of a cache of four taken from a 12-foot deep river. Beautifully chipped, no use-wear is evident. It has superb workstyle and condition. Examples of this quality can be worth thousands of dollars. Photo courtesy CTA Collection.   Museum quality

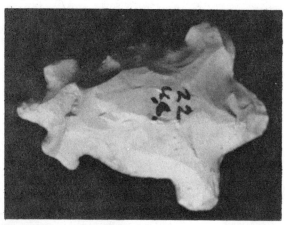

TURTLE EFFIGY, found by the collector in Upshur County, Texas, near the town of Kelsey. Several projectile points were also found on the site. Authentic effigy flints are quite rare. $100
Courtesy Doug Pilcher collection, Texas

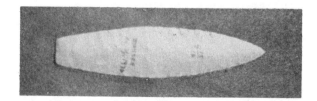

AGATE BASIN POINT, found by collector on Salt River, Mercer County, Kentucky in 1970. At 4 13/16 inches, this may be the best of type from the County. Pieces of this high quality may at times have served an ornamental purpose. $800 plus
Courtesy Michael Darland, Kentucky

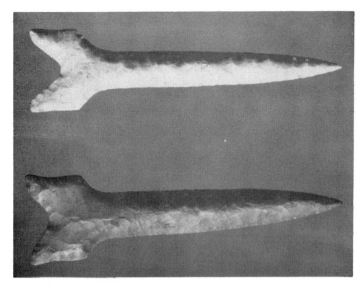

DALTON "DRILLS", actually probably hairpins or clothing toggles. These are from a lake region several states West of the Mississippi. The white example is 3½ inches long. These do not appear to be true drills, and are very finely made, with grinding on the edges. Beautiful pieces.   Each, $250-300
Courtesy Larry G. Merriam collection, Oklahoma

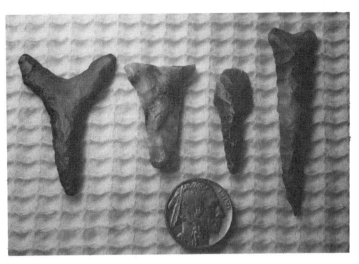

ORNAMENTAL FLINT ARTIFACTS, all from Cass County, Texas. Longest example, on right, is 2¼ inches long. Material is novaculite in many different colors. None of these objects, several salvaged from points or blades, show any actual use and may have served as pins or bodkins.   Unlisted
Courtesy Willie Fields collection, Texas

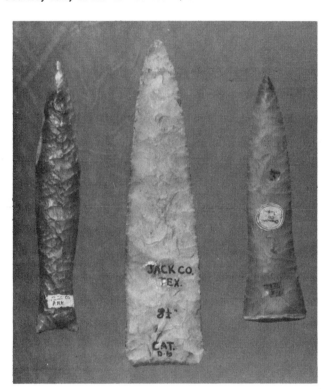

CEREMONIAL Caddoan blades, left to right:
Pike Co., Arkansas $500
Jack County, Texas, 8½ inch. $500
Brown County, Texas. $350
Often blades of this size and fine material/workmanship are decorative or ceremonial in purpose.
Courtesy private collection.

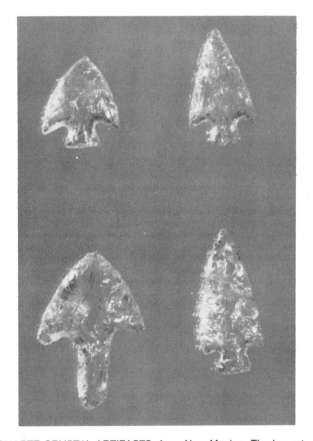

QUARTZ CRYSTAL ARTIFACTS, from New Mexico. The largest point is 1¼ inches long. Often quartz crystal was used for non-utilitarian purposes, and these do not have use-damage; these may be decorative or ceremonial. Scarce items, and quite attractive.
                    Each, $50-75
Courtesy Larry G. Merriam collection, Oklahoma

5

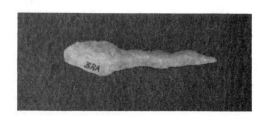

FLINT ARTIFACT, probably too large to be a drill; some objects of this type were used as hairpins. This piece is 5⅜ inches long, and is from Randolph County, Arkansas. $100
Photo courtesy James M. Dethrow collection, Arkansas

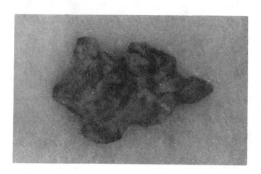

ECCENTRIC FLINTS, larger banded piece 2 inches long. Found in a south-central state, these have both been authenticated. True eccentrics are quite rare anywhere in the county. Note that these do not seem to represent anything in particular.

Smaller, $60
Larger, $100
Courtesy Larry G. Merriam collection, Oklahoma

ECCENTRIC FLINT, pinkish-red Flintridge material, from Fairfield County, Ohio. It measures 1x1½ inches and may have been suspended from the smaller, tapered end. It has no use-signs as a tool. $25
Courtesy private collection

CEREMONIAL POINTS AND BLADES, several Southwestern states. The two double-notched Agee types were found side-by-side. The other points, AD 1200, show extremely fine workmanship, in high-quality material.   Group, $1500
Courtesy Larry Shaver collection, Oklahoma; Larry Merriam, photographer

Chapter 3
ATL - ATL WEIGHTS

Certain classes of ornamental objects, found across North America, have long been termed *Atl-atl* weights. This means – after discoveries in a very few Archaic sites, especially in Kentucky – they were affixed to the launching board in pre-bow centuries to propel a light lance. Such wooden sticks, about 18 but up to 24 inches long, acted as an extension of the human arm. This provided more leverage and a longer throw, increasing distance from 30% to 50%, depending on which experiments one cares to consult.

Conventional wisdom has long been that such "weights" provided more momentum to the *Atl-atl* which transferred to the lance during the throw and allowed a longer case. However, some weights weigh only an ounce or two and would add little if anything to increased power. And, a matter that experimenters have not really considered, if one operates a lance-thrower with maximum power with each cast, the matter of inertia comes in. A weighted *Atl-atl* will move slightly less fast than an unweighted one, cancelling out any advantage the weight might have provided in the first place. And if additional momentum in fact is wanted for some reason, this could more easily have been achieved simply by cutting away less wood and having a heavier *Atl-atl*. If this were done, one had an *Atl-atl* that was less difficult to make, was stronger, and it would not have been necessary to make and attach a weight.

Prehistoric hunters knew very well that their survival depended on tools that were workable, like the *Atl-atl*. We should credit the early hunters and warriors with full knowledge of what they were doing with most phases of their lives. This means doing away with the established weight theory, or at least we should strongly question the assumption.

Weights probably had only one practical function. And this was to counter-balance a lance in position, ready to be thrown. Even this result could have been more easily achieved simply by leaving a knob or heavy wooden mass or thicker portion on the throwing board itself. So weights must have served another function as well. This purpose was certainly ornamental, for even some of the oldest weights from the Early Archaic period (8000 - 6000 BC), while rather plain, are surprisingly well made, even roughly beautiful.

Additional purposes for having weights on the *Atl-atl* may have gone beyond ornamental and engaged elements of ownership, family or tribal affiliation, or even magic. These things we really don't know and perhaps may never know. What is known is that very old sites have produced worked stone objects that are almost certainly *Atl-atl* associated.

Early *Atl-atl* stones – it is safe to refer to them in this way, stating association but not reason-for-being – are generally long and narrow, up to 5 or so inches in length, up to 2 inches wide depending on the specimen. Long *Atl-atl* stones may be narrow and thin, shorter stones may be wider and thicker. All were attached on the under-side of the lance-thrower, on the face away from the lance when in position and ready to be thrown. It was there, but totally out of the way.

Very little data is available as to whether Paleo Indians in the pre-8000 BC period used *Atl-atl* stones, or even the lance-thrower itself. Opinions vary and little proof one way or another has been forthcoming. The weight of evidence on the existence of weights at this very early time is that the lance-thrower was probably in use, and the concept may even have come across the Bering Strait with some of the earliest migrants to the New World.

If they indeed did, there is one general *Atl-atl* stone class that would seem to "belong". These stones tend to be isolated finds, as are the famous fluted points made by Paleo Indians. Most of the stones are oblong, and one side (possibly the "bottom") may be flattened.

Most of these "pebble" weights tend to be of fairly soft material that did not require a great deal of work to shape and could easily be carved with the chipped tools at hand. And, some are decorated with deeply-cut lines or marks on the sides, as if sawn into the stone with flint blades. While some are fairly well made, most have a somewhat crude or semi-finished appearance.

In the Early Archaic, *Atl-atl* stones are both more developed and better finished. It is unknown when the first stones were attached, but the lance-thrower was certainly in use at a very early period. An *Atl-atl* spur (end-hook, used to engage the butt of the lance) was found in Oregon's Fort Rock Cave, and was dated to ca. 6500 BC. Several other ancient spurs also came from near The Dalles, at the Five-Mile Rapids Site in Oregon.

The oldest known counter-balance weights tend to be simple. If there is a method of attachment to the wooden shaft, the stone is merely grooved. Such grooves or deeply cut channels may be across the center, at each end, or a combination. At times, the *Atl-atl* stone is also decorated with smaller grooves or incised lines, often in a basic geometric pattern.

Such elementary weights are found all across North America and regional types were fully developed from the earliest simple forms. These early forms, for the most part, lack a large longtitudinal hole for thick stones and smaller (often matching pairs) sets of holes for thinner types. While some of the early lance-thrower stones may be carefully flattened for attachment on one face, and are fairly well polished, this is about the usual extent of refinement.

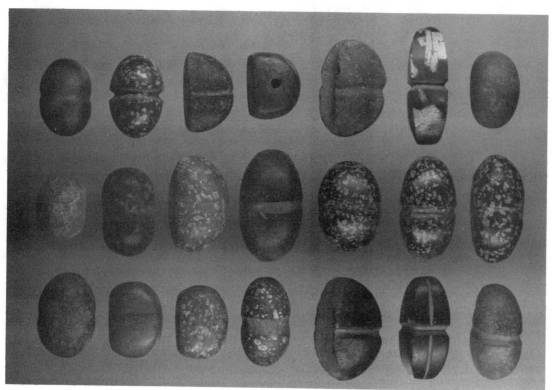

EXTENDED BAR WEIGHT, grey hardstone, size ¾ x 3½ inches. This type is found sparingly over most of the United States. This is a nicely formed and polished piece from Archaic times. It was found in 1959 and came from Franklin County, Tennessee.
$500
Courtesy Lawson Corley collection, Alabama

ATL-ATL WEIGHTS, made of porphyry and other dense, colorful hardstones. All are polished except on the flattened side where they were attached to lance-throwers. Weights, 3¼ to 6 ounces; this is a fine assemblage of Pacific Northwest Atl-atl stones.
Each $100-250
Photo courtesy Harold Grubenhoff collection, Washington

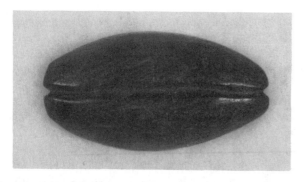

LOAFSTONE, a decorative ATL-ATL stone, 1⅛ x 2¼ inches. The longtitudinal groove bisects the top and continues through the flat reverse. Material may be black steatite and a trace of green suggests attachment by copper wire. These were made in the Archaic and Early Woodland periods. Lar Hothem collection, Ohio. $125

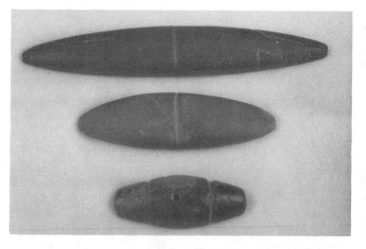

ELLIPSOIDAL BAR WEIGHTS. Top, black slate, 1 x 6 inches, from Franklin County, Ohio.
Middle, micaceous schist, Delaware County, Ohio.
Bottom, steatite, with central drill-hole, Ross County, Ohio.
These are all good examples of a hard-to-find weight type. $150-750
Courtesy Len & Janie Weidner Collection, Ohio

BAR-WEIGHT, red hematite, ½ x 1 x 2¾ inches. These are early in the Archaic period, one of the first decorative weight forms. This piece, flattened on the reverse, is from Fairfield County, Ohio. Private collection. $75

BOATSTONES, all left to right:
Cannel coal, KY, ⅝ x 3⅞ in. $125-225
Cannel coal, KY, 1½ x 3⅛ inches $150-250
Slate, Kentucky, 1 x 5 inches. $200-300
Cannel coal, Calloway County, KY, 1 x 6¼ inches, two-hole
$300-500
Courtesy Marguerite L. Kernaghan collection; photographers Marguerite L. & Stewart W. Kernaghan

8

Chapter 4
EFFIGY STONES

Prehistoric North America had a number of Indian-made effigies that ranged from life-size to larger or smaller. Probably the most common effigy size is considerably smaller than life. Related to this area are the numerous small objects made by Eskimo craftspeople from bone, steatite and ivory. Many of these objects may have been charms or fetishes or talismans, all with supposed magical or mystical or supernatural powers or properties. Whatever the original intent or purpose, they remain fascinating objects today.

Whale-shaped stones have been found in the coastal regions of both the Northeast and Northwest. California has the "pelican" stones, which seem to portray part of a body, long neck, head, and long, tapered beak. Seal and otter and bear effigies are known. Probably the largest remaining effigy in the world is Ohio's Great Serpent Mound in Adams County, certainly made in Early/Middle Woodland times, and over 1400 feet in length.

One of the widest-spread and best-known effigy forms is the so-called "lizard" effigy of the Eastern Midwest, with the main center of distribution in Indiana and Ohio. These artifacts average about 5 inches long, and the range is from just over 3 inches to more than 6 inches. Most are about 1½ inches wide. While about 10-15% were made in hardstone, most were pecked and ground from colorful glacial slate which was readily found in the glacial drift of the region.

It is not precisely known when the lizard effigies were made. From the fact that they are random surface finds, degree of workstyle and finish, it is probably safe to assign them to the Middle Archaic, ca. 5000 - 2500 BC. For various reasons – size, shape, width, flat bottoms – they may well be the predecessors of the famous birdstones of Late Archaic times.

The name "lizard" is somewhat of a problem, but they have been assigned this term for many years so it is probably here to stay. First, there are no true lizards (reptiles) in the geographic area, although the word was once used to designate salamanders (amphibians). However, only a minor number of lizard effigies ever resemble the long, thin salamanders in any way. So even if the name lizard is incorrect, it must also be said that the correct name for the objects is totally unknown.

There is a large variety of styles for this artifact form. Some are fairly roughly made, almost crude, but the majority are well-shaped and well-finished, which is the reason they are so admired by collectors today. A few are elongated bars, but with differently treated ends. One will be shorter, or wider, or thicker, or shaped differently. This gives the lizard a definite front and rear portion.

Most often, there is a "head" end which is shorter and that terminates in a squared, rounded or oval configuration, the region sometimes enhanced by a thinner "neck". This short area in turn usually expands fairly abruptly to the "shoulder/body" section, and this often is a dramatic expansion of artifact width or thickness or both.

The "body" may be rounded or oval, but usually tapers to some degree toward the "tail", which is one of the longest parts of most effigies. This in turn terminates in a rounded or squared or pointed shape. Usually, but not always, the head-end and tail-end are treated in similar fashion.

Viewed from the side, most effigies are highest or thickest in the shoulder/body area, and this thickness is usually nearer the head end. The base is usually both straight and flat. An interesting aspect of a very small number of lizards is that the head sides or front may have rough depictions of eyes and/or a mouth. This suggests that the lizard effigy at least is supposed to represent a living creature of some sort.

A fairly large number of these fascinating objects have attachment places. Usually this is a thin groove that may be around the center of the body, or if in two places, around the neck and the tail. Probably all were secured to something at one time, and the most common and logical method was fastening with cord or sinew at each end.

These objects are almost certainly *Atl-atl* stones, and once associated with the lance-throwing board. They may have served as balance-weights, or even as parts of handle grips or positioning indicators for giving the lance-welder the proper handhold. And as to what these puzzling objects really represent, in the Author's opinion they are snake symbols. Not only are they probably snake effigies, but of snakes that have seized and swallowed prey. A few examples even have twin protrusions on either side of the head end, perhaps indications that the snake depicted is a poisonous type.

These effigies may be highly stylized representations of successful hunters. No doubt the symbolism of a hunting or waiting snake that strikes suddenly and accurately and fatally was not lost on the long-ago human hunter who went out for food for himself, his family, or his group. It is known that two of the more common hunting techniques of American Indians was the stalk and the ambush, both of which are also done by hunting snakes.

If this is indeed accurate, lizard effigies can be considered primarily as hunting charms or magical stones. Fascination, or respect, for snakes appears frequently in Amerind works, and Ohio's Great Serpent Mound is perhaps the best surviving example. By the way, there was (is?) another snake mound in Warren County, Ohio, between Morrow and South Lebanon. Built along a stream on a foundation of stone, it was three feet high, 15-20 feet wide, and about 1380 feet long. Even in the late 1800's it suffered from erosion.

Some of the lizard effigy forms are indeed snake-like. Others are so highly stylized (probably later-made examples) that it is necessary to be aware of the complete artifact family to know that such examples are really part of it. A good questions is why more life-like depictions were not made, for the majority of these pieces range from slightly to decidedly abstract. They obviously were made to represent something living, but the design was usually not too clear-cut or obvious.

No style evolution is really known for this class of effigy artifacts. If the usual process holds true, the rougher forms are early, the better-designed and more highly finished and polished examples are later. However there may have been a certain intermixing to some extent. The artifact type may have lasted for several thousand years, but even this is only an estimate. For a lesser period, there would not have been as many variations, and for a longer period there should have been more major differences.

Whatever lizard effigies once really were, these artifacts are among the most mysterious and beautiful in all of North American prehistoric art.

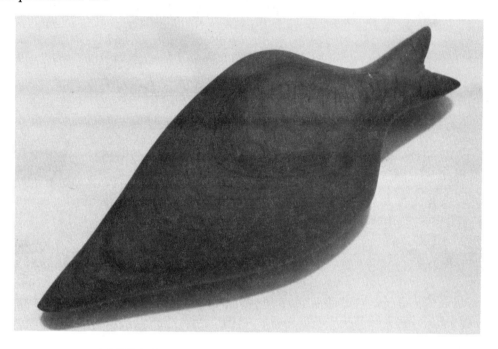

LIZARD EFFIGY, probably ca. Middle Archaic, an excellent example of a top-grade artifact. Blue-black slate, with concentric banding that focused on the top or shoulder/body region. Size 2¹⁄₁₆ x 5 inches, ex-coll. C.C. Smith, from Clark County, Ohio.

$2500-3500

Courtesy Dennis Bushey collection, Alabama

SHAMAN'S CHARM(?), tan and grey basaltic rock, weight 4¾ ounces. Size, 1x1¼x3¼ inches. Besides the lightly grooved pattern on "top", there is a face-like design on the front of one end, possibly that of a seal. Origin, Pacific Northwest. $150-250
Photo courtesy Harold Grubenhoff collection, Washington

Chapter 5
BIRDSTONES

While the lizard (snake) effigies are largely restricted to the Eastern Midwest, birdstones are found in most of Eastern North America, including lower Canada. Various cultures – such as the Glacial Kame and Meadowood – made birdstones in one form or another. The artifact type probably lasted at least 1500 years.

Birdstones are mainly from the Late Archaic period, probably pre-1000 BC and several forms lasted into Woodland times, ca. AD 500. Surprisingly, though there are a few less well-designed and haphazardly finished "birds", by far the majority of examples are finely formed and highly polished overall. In length, most range from 3 to 6 inches (similar to the earlier lizard effigies).

While various birdstones have different characteristics according to sub-groups within the class, a very high percentage have features in common. The base bottom is flattened, and holes are drilled at each end for attachment. There is a well-defined head end that is higher, and consists of a neck, head and pointed beak. The body is usually elongated, often ridged, extending to the raised tail region which is treated in a number of ways. The last of the birdstone lineage, the bust type, lacks a tail entirely.

Birdstones, as the name accurately suggests, do seem to look more like birds than anything else. Wings are not depicted, so the birds seem to be resting or setting on a nest. They are not birds in motion or flight. Here are some of the major birdstone types.

Birdstone Preforms

Birdstones, like most other slate ornaments, were rough-pecked into shape with a hammerstone. This first stage or birdstone preform was then further ground into shape with abrasive material. A final polish was applied, probably with the use of leather, grit and animal fat. Finally, the attachment holes were drilled.

The early stages of birdstone production are collected for several reasons. There is no doubt as to authenticity, and each example provides a thousands-of-years-old glimpse of what material was selected and how it was worked. Often the preforms are several times the size and weight compared with finished examples, and of course do not have the fine shape or high value that finished "birds" do. They are yet completely valid examples of prehistoric ornamental art.

Animal Type

Possibly these are the first birdstones to follow the earlier lizard effigies. Though relatively small in number, they have little that resembles the earlier elongated effigies or the later classic types. Most of the animal birdstones have a main distinguishing feature, holes drilled at each end of the rectangular, flattened base, that completely separates them from the lizard forms. They are also higher and may lack the smooth, flowing contours of the lizards or snakes.

The bodies are generally rather short and chunky, and the rear may terminate abruptly or have the rudimentary shape of a tail. Often the head region is fairly well defined, and a mouth and/or eyes may be depicted in some fashion. Many somewhat resemble a bear or a badger, but it is not really known what they in fact represent. What this class sometimes lacks in artistry, individual examples more than make up in rarity. The material is usually any grade of slate.

One characteristic often noted in the animal type is the widely different manner in which the neck and head area is presented. Some extend simply forward from the body, some are raised at an angle as if leaning forward, and some are both extended and raised. Most also are narrow and tapering, especially compared with the rather heavy body area. Some bulge upward in the head area while other diminish in that portion. Only a few animal types have narrow, ridged backs, and most are wide and rounded in the body area. The material is usually any compact grade of glacial slate, and the colorful banded varieties are rather rare for the type.

Elongated-bar Type

Diagnostic (along with the shortened-bar type) of the Glacial Kame peoples, these birdstones have clean and flowing lines. The type is classic for the culture, and examples are among the most beautiful "birds" ever made.

The tail area is of medium height, rounded to squared; a variety has a larger, flared tail and is called the "fan-tail" birdstone. Relatively narrow for size (usually 5 to 7 inches in length) the body is somewhat triangular in cross-section with a top ridge that runs from the head to the tail. The neck and head area flow forward gracefully and are usually the highest part of the type, except for examples with exceptionally high tails.

The head and beak areas are still lightly ridged and forward-extending, coming to a rounded point at the beak terminus. The under-neck area is usually rounded, but may be somewhat angular. Eyes are sometimes indicated by slight knobbing, but more often by concentric banding in the slate material itself.

Often the highest grades of banded glacial slate were selected, and the birdstones were worked sometimes so that this banding added to the overall attraction of the piece by emphasizing certain portions or features. The birdstone was drilled at each end of the rectangular base in the most common birdstone fashion, with small, interconnecting holes that form an "L"-configuration.

Shortened-bar Type

Probably the most common of the slate birdstone forms, this is the "basic bird". It is widely found throughout the birdstone region, but the main distribution area is probably the Eastern Midwest. The tail is rarely flared and is usually short and upright. The back is often ridged. The neck and head region usually do not extend as far as the elongated-bar type. Good grades of banded slate were almost always used, but as with other birdstones some are monochrome in red, green, black, brown or yellowish slate.

Long-necked Type

Probably a variety of the shortened-bar type, these artifacts have extraordinarily long raised necks. In terms of overall body length, the necks may contribute nearly 50% of that length. The head usually terminates rather quickly with a down-thrust, rather short beak. This birdstone type is quite scarce.

Elongated Eyes

A probable variant of the elongated-bar type, these birdstones all have eye protrusions. These range from tiny bumps to cylindrical to button-shaped. At times the head is raised to a normal height, while in others the head is lowered. Some of these "birds" have extremely long bodies; a large number of them seem to come from New York state and southeast of the province of Ontario, Canada.

These bar-type birdstones with well-indicated eyes seem most common in the U.S. Northeast, and there are a number of sub-types. A variant even has a single eye or knob atop the head.

Pop-eyed

This shape, while still obviously a birdstone, seems to have enhanced features. The head is erect, the beak points out and up, and the lower jawline has a large indentation at the neck. Eyes are extended from the head and are on stalks, somewhat mushroom-shaped. The body is short and rounded, the tail wide and flattened. A number have come from glaciated regions all across the Northeast and Upper Midwest. Those with oval bases may have a front and rear base-bottom ridge, and the drill-holes go through these ridges.

One aspect of interest for the pop-eyed type is that while some are made of high-quality glacial slate, others are made of hardstone. The most preferred stone, if surviving examples are any indication, is porphyry. This extremely durable material has light-colored inclusions against a darker background.

Moorehead (*The Stone Age In North America*, Vol. II, p. 10) refers to one pop-eyed birdstone as being made of diorite with feldspar crystals. Most inclusions are white, cream or yellow, and provide an attractive contrast and appearance. This type is certainly the rarest of all birdstones, even though it is found across a very wide area. When damage is done to one of the class, usually one or both of the relatively delicate eyes sections is missing, though occasionally the head also is gone.

Non-bird Type

This is a fairly large category, and some examples are extremely well-made and highly artistic. Many examples have little or no tail, and heads of many different configurations. The body is very wide and quite flat; drill-holes (usually two) may go through the body from the back mid-line to the flat base. This drilling is non-birdstone-like, and such stylized forms may not even be in the birdstone family. Materials are almost always a high quality glacial slate.

Bust Type

From Woodland times (1000 BC - AD 500) these are unusual birdstones and may be the last of the line. Some have large eye-protrusions, while others do not. The base, like that of certain of the pop-eyed family – is oval, and drilling may be present front and back. As the name suggests, the effigy portrays the bust only, or the upper body, the neck and the head. Most of the lower body and all of the tail are missing. At least one example with two heads, one at each end of the oval base, is known.

A variety of the bust-type originated in Ohio, and the material is colorful pipestone from the Lower Scioto Valley region. The eyes for this variety may be large and flattened. Ohio pipestone is actually a very unusual material for birdstones, so use of the material for this sub-type is rather unique.

Salvaged Types

Birdstones were evidently very important to their makers and users. There are many examples of artifacts that were salvaged or repaired or reworked in some fashion so they could continue in use. On nearly intact birdstones, a missing head may have the break area ground off and smoothed. Sometimes the damage occurred at each end, and both areas were similarly treated, and the body only being salvaged.

Broken-out attachment holes are very common. At times the holes were redrilled at each end of the base, though occasionally the repair holes are on the lower body sides. In cases where a birdstone was broken apart, repair holes might be made along the break area so the pieces could be fastened back together.

Birdstone heads seem to have had a special significance or fascination to prehistoric Indians. At times, when the head was broken from the body, the surviving head-piece may have become a charm or pendant. The neck portion may be drilled or grooved for suspension. Once made, a birdstone seems to have retained value whether in whole or in part.

A few birdstones were further treated. When complete, basal edges or the tail region might be tally-marked. This is a series of cut-in lines, usually short and uniform, and done at regular, close intervals. Their purpose is unknown. And a very few whole birdstones were incised, or have designs on the surface scratched in with a sharp-tipped flint tool. This was more often done on damaged or broken specimens, however.

While it is known with some certainty where and when birdstones were made, very little is known about how they were used. Numerous theories have arisen, but they remain only theories. In the Author's opinion – based on birdstone size, height, length, basal holes and polish over the back areas – birdstones served as handle-grips for *Atl-atls*. Some, such as the pop-eyed type, may have been merely handle-grip guides for positioning the hand. If used in this manner, birdstones would have been fastened on the underside of the lance-throwing board in the usual manner of *Atl-atl* stones, but in a different position. Some of the final forms, like the bust-types, may have "migrated" entirely away from the lance-thrower and were used for other ceremonial/status purposes. It is at least a highly interesting coincidence in time that about when birdstones ceased to be made, the bow and arrow had arrived and the lance-thrower was on the way to becoming obsolete.

Whatever their original purpose and actual use, birdstones are among the most sought-after ornamental artifacts from prehistoric times.

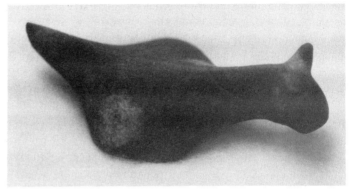

POPEYED ANIMAL-TYPE BIRDSTONE, made of porphyry. It is from central Illinois, and 1⅜ x 3½ inches long. An artifact that is finely made, it is also interesting in that it looks more like a snail than a bird. Very unusual, and made of a scarce and attractive material.
$2900-3700

Private collection, Ohio

BIRDSTONE, pop-eyed bust type, found along the east branch of the Little Pigeon River, Sevier County, TN. It is steatite and well-polished; site while producing few artifacts is mainly Archaic through Late Woodland. Size, ⅞ x 1⅜ x 1½ inches. A well-made piece.
$1200-1800

Photo courtesy Blake Gehagan, Tennessee

POPEYED BIRDSTONE, speckled porphyry, a finely made example with intact eyes and unblemished features. From Henry County, Ohio, it is a 1⅝ x 3½ in. long. This is a highly developed type and a very desirable artifact.
$3500-4500
Private collection, Ohio

POPEYED BIRDSTONE, made of a very unusual quartzite-greenstone conglomerate. From Fulton County, Ohio, it is a 1⅝ x 2⅝ inches long, and a fine, attractive little piece. $2100-2750
Private collection, Ohio

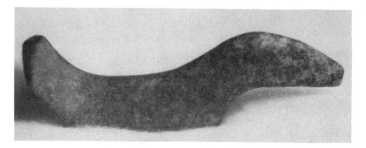

BAR-TYPE BIRDSTONE, material is a tan and black speckled granite. From Green County, Indiana, it is a 1⅜ x 4½ inches long. Beautiful lines, good size and high polish make this a very fine fantail birdstone. $2800-3400
Private collection, Ohio

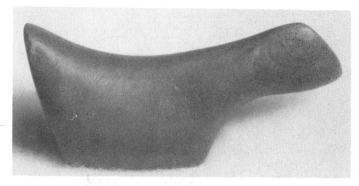

BAR-TYPE BIRDSTONE, it is made of dark green and brown banded quartzite, a very unusual artifact material. It is from Lynn Township, Hardin County, Ohio, and is 1⅝ x 3⅝ inches long. The drilling at base was started but is incomplete; otherwise this is a well-finished and fine piece. $1500-2500
Private collection, Ohio

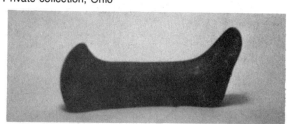

BIRDSTONE, possibly from the Eastern Midwest but found in Davidson County, Tennessee. Finder was Dr. T. Hugh Young prior to 1910, and the site was a few miles south of Nashville. This bird is ex-coll. Parks and is pictured in Townsend's book on page 671 figure B. Size, 1 x 1⅜ x 3½ inches; material is black-banded green slate. Piece was salvaged after head broken. $600-900
Photo courtesy Blake Gahagan, Tennessee

BIRDSTONE, made of porphyry, and found by a farmer near Forbest, Missouri. It is drilled on the underside in 4 places, and tail tip has been broken. Size, 1⅛ x 4¾ inches long. This is an attractive piece in a highly stylized form. $1300
Photo courtesy Mike George, Missouri

BIRDSTONE, from Montgomery County, Pennsylvania. Made of a speckled hardstone, it is 2 in. high and 6 in. long. Birdstones are very rare in the area where found. $350-450
Photo courtesy Lee Hallman, Pennsylvania

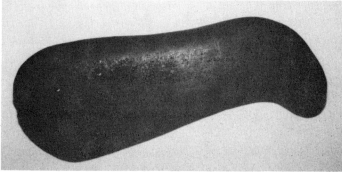

BIRDSTONE, a rare form positioned to be flat rather than as a nesting form. It is made of hematite, is highly polished, and 6¾ inches long. It was found near Youngstown, Ohio. Such pieces are nearly one-of-a-kind. $750-1000
Photo courtesy Steven R. Dowell collection, Kentucky

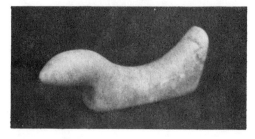

BIRDSTONE, from Randolph County, Arkansas. This is a beautiful hardstone example, drilled front and rear at the base. It measures ¾ x 4¼ inches and is in fine condition. These are very rare artifacts. $1000-1800
Photo courtesy James M. Dethrow collection, Arkansas

14

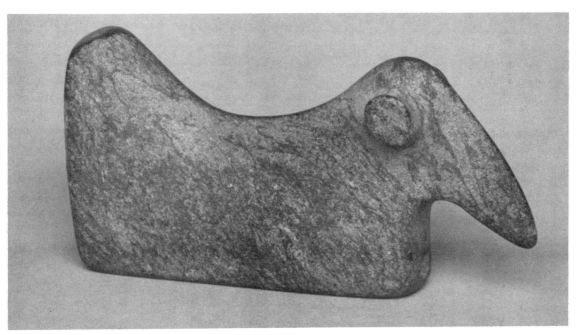

BIRDSTONE, green and black hardstone, from Indiana. Size, 32 x 103 mm and 52 mm high. This stately, high-bodied bird is unusual in that glacial slate was the more common material. Ex-colls. Guftafson (IA) and Dyson (LA). $1000-1500
Photo courtesy Chris Callaway collection, Louisiana

BIRDSTONE, unfinished or preform example. This bird was found 5 miles east of Dale Hollow Lake on the KY-TN line, Pickett County, Tennessee. Material is a speckled hardstone, and size is 1½ x 1¾ x 3¾ inches. $300-450
Photo courtesy Blake Gahagan, Tennessee

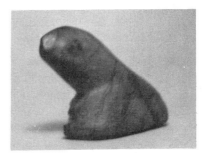

BIRDSTONE, bust-type, from Early or Middle Woodland times. It was found along the French Broad River, Cocke County, TN. Material is light and dark grey banded slate; base is drilled and base and beak area have slight damage. Eyes are mildly raised. Size, 1½ x 2 x 2½ inches., a fine specimen. $800-1500
Photo courtesy Blake Gahagan, Tennessee

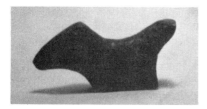

BIRDSTONE, unperforated, found on the Carter farm, Tennessee River, Hamilton County, TN. Material is reddish-brown steatite. Size, ⅝ x 1¼ x 2½ inches. Ex-coll. Cassell (MN) and Petrie (WI). This piece is pictured in Townsend's birdstone book on page 671 figure A. An artistic small bird with a fine pedigree. $1200-1800
Photo courtesy Blake Gahagan, Tennessee

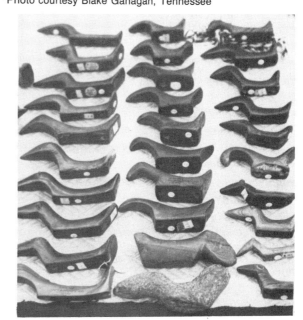

Unusual photograph of long- and short-bar birdstones, side/bottom views. An unfinished or preform birdstone is at bottom center. Ex-coll. Cameron Parks, Indiana and ca. 1975. Lar Hothem photo.

15

Chapter 6
BANNERSTONES – HARDSTONE

The term bannerstone means a certain class of artifacts that seems to be associated with *Atl-atls*, at least in a few, proven instances. Some bannerstone types are usually, in some cases almost always, made of higher grades of hardstone. Hardstone bannerstones or banners are most often found in the Eastern U.S., and they are most common in the Upper Mississippi watershed region.

Bannerstones for the most part seem to be Middle and Late Archaic in time, or ca. 5000 - 1000 BC. In this four-thousand-year period a great variety of banners was made, and only the basic hardstone types are covered in this chapter. Due to the density and weight of hardstone, most banners made of this material are not large. While size varies both with individual specimens and the type or class, an average size would be about 2 x 3 inches.

Manufacture methods were simple and effective. A hardstone of suitable size was selected, and often a colorful material was chosen. Care was taken in selection, and most banners do not have major fault-lines or inclusions of inferior material. The stone was rough-shaped by pecking with a small hammerstone, each was contoured by grinding against a larger rock of sandstone, and sandstone slabs were undoubtedley employed for out-of-the-way places.

Polishing was accomplished in a different way, probably with grease or fat, fine grit, and leather. Most banners were drilled as a last step. There are many bannerstone examples in collections that are entirely finished except for drilling the center hole. This may be partially accomplished, or, for whatever reasons was never begun. The holes range slightly in diameter from ½ to ¾ inches, with an average of about ⅝ inch.

Drilling was done last for several reasons. It was so laborious and time-consuming that the banner-maker wanted to be certain that the rest of the stone was sound and satisfactory before devoting dozens, sometimes hundreds, of hours to drilling the hole. And a drill-hole made before the banner was entirely pecked into shape would have weakened the body and resulted in much breakage.

Depending on time and place, one of three drilling methods was used. Perhaps an added bit of information to those who do not have an extensive banner collection, flint drills seem to have been rarely used. These were more often employed to make smaller holes in material other than hardstone. Instead, hardstone banners were drilled mainly with either a hardwood wand (solid drilling) or a section of cane (hollow drilling).

The hardwood wand bored out a hole the diameter of the stick being used. The softer cane bored a hole the diameter of the stick, but cut only on the edges, leaving a protruding hardstone core. Occasionally these cores are found on an Archaic site, showing not only that bannerstones were made there, but proving how they were drilled and the material that was used.

Both methods used, in conjunction with the drill-stick, very fine sand as an abrasive to actually cut the hardstone. The drill provided only the pressure and guided the cut. The process was a very gradual wearing away of the stone. Probably dozens of hardwood drills and hundreds of cane sections were used up before a typical hardstone banner hole was completed. It must have been a great moment for the Indian artisan when the drill finally wore through to the other side and the bannerstone was complete.

As for bannerstones themselves, the most complete book on the subject was written by Byron W. Knoblock, Illinois, in 1939. It is *Bannerstones Of The North American Indian*. This 596-page hardback, now a collector item in itself, has gone through a number of printings and is still the main reference to have on the subject. The classification of hardstone banners in this chapter largely follows Mr. Knoblock's ground-breaking effort.

Here is a brief summary of basic hardstone banner types. It should be noted that there are also a number of offshoots, blending forms and one-of-a-kind pieces.

Bottle
The type has narrowed ends and a larger center which may expand gently or abruptly. Most examples are extremely well made, and the classic material is a quartzite in pinks and/or orange and/or red. The central hole is drilled longtitudinally. A bi-face group has extremely pronounced side protrusions and is a sub-variety.

Hinge
Indeed hinge-like, there is one flat or flattish face, with the opposite face raised or ridged in the hole area. The wings are short and blunt, and the type when made of hardstone tends to be of materials like granite or steatite.

Hourglass
The type has a more narrow center, which expands at each end. The end-edges tend to be excurvate or convex, and there is a central ridge which strengthens the drill-hole region. Quartzite of many different shades, some translucent, was the material of choice.

Humped
Here, one face is somewhat flat (but may be flat, concave or convex) while the other face is definitely humped. Sides are usually straight, but some examples are slightly excurvate. Known materials include granite, steatite, and hematite, with the former the most likely.

Pick

Somewhat similar to the slate pick family, the hardstone type tends to be shorter and thicker, and with less curve. A preference was shown for certain materials, and chlorite (a green, yellow, black or greenish-yellow secondary mineral) was apparently used when it could be obtained.

Quartzite Butterfly

The central section (drill-hole area) is narrowed and rounded. The wings project a medium distance and are always greatly excurvate; the type is always considerably wider than length. These are among the best-made artifacts of the hardstone banner family, and sometimes have a very high polish. As the name suggests, the classic material is ferruginous (the color of iron rust) quartzite, in various reddish shades, pink to deep red.

Rectangular

This is a basic banner family and it has a large variety of related forms. The factor in common is that most are somewhat rectangular in shape. However, there may be some proportional variations in length and width. The central hole is usually ridged or at least raised, and a tremendous variety of materials was used in manufacture. Wings may be rounded, squared or incurvate.

Saddle

Basically a triangular form, the face with the drill-hole ridge is further worked. Each end of the ridge has a small protrusion, which ranges from a small bump to a relatively large area that at times is almost hook-like. Whatever the artifact, each ridge-peak is treated in the same fashion so that they match. High-grade materials of many kinds were used, especially porphyry and quartzite.

Shuttle

This form is fairly thick and does not have ridged drill-holes. It is wide in the center and tapers rapidly toward the wing-tips, which in a few cases are almost pointed. The thinnest portion is at the wing-ends and both faces are usually smooth. A wide range of materials was used.

Triangular

Seen from the drill-hole side, this type forms a wide triangle, usually wider than high. Faces have dissimilar treatment with the bottom somewhat flattened or excurvate, the top peaked. Sides are straight and slightly incurvate or excurvate. Most examples are longer than wide. Serpentine, diorite, steatite and granite were widely used.

Wisconsin Winged

This type exists in both drilled and undrilled configurations. It has a narrowed center and expands rapidly to wide wings; if drilled, the hole area may have a rectangular ridge. Wing-tips may be pointed, and wing sides are excurvate. Sometimes informally called a "bow-tie" banner, the type is found mainly in Wisconsin, plus Iowa, Illinois and Missouri. Porphyry and other quality hardstone was used.

Other Banners

Besides the major families or groups mentioned and described here, made entirely or largely of hardstone, other bannerstone groups may occasionally have a hardstone example. And, there are also few-of-a-kind or one-of-a-kind examples that do not fit easily into any of the major categories or classes. Most, however, have the single large drill-hole at center and equal protrusions of whatever size and shape to either side of the hole.

For more than a century, these fascinating artifacts (including the slate forms) have been called bannerstones, in the belief that they served as a standard or symbol of rank or importance. Banners have had alternate names as well, among them "problematicals" (Moorehead, *The Stone Age In North America*, 1910), "badges of authority" (MacLean, *The Mound Builders*, 1879), and "badges or wands" (*Ohio Centennial Report*, 1877).

The latest theories, based largely on a number of finds in Kentucky at such sites as Indian Knoll and the Read Shell Midden, and elsewhere, postulate that banners were *Atl-atl* weights. However, these bannerstones were probably far more than mere weights, for they are as a class among the best-made artifacts of Archaic times in Eastern North America.

A very quick look at *Atl-atl* development bears this out. The first known lance-throwing board, the oldest, is of the compound type. These had a wooden shaft and a separate, attached hook to engage the lance-butt. Some examples are extremely early. A shell *Atl-atl* hook from Warm Mineral Springs, Florida, was Carbon-14 dated to 8300 BC as reported by Fagan, *The Great Journey*, p. 161. That's 10,300 years ago.

Rather perplexing, at least at first thought, is the next stage of development, the simple form. This was an all-wood *Atl-atl* which one would think should have come before the compound type. However, this is explained by the obvious fact that later peoples were likely more skilled at working wood. They simply did away with the potentially weak point of a separate hook and created the whole throwing-board in solid wood.

The final *Atl-atl* form, one that seems always associated with bannerstones, is the complex type. (See Webb, *Indian Knoll*, University of Kentucky, Vol. IV, No. 3, Part 1, p. 323.) This consists of three separate and distinct sections: a handle, usually of antler-base; an antler hook-end; and, connecting the two was a narrow rod, apparently of hardwood.

The weight fitted around this central *Atl-atl* rod. Interestingly, other *Atl-atls* of the complex type and with fitted and matched shell discs as "weights", also were found at Indian Knoll. Other observations came from this site, among them the fact that five *Atl-atls* had hooks and handles remaining, but no weights (*Indian Knoll*, p. 326). Asphalt (mineral pitch, obtained from natural deposits) was sometimes used to aid in securing the various parts together.

The Author's opinion on all this is that such *Atl-atls* of the complex type – being rather prone to easy breakage at the central rod and very likely to fly apart if actual use was attempted – were never actually employed as lance-throwers. They were simply too fragile for rigorous use on the hunt or in battle, and the bannerstones too precious to risk damage, breakage or loss.

Such *Atl-atls* may well have been ceremonial or symbolic objects of power or prowess and ornamental in every way. So the old term "bannerstone" may still have great validity and may continue as an accurate description.

HARDSTONE BANNERSTONES, all l. to r.: Mottled hardstone, saddleback type, from Illinois, 2 x 3 inches. $800
Mottled hardstone, humped type, Illinois, 1⅞ x 2½ inches. $600
Mottled hardstone, saddleback type, Peoria County, Illinois;size, 2½ x 3 inches. $900
Courtesy Gerald Bernacchi collection, Indiana

INCISED BANNERSTONE, short-winged type, with central ridge above the drill-hole. Incised banners are rare. Made of highly polished dark hardstone, this piece is in the Silvagne collection and is from Lycoming County, Pennsylvania. $350
Photo courtesy Lee Hallman, Pennsylvania

D-HUMPED BANNERSTONE, material a black and white quartzite. From Logan Co., Ohio, size is 1½ x 2 inches. Ex-colls. Burdett and Wachtel, the artifact is pictured in *Who's Who #1*. Material and workstyle make this piece one of the best examples of primary humped Ohio banner forms. $1500-1800
Courtesy Len & Janie Weidner Collection, Ohio

CURVED PICK BANNERSTONE, in bright light green micaceous chlorite. It is from Medina County, Ohio, and is 1¼ x 4³⁄₁₆ in. wide. The form and color make this banner a very attractive artifact, with good lines and fine taper. $2250-3000
Private collection, Ohio

BOAT-TYPE PICK BANNERSTONE, hardstone, green granite with tan and black specks. Found in state of Michigan, it is 1¾ x 4⁷⁄₁₆ in. wide. Color, workstyle and symmetry are excellent for this fine artifact which is quite attractive. $1200-1500
Private collection, Ohio

BANNERSTONE, fluted-ball variant that is heart-shaped, from Berks County, Pennsylvania. Made of a green-tan material with full polish, this piece is in the Bower collection. $500
Photo courtesy Lee Hallman, Pennsylvania

18

SADDLE-FACED PRISMOIDAL BANNERSTONE, made of tan and black speckled granite. From St. Clair County, Illinois, it is 2⅜ x 3½ in. long. This is a highly developed type, is well-polished and has graceful, flowing contours. Top piece. $2100-2800
Private collection, Ohio

SADDLE-FACED PRISMOIDAL BANNERSTONE, made from porphyry. Found along the Spoon River, Knox County, Tnnessee, it is 2⁵⁄₁₆ x 3⅛ in. long. This is a well-made piece with fine type lines, very attractive in this scarce artifact material.   1200-2000
Private collection, Ohio

WISCONSIN-TYPE WINGED HARDSTONE BANNER, made of beautifully patterned prophyry. Found in the vicinity of Navyoc, Illinois, it is 2¹³⁄₁₆ x 3⁹⁄₁₆ in. wide. This is a finely made piece with good lines; a very collectible specimen. $1800-2300
Private collection, Ohio

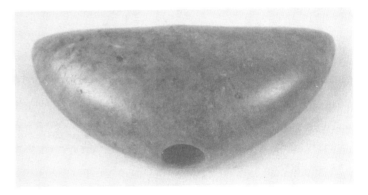

PICK BANNERSTONE, pale green chlorite, from Franklin County, Ohio. It is 1⁹⁄₁₆ x 3½ in. wide. This banner has four shallow holes drilled parallel with the center hole, possibly for insetting small pearls. There are four tally or hash-marks on the top right side of the banner. A fine piece. $3000-4500
Private collection, Ohio

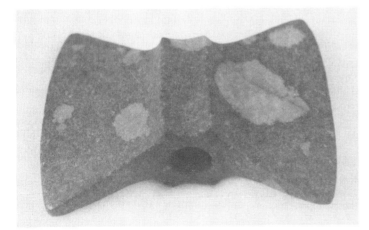

WISCONSIN-TYPE BIFLUTED WINGED BANNER, hardstone, made of porphyry. From Winnebago County, Illinois, it is 2 ¹³⁄₁₆ x 3⁹⁄₁₆ in. wide. This is a very highly developed form for the type, and is wonderfully made in an attractive material. A truly top piece in all aspects. $2100-3000

Private collection, Ohio

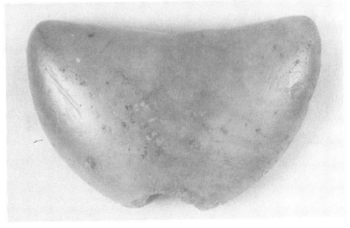

PICK BANNERSTONE, tan and yellow chlorite, from Miamisburg, Ohio. It is 1⅞ x 3⅛ in. wide and ex-coll. Dr. Gordon Meuser. Fine workstyle and color make this polished piece very collectible. $2800-3500

Private collection, Ohio

19

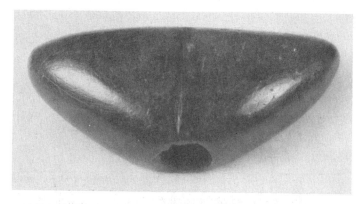

PICK BANNERSTONE, dark olive-green chlorite, 1⁹⁄₁₆ x 3¹¹⁄₁₆ in. wide. It is from Meigs County, Ohio, and ex-coll. Dr. Gordon Meuser. It has one long distinct vertical groove at the banner center in line with the hole and two shorter grooves to each side. Fine configuration and high polish. $2400-3100
Private collection, Ohio

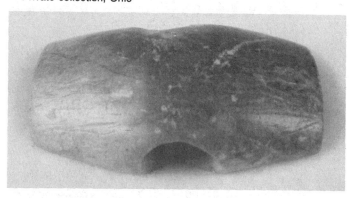

PICK BANNERSTONE, pale to dark green chlorite. Size, 1⁵⁄₈ x 3 in. wide, it is from Clermont County, Ohio, and is ex-coll. Dr. Gordon Meuser. The blunt ends are likely the result of repair in an attempt to make the banner symmetrical after damage in use. An interesting, attractive piece. $1850-2650
Private collection, Ohio

PICK BANNERSTONE, pale green chlorite, from Knox County, Ohio. It is 1⁵⁄₈ x 2⁵⁄₈ in. wide, and ex-coll. Dr. Gordon Meuser. This is a well-made, compact banner with excellent polish. $2100-2600
Private collection, Ohio

PICK BÁNNERSTONE, in bright light to dark green chlorite. This artifact is unusually large at 1⁹⁄₁₆ x 5 inches, and the provenance is Ohio. Specimen has crisp, clean and elegant lines, with a pleasing materials mixture. A top piece. $4500-6000
Private collection, Ohio

SADDLE-FACED BANNERSTONE, dark, well-polished hardstone. Size, ¾ x 2¼ x 3 in. long. Interior hole is ⁷⁄₁₆ in. diameter.
                                                                    $850
Courtesy Cliff Markley collection, Alabama

HINGE-TYPE BANNERSTONE, made of granite in light and dark green with pink mottling. From west-central Illinois, it is 2¹⁄₁₆ x 2¹¹⁄₁₆ inches, and ex-coll. John F. Neil. This piece has excellent lines, good coloring and top workstyle. Very desirable artifact. $1200-1450
Private collection, Ohio

PICK BANNERSTONE, dark greenish-brown chlorite, 1⁹⁄₁₆ x 4¾ inches. It is from Newago County, Michigan, and has fine form and superb polish. The mixture of fine material is of interest as well.
                                                                    $3500-4500
Private collection, Ohio

20

SADDLE-FACE/CONVEX-BACK PRISMOIDAL BANNER, made of very dark green hardstone with tan inclusions. From Bennington Township, Licking County, Ohio, it is 2⅝ x 3¼ in. long. Ex-coll. Dr. Gordon Meuser, this piece is unusual in that the wings come to a thin chisel edge. Well developed and attractive artifact.
$1350-1700
Private collection, Ohio

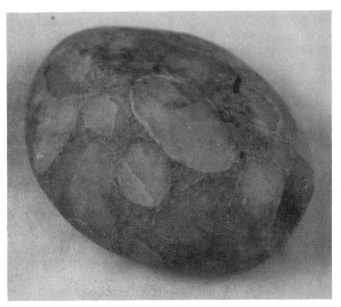

ELLIPTICAL RIDGED BANNERSTONE, made of a rare material, quartz conglomerate. It is from Lorain County, Ohio, and is 2½ x 3¹/₁₆ inches measured along the central hole. This is a finely made piece, and overall very attractive.
$1500-2500
Private collection, Ohio

WISCONSIN-TYPE WINGED BANNERSTONE, made of grey and cream-colored mottled granite. It is from Kane County, Illinois, and 2⅝ x 3⅝ in. wide. Ex-coll. C.T. Love, this is a top piece in workstyle, material and finish. Note fluting over the drill-hole area.
$1800-2400
Private collection, Ohio

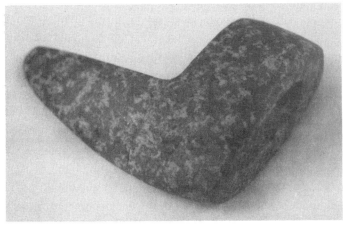

GENICULATE HARDSTONE BANNER, made of black, cream and pink speckled granite. From Clinton County, Ohio, it is 2¼ x 3³/₁₆ in. long. Ex-coll. J. F. Neil, this is a rare bannerstone type with rarity enhanced by the hardstone material. Fine artifact.
$2100-2700
Private collection, Ohio

SHUTTLE BANNERSTONE, material a light red jasper with pink mottling. It is 1¾ x 3⅛ in. wide, and is from Mexico, Missouri. This is a rare banner type, with good workstyle and in top condition, fine piece.
$800-1250
Private collection, Ohio

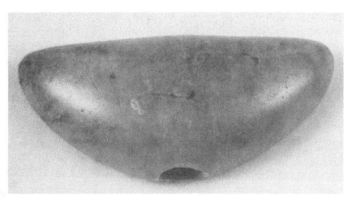

PICK BANNERSTONE, tan and light green mottled chlorite. It is 1⁹/₁₆ x 3¾ in. wide, from Licking County, Ohio, and ex-coll. Dr. Gordon Meuser. Fine shape, beautiful polish and a rare material make this exceptional.
$3000-3600
Private collection, Ohio

21

SHIELD-SHAPED DOUBLE-RIDGED BANNERSTONE, from Perry County, Indiana, and 1¹¹⁄₁₆ x 3 inches long. Material is a light, bright green chlorite with dark green mottling, quite unusual and beautiful. Both sides of the shield's large end were broken and salvaged in prehistoric times. $1500-2150
Private collection, Ohio

WINGED BANNERSTONES, both from Pennsylvania.
Left, damaged piece, Berks County, broken-out drill-hole $30
Right, ex-coll. Vanderpoel, Bradford County, a fine piece. $400
Photo courtesy Lee Hallman, Pennsylvania

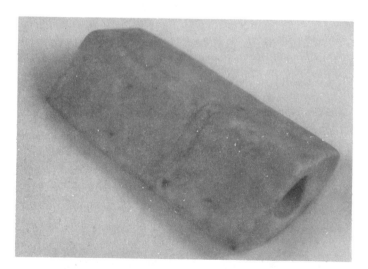

TRIANGULAR FLUTED-FACE BANNERSTONE, in cream, tan and brown quartzite. From Harrison County, Indiana, size is 1⅞ x 3⅛ inches. Ex-colls. Stephens, Gerber, Sailor and Gardner. This is a top example of a very rare type in a scarce material and is fluted both front and rear. $2000-2500
Courtesy Len & Janie Weidner Collection, Ohio

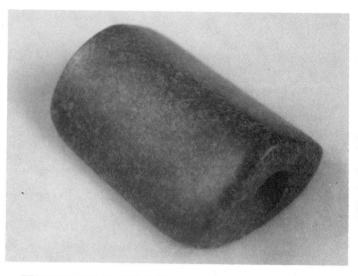

TRIANGULAR BANNERSTONE, dark speckled granite, from Ohio County, Kentucky. It is 1⅞ x 2½ inches, ex-coll. Stan Copeland, and found by Charles Gillam. This is a highly polished rare complete example with red ochre stains. $900-1200
Courtesy Len & Janie Weidner Collection, Ohio

TRIANGULAR BANNERSTONE, in black, pink and green granite. Size 1⅞ x 2½ inches; it is ex-colls. Carter, Gerber and Shenk. From McLean County, Kentucky, this is an excellent primary form with fine polish and a quality material. $900-1200
Courtesy Len & Janie Weidner Collection, Ohio

CONSTRICTED-CENTER BANNERSTONE, made of steatite. Size is 1¼ x 3 inches, and the artifact is from Tennessee. It is pictured in Knoblock's *Bannerstone* book. Not only well-made, this is rare because it is a one-of-a-kind form. $1200
Courtesy Len & Janie Weidner Collection, Ohio

22

HOURGLASS / LENS-SHAPED BANNERSTONE, made of translucent rose-colored ferruginous quartzite. Found along the Green River, Ohio County, Kentucky, it is 2³⁄₁₆ x 3³⁄₁₆ in. long. This piece is beautifully worked and polished, a true fragile artwork.
$1500-2500

Private collection, Ohio

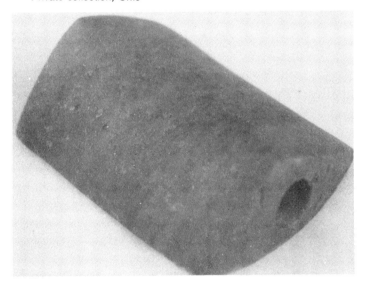

SADDLE-FACE BANNERSTONE, made of green quartzite. Size is 2¼ x 3 inches, this piece is from Harrison County, Indiana. This is a classic banner form, in a rare material, in top condition, and beautifully made. $1800-2200
Courtesy Len & Janie Weidner Collection, Ohio

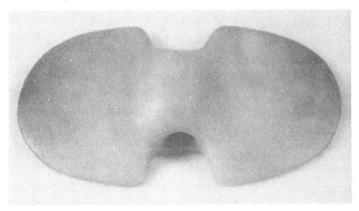

NOTCHED OVATE WINGED (BUTTERFLY) BANNER, made of translucent yellow and rose-colored ferruginious quartzite. From Muhlenburg County, Kentucky, it is 2⅜ x 4³⁄₁₆ in. wide. Ex-coll. Judge Claude U. Stone, this is a wonderfully formed and finished piece.
Private collection, Ohio $2500-3000

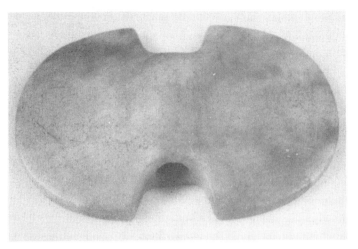

NOTCHED OVATE WINGED (BUTTERFLY) BANNER, material is a translucent cream and rose-colored ferruginous quartzite. From LaSalle County, Illinois, it is 2¹⁵⁄₁₆ x 4⁷⁄₁₆ in. wide. This is a colorful and well-made and desirable artifact with good size. $2700-3600
Private collection, Ohio

BOTTLE BANNERSTONE, made of translucent rose-colored ferruginous quartzite. From Jersey County, Illinois, it is 2⅛ x 2⅜ inches. This is a rare banner form, well-made and nicely finished. $1900-2400
Private collection, Ohio

HARDSTONE GROOVED BALL BANNERSTONE, tan-colored quartzite. It is ¹⁵⁄₁₆ x 2³⁄₁₆ in. wide, from Morrow County, Ohio, and ex-coll. Roger Mayne. Most banners of this type were made of glacial slate, so the form is very rare in this material. $1500-2200
Private collection, Ohio

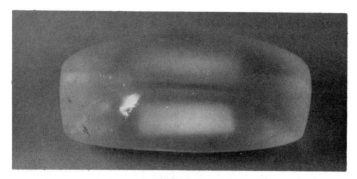

ROCK-CRYSTAL BOATSTONE, shaped from clear quartz crystal. It is 1 x 2⁵⁄₁₆ in. long, from Hardin County, Ohio, and ex-coll. Judge Claude E. Stone. The concave base is deep and highly polished. While small, this is a very rare piece. $700-1250
Private collection, Ohio

TUBULAR BANNERSTONE, made of red jasper. It is 1⅜ x 2⅛ in. long, and from Logan County, Ohio. This is a very well-made artifact with high polish, and in rare material for the type. Very collectible.
Private collection, Ohio $750-1100

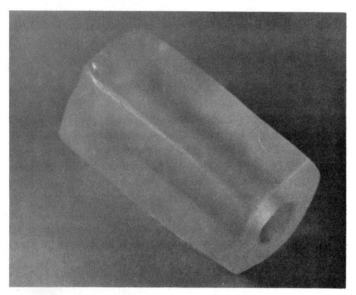

ROCK-CRYSTAL TUBE BANNERSTONE, shaped from clear quartz crystal. It is 1⁷⁄₁₆ x 2⅜ in. long, from Mercer County, Ohio, and ex-coll. John F. Neil. The prehistoric maker utilized the original crystalline structure in making this piece; the quality is so high the fully drilled hole can be seen through the sides. $2100-3000
Private collection, Ohio

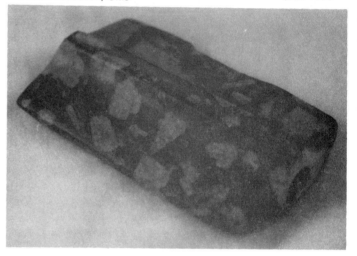

FLUTED FACE / CONVEX RECTANGULAR BANNER, made of por-phyry. It is 2³⁄₁₆ x 3⅝ in. long and from southern Michigan. This is a very highly developed form that is quite rare. In addition to the great care evidenced in the making, the piece is beautifully patterned in well-polished stone. Top piece. $3100-3800
Private collection, Ohio

ELONGATED BALL BANNERSTONE, made of grey and white speckled quartzite. It is 1⅜ x 1¾ in. long, from Erie County, Ohio and ex-coll. Harold Engle. This is a well-made artifact, nicely drilled, and in unusual material. $700-950
Private collection, Ohio

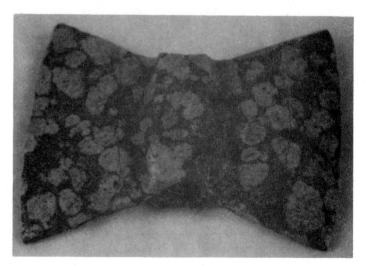

WISCONSIN-TYPE WINGED HARDSTONE BANNER, done in por-phyry. It measures 3 x 3¾ in. wide and is from Winnebago County, Wisconsin. The material has a very attractive pattern and the artifact is wonderfully made. A superb specimen. $3200-3800
Private collection, Ohio

FLARED-WING BANNERSTONE, grey hardstone, probably from late in the Archaic period. Size, 2 x 3¾ inches, and found along the Coosa River, Alabama, in 1937. This is a rare form, in perfect condition.
$500-750

Courtesy Lawson Corley collection, Alabama

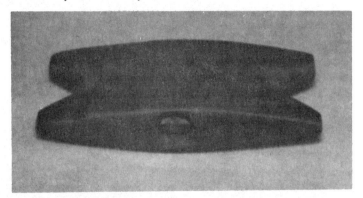

REEL-TYPE BANNERSTONE, brown material, size 1⅝ x 4 inches. Provenance of this piece is unknown, but the type is typically found in the upper Eastern Midwest. The hollow-drilled (cane drill) hole was just begun, and the core still remains, very unusual. $400-500
Courtesy Lawson Corley collection, Alabama

SOUTHEASTERN U.S. ARTIFACTS:
Top row, l. to r.: One-half bannerstone, $25; hematite banner, $50; effigy banner (?), broken, greenstone, $20
2nd row, l. to r.: Brownstone banner, $40; saddle-type banner, drilled and polished, MS, $100; barrel hematite banner, MS, well-drilled, $75
Bottom, scooped boatstone with effigy head, green hardstone, MS, $450
Courtesy Wilfred Dick collection, Mississippi

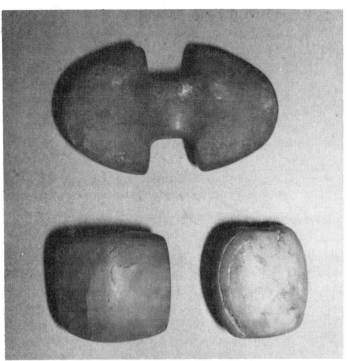

QUARTZITE BANNERSTONES, top, Butterfly-type, 1½ x 3 inches, Livingston Co., KY. $900-1500
Bottom left, diamond-shape, 1¼ x 1½ inches, Clark County, Indiana, off-center drill. $600-1000
Bottom right, round form, 1¼ x 1¼, Marshall County, KY $400-900
Courtesy Marguerite L. Kernaghan collection; photographers Marguerite L & Stewart W. Kernaghan

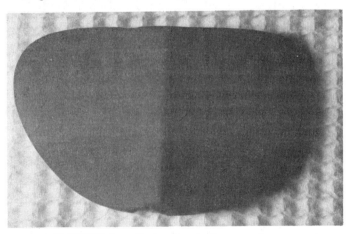

BANNERSTONE, from Upshur County, Texas, and an unusual artifact for the area. Material is a brown hardstone and size is ¾ x 2¼ x 3½ inches. This winged banner has fine form and is in top condition. $500
Courtesy Willie Fields collection, Texas

BANNERSTONE, rectangular barrel type, from Boone County, Missouri. It is made of well-polished black material and measures 2½ x 3½ inches. This piece is pictured in Who's Who Vol. 7, p. 13.
Photo courtesy Zell Adams collection, California $400

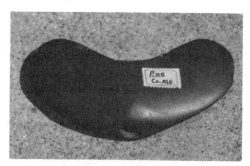

BANNERSTONE, crescent-type, made of black hematite. From Pike County, Missouri, this piece is 2½ x 3 inches wide, fully drilled. Ex-coll. Willard Johnson; pictured in *Who's Who* Vol. 7, p. 14. $450
Photo courtesy Zell Adams collection, California

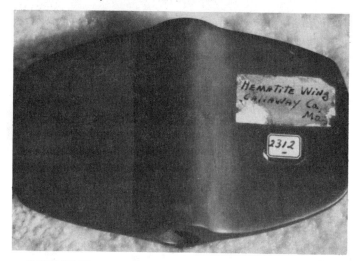

BANNERSTONE, winged type, made of grey hematite. It is from Callaway County, Missouri and measures 2¾ x 4¾ in. wide. Ex-coll. Knoblock. $500
Photo courtesy Zell Adams collection, California

CLASS C HINGE-TYPE BANNERSTONE, from Lawrence County, Indiana. Size is 52 x 62 mm and material is grey, green and black conglomerate. Old label with origin is dated 7-10-36. Ex-colls. Stuart (IN), Meeks (IN), Ritter (IL) and Callaway (LA). A highly developed banner form, these are typically found in IL, IN OH and KY.
$1200-1800
Photo courtesy Chris Callaway, Louisiana

HINGE-TYPE BANNERSTONE, from Brown County, Illinois. Size is 60 x 77 mm and material is a light tan and black speckled hardstone. This Class C specimen is ex-colls. Gustafson (IA) and Callaway (LA). According to Knoblock (p. 162) this type is based on the Southern triangular primary banner form. $600-plus
Photo courtesy Chris Callaway, Louisiana

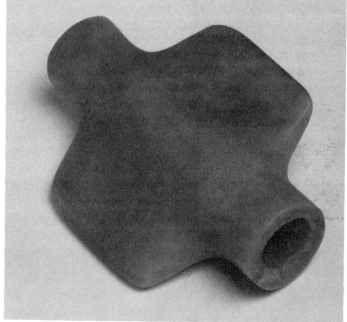

CLASS C BOTTLE-TYPE BANNERSTONE, from Lincoln County, Missouri. This piece was found in a field ditch by Seth Grimes in 1929. Size is 59 x 88 mm, and material is a white ferruginous quartz with excellent patina. Ex-colls. Gustafson (IA) and Callaway (LA). The type is found south of the Great Lakes, along the Mississippi and Ohio watersheds. A top piece. $1000-plus
Photo courtesy Chris Callaway, Louisiana

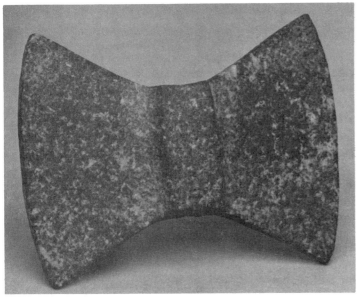

CLASS C WISCONSIN WINGED BANNERSTONE, from Missouri. Size is 65 x 90 mm and the central perforation is complete. Material is a black and white speckled hardstone. Ex-colls. Gustafson (IA) and Dyson (LA). This type (Knoblock, p. 165) is found in WI, IL, MO and IA. A beautiful piece. $750-1000
Photo courtesy Chris Callaway, Louisiana

CLASS C WISCONSIN WINGED BANNERSTONE, from Wayne County, Illinois. From the estate auction of Dr. John Neil (PA), it is also ex-colls. Wachtel, Stephens, Huff, Weidner and Callaway. Size is 76 x 97 mm, and material is gray-green hardstone. There is a groove or flute on both obverse and reverse that follows the perforation. This is a rare and superb piece. $2000-plus
Photo courtesy Chris Callaway, Louisiana

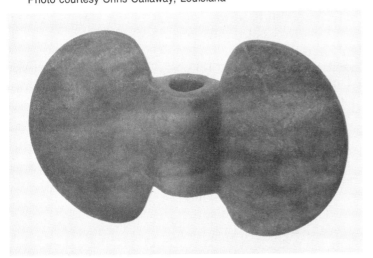

BUTTERFLY BANNERSTONE, from Hancock County, Mississippi. Ca. 3000-1000 BC, Knoblock (p. 164) places the distribution in the Mississippi watershed area. This piece was found at the Cedarland site, C-14 dated at 2500 BC. Part of a cache, also found were 5 jasper beads, a polished jasper point and two rose quartz bottle-type bannerstones. Ex-colls. Shiyou (MS) and Callaway (LA). Size 81 x 128 mm, rose quartz. $4000-plus
Photo courtesy Chris Callaway, Louisiana

Chapter 7
BANNERSTONES – Slate

Important and beautiful and valuable as the hardstone banners are, far more bannerstones were actually made of slate. While some native layer slate was utilized, a very high percentage of bannerstones was made from glacial slate. Often this is mottled or banded and striped and swirled. Both bands and background were formed in a limitless number of combinations in regard to number, thickness and colors.

Slate bannerstones, like their hardstone counterparts, are mainly Middle and Late Archaic in origin. Some of the simpler forms like the drilled pebbles are undoubtedly quite early, but it is not known which type was truly first or the original bannerstone. Slate banners are found throughout Eastern North America, though it is extremely unusual to find a large bannerstone in perfect condition anywhere. In fact, slate banners are encountered to some degree in most glaciated regions of the adjoining 48 states and into lower Canada.

Manufacturing a slate banner was similar to that of hardstone banners, except that some slate banners – especially of layer or quarried slate – evidence rough chipping-to-shape as a preliminary step before pecking and grinding.

There is another major difference. With hardstone, the overall color and quality of the stone was often important. With slate banners, banded slate was often selected, especially examples with attractive banding. Further, the bannerstone was often worked so that the color bands were arranged in an artistic manner, or converged to emphasize an area like the banner center. Frequently a great deal of thought seems to have gone into just how the raw material was to be worked.

Slate bannerstones have a very extensive number of family types. These range from small (ball) to quite large (knobbed crescent), and some highly imaginative forms were eventually developed. Slate banners have a much larger size and type variety than the hardstone examples. While some forms were also made in hardstone (plain crescents, picks), only slate was used to create the double crescents and notched ovates and reels.

In listing many of the major slate bannerstone types, again reference is made to Mr. Knoblock's *Bannerstones Of The North American Indian*. Though the cost of an original copy of this book today equals that of a minor bannerstone, the serious banner collector should have, or at least have access to, this book.

Butterfly - Plain
There are many general butterfly forms, all with extended, relatively thin wings on either side of the drill-hole. The wings taper to angular or rounded tips, and the drilled area is usually the thickest portion of the artifact, which reinforces the hole region. Such winged banners have an unbroken contour or profile from one side of the wings to the other, often with small straight sections at each end of the drill-hole.

Butterfly - Notched
Probably a development of the plain form, there are two notched types. One is the single-notch, with the body cut back at one end of the drill-hole. The double-notch is cut back at both ends, leaving only a thicker central portion. This section may be rectangular, rounded or ridged. Some of the notched forms are very advanced designs with ultra-thin wings, overall finely made and highly polished. Notches were sawed into the slate, probably with thin sandstone slabs or even flint flakes, and the area was later ground and polished.

Butterfly - Undrilled
Most of the undrilled types are double-notched, and many examples have come from Michigan. Despite lacking a central drill-hole, an attachment contour was usually put on the artifacts. This, at the center, is in the form of a long groove or channel that runs across both faces in the exact area where other butterflies have a drill-hole. Some undrilled butterflies lack this lashing or attachment channel, and are smooth-faced from wing-tip to wing-tip.

Crescent - Plain
This was apparently one of the popular bannerstone forms in prehistoric times, for there are a large number of them, and they exist in many forms. The central drill-hole is present, and as in most banners the wings project to the sides the same distance and in the same configuration. The edge formed by the wings on one side, however, is nearly straight or concave, while the opposite edge is usually quite excurvate. In no case are the configurations identical. A few unusual forms may be single-notched at the center of the excurvate edge.

Crescent - Knobbed
Also called a "knobbed lunate," this type is among the most spectacular of all banners. The form is difficult to describe, but some examples look like boomerangs or kayaks. Other forms are so "bent" or highly curved that they are U-shaped. All have the central drill-hole. The ends terminate as points, or are squared, or have enlarged knobs or expansions, sometimes markedly so. While these objects have always been classed as bannerstones, perhaps rightly so, in the Author's opinion this particular type may have been cross-pieces for pump-drills.

Crescent - Double
Double crescents may be the rarest of all slate banner forms; well-made, large and complete specimens certainly are. Each half resembles a crescent that has been joined or merged so that four separate prongs extend out and away from the body. Some prongs terminate in a slight hook. The region of the central drill-hole is always thickened and is usually ridged. Some examples are quite large, up to 8 inches wide. Areas between the prongs are deeply

indented, and sometimes notched as well. Here again, instead of a "fancy" banner, this class may have been pump-drill cross pieces.

Double-bitted Axe

An appropriate name, many of the more developed forms do resemble axes with opposing blades. Most are thickened in the center, and a very few are ridged. In most cases the wings expanded out from the drill-hole, and the lines may be straight or incurvate. The wing sides (the "axe edges") are slightly to very excurvate. On highly advanced forms, wing sides may terminate in hooks. This form may in fact be a ceremonial or stylized depiction of an axe, done in the form of a bannerstone.

Fluted Ball

This is a thick and rounded bannerstone. Some are indeed ball-shaped, while others in outline resemble apples, hearts or short tubes. The central hole is round. While a few ball banners lack the side-flutes, most have a channel or groove that extends across the face, parallel to the central hole. The flute may be narrow and shallow or wide and deep. In some cases, it is so wide that the ball is flattened or slightly concave for a considerable area. And a few rare examples have two flutes, on opposite sides; in this case, there is usually a larger and a smaller flute.

Geniculate – Angular

Geniculte means bent at an abrupt angle, or knee-like. This is a highly unusual banner form, for two reasons. One is that a portion (here, with rectangular or squared cross-section) extends beyond the opposite side, giving an unbalanced appearance, at least when seen from the side.

Another reason is the hole configuration. Instead of being round it is oblong. Study indicates that the original hole was further reamed out to the oblong shape. The portion that extends on one side may be somewhat fluted as a continuation of the hole.

Geniculate – Rounded

Essentially the same highly bent configuration, this type has rounded instead of angular edges. The unusual ovoid hole is retained, and the extension of one side may be extreme in some examples. While it is thought that geniculates were a form of *Atl-atl* ornamental stone, it is not known precisely how they were fitted. There is a possibility that they were handle-related.

Humped

A very basic bannerstone form, this is usually about twice as long as wide. The "top" is high and rounded, while the opposite side or face has a number of different configurations. This may be flat, somewhat fluted, concave, convex, or indented with two parallel flutes to either side of a raised portion along the drill-hole area. Seen from one end, simpler forms are somewhat semi-circular in shape, with the drill-hole centered.

Notched Ovate

One of the largest (in size) bannerstones, some rounded examples were also made of hardstone, especially in the Southeast. In and near glaciated regions, banded slate predominates as the material of prehistoric choice. The basic form is oval and the drill-hole is through the longer axis, which area may be raised or ridged.

Wing sides are gently excurvate. Both terminate near each end, well beyond the drill-holes, which are deeply inset. The hollowed or cut-out region may be rounded or angular. Ohio, Indiana and Michigan have produced fine examples, but the form is rare wherever encountered.

Panel

A wide-variety bannerstone family, panels are somewhat rectangular, but one end may be wider than the other. When such examples occur, wing sides are slightly incurvate or excurvate, rarely straight. The drill-hole area may be ridged, and a few forms are worked down on at least one face, leaving a border-like raised section. Wing-edges are sometimes tally-notched. As with the geniculates, the hole is ovoid or egg-shaped.

Pick - Curved

Perhaps a development of the straight type, or simply another variety, these artifacts in some cases are more detailed. The straighter side may be wider, and the tips of the picks less pointed than the straight type. A number were made wider or thicker through the drill-hole region, mainly due to the excurvate or even angled opposite side. A few examples are nearly 8 inches wide.

Pick - Straight

These are relatively long and narrow, pointed at both ends, rounded, and with a hole through the center. There is a wide range of size for straight picks, and a number are fairly short and thick. Frequently slate with bold and distinctive banding was selected. Indiana, Michigan and Ohio have produced excellent specimens. Some examples are wider at one end than the other. Materials other than banded slate, such as quartzite and steatite, were sometimes used.

Tubular - Plain

The plain tubes may be equi-sized at each end, or, one end may be larger. They are drilled the entire length, and some examples are 8 inches long. Some confusion reigns here, because some shorter, thicker pieces may indeed be banners, while others may be tubular pipes of the "cloud-blower" type. Some forms are rounded, while others are squared in end-view.

Other Bannerstones

There are a number of other bannerstones that do not fall readily into the major categories or classes listed here. Some have features of several groups, while others appear to be one-of-a-kind.

While it is known that some bannerstones did serve as *Atl-atl* stones, these are mainly the smaller, compact forms. Large and ornate banners, and those with relatively fragile wings, may have several other purposes. What these once were is difficult to say with certainty.

Without expounding on various theories, bannerstones do tell part of the overall story. Finds of banners made of banded slate well outside the standard natural distribution areas suggest prehistoric trade in raw materials, finished artifacts or both.

There is no mystery, either, as to why banded slate was a favorite, even preferred, material in prehistoric times. It was readily available, at least in glaciated areas or from trade sources. The slate was quite durable, yet worked and drilled fairly easily, at least compared with some of the hardstone materials. Perhaps most importantly, it was an attractive stone and added even more beauty to the finished form.

If one stops to think about it, what an amazing thing that these banner forms do not appear out-dated or old-fashioned or primitive or crude. Most of the forms are made in a highly artistic manner that follows the timeless rules of good art. These artifacts, thousands of years old, will be just as attractive thousands of years from now.

BALL-TYPE BANNERSTONES, left to right: Brown banded slate, LaPorte County, Indiana; 1¾ x 2⅛ inches. $175
Brown banded slate, Clinton County, Ohio; 2¼ x 2⅝ inches. $300
Green banded slate, Delaware County, Ohio; 2 x 2 inches. $300
Courtesy Gerald Bernacchi collection, Indiana

TUBULAR BANNER, Archaic period, in a green and black banded slate, with centering bands on the faces. It is 1⁵⁄₁₆ x 3⁵⁄₁₆ inches, good size for the type, and from Ohio. Fine example. $500-750
Courtesy Dennis Bushey collection, Alabama

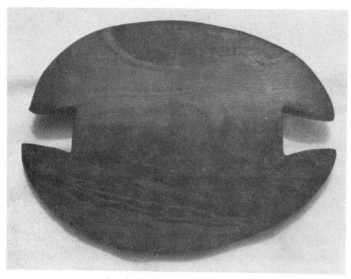

NOTCHED OVATE BANNER, Archaic period, and one of the rarest bannerstone family members. Made of green and black banded slate, it is 3⅝ x 4¹⁵⁄₁₆ inches. From Marion County, Ohio, and ex-coll. Dr. Meuser. This is a fine example. $3500-5500
Courtesy Dennis Bushey collection, Alabama

PANEL BANNER, Archaic period, from Miami County, Ohio. It is 1³⁄₁₆ x 3¼ inches, made of green and black banded slate. This example has the elongated or oval central hole instead of the round hole in most other bannerstones. Ex-coll. Steere, and a classic piece. $1200-2500
Courtesy Dennis Bushey collection, Alabama

BALL BANNER, Archaic period, nicely banded in green and black slate. It is 2 x 2¹/₁₆ inches, from Ohio, and ex-coll. C.C. Smith. This is a scarce bannerstone form. $350-750
Courtesy Dennis Bushey collection, Alabama

REEL-SHAPE BANNER, Archaic period, a rare bannerstone form. Made of green and black banded slate, this piece has fine shape and excellent banding. It is 1⁷/₁₆ x 4⅝ inches, is from Ohio, and ex-coll. Steere. It is classic for the type. $2500-5000
Courtesy Dennis Bushey collection, Alabama

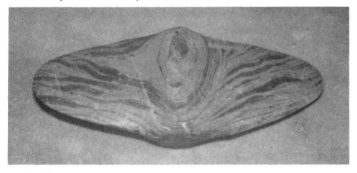

WINGED BANNERSTONE, provenance unknown, brownish slate with black markings. This piece, 3 x 5½ inches, is completed except for the central drill-hole. The left wingtip has been restored. This type is usually found in a large area south of the Great Lakes.
Courtesy Lawson Corley collection, Alabama $250-300

PICK BANNER, excellent banding pattern, probably ca. Middle Archaic. From Ohio, this piece is ex-coll. C.C. Smith. Material is green and black banded slate, and size is 1³/₁₆ x 3⅝ inches. This is a fine example of a scarce bannerstone form. $400-800
Courtesy Dennis Bushey collection, Alabama

ELLIPTICAL WINGED RIDGED BANNERSTONE, made of banded slate. It is 2⅞ x 4⅞ in. wide, from Richland County, Ohio, and ex-coll. Dr. Gordon Meuser. The banding pattern has been kept in regard during manufacture to accent the beauty of the artifact itself, adding to total attractiveness. Fine piece. $3500-4200
Private collection, Ohio

FLUTED-BALL BANNERSTONES, all Ohio, all banded slate. Bottom example, 2¾ x 2⅞ inches. Banner on left is pictured in Knoblock's *Bannerstone* book, while others are ex-colls. Parks, Wehrle and Knoblock. These are highly sought-after specimen with good banding. $250-850
Courtesy Len & Janie Weidner Collection, Ohio

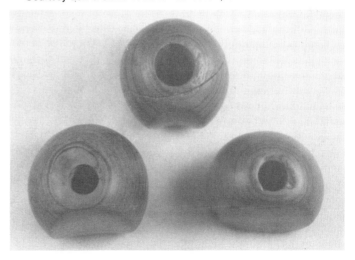

FLUTED-BALL BANNERSTONES, all Ohio, all made of banded slate. Left example, 2½ x 2¾ inches. From old-time major collections, Copeland, Wehrle and Shipley, these are classic examples. Top center specimen has been broken and glued, but is still a fine piece.
Courtesy Len & Janie Weidner Collection, Ohio $250-850

31

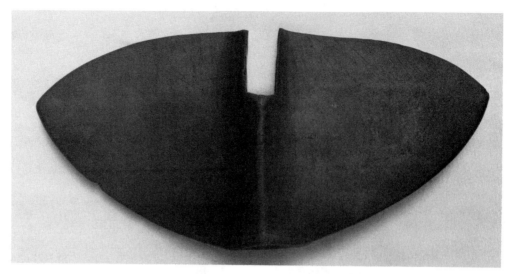

SINGLE-NOTCH BUTTERFLY, one of the rarest bannerstone forms. At 3⅛ x 6½ inches, it is above-average in size. Material is black banded slate. From Pickaway County, Ohio, it is ex-coll. Copeland. This has classic shape, is a highly refined form, and is one of the finest examples ever found. $4000-6000
Courtesy Dennis Bushey collection, Alabama

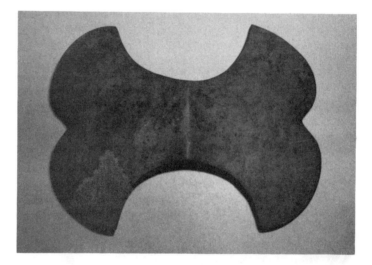

NOTCHED OVATE BANNERSTONE, 4½ x 6 inches, mottled slate material. It is from the Harkis Farm, Orange County, Indiana. Ex-coll, Ed Parks. This is a large and fine speciman. $2000-$4000
Courtesy Marguerite L. Kernaghan collection;
photographers Marguerite L. & Stewart W. Kernaghan

Chapter 8
GORGETS

The word gorget means an ornamental collar or section of armor that protects the throat (gorge). Gorget is a perfectly good word, and as employed to describe Amerind artifacts, it is correct in two of three applications.

One is when the prehistoric decorated shell gorget-pendant of the Southern U.S. Mississippian peoples is meant. Another is when the historic trade-era metal (copper, sheet-silver, brass) gorget is meant, this copied from European military officer's accoutrements. Other true gorget forms also exist.

However, the word gorget used to describe a great class of prehistoric artifacts is almost certainly incorrect. Early investigators and writers had other names for gorgets. They were also called shuttles in the belief they were once used in weaving. Other names included sizers, for thread (supposedly pulled through the holes), and gauges (supposedly for net-making). Still another use was guessed to be rope-makers, with the gorgets whirled to wind together cords passing through the holes. No one has seriously proposed such uses for at least half a century. Some of the more objective early explorers simply reported the artifacts as ''drilled panels'', ''perforated tablets'' or words with similar meaning.

Gorgets, and the word seems to be with us for good, tend to be long, narrow and flat, at least on one face. Ends, except for a few rare classes – and whether squared, rounded or somewhat pointed – tend to be similar. One or more holes, but usually two, are drilled in the center and equidistant from the ends. Both faces are usually treated the same, but one may be more flattened, or even somewhat concave. Engraving is present on a few complete specimens, but this was more often done on broken gorget pieces or on damaged specimens.

Many different materials were used to make gorgets, and slate is the most common. This may be quarried material from the area, or beautiful banded or striped slate in a wide variety of colors. Hardstone was also used, though rarely, plus shales, ivory, shell and bone. In the Eastern U.S., steatite (soapstone) was often used, and in the Southeastern U.S., greenstone was sometimes employed.

Gorgets in one form or another are widely found across North America. Beyond the basic form described, there are dozens of types, some of which are quite thick and asymmetrical. Most tend to have at least one flat face. Many of the gorget forms are from Late Archaic times through Woodland times, or, 2500 BC - AD 1000 or so.

Here is a partial listing of some of the major gorget types. It should be noted that many of the plainer forms can only be generally assigned to the 3500-year gorget period; they are not otherwise sufficiently diagnostic of any one culture or time-period.

Biconcave
An Adena (Early Woodland) gorget type, this form has incurved sides and ends that are slightly to very excurvate. Some forms may be rather thick. Banded slate is the common material in glaciated areas. A few forms seem to have definite top and bottom, the top surface being somewhat excurvate, the bottom incurvate. Most biconcaves are drilled with two holes. A few examples were made of highly unusual material, such as native copper pounded into shape.

Boat-shaped
From Middle Woodland and Hopewell times, this gorget form does look like a double-ended watercraft. It has excurvate sides that taper to rounded ends. Two-hole verions are the most common type, and these may be drilled close to the ends. The top face is rounded, the bottom face flat. Note that boat-shaped gorgets are a different artifact class than are boat-stones, another type altogether and which was made from Archaic through Woodland times.

Clipped-corner
Hopewell in origin, these are a minority type though basic and rectangular in form. The distinctive feature is that one pair of diagonally opposing corners has been cut off at an angle. The other corners terminate in somewhat squared configurations. Sometimes instead of being clipped, one pair of opposing corners is notched.

Concave-ended
Sides for the gorget form may be nearly straight but more likely are a bit excurvate. Both ends terminate in rounded points, and the area between the ends is slightly to deeply concave. This form may be smaller in size than average, some specimen being only three inches long. Two holes are typical for the concave-ended type.

Eliptical
Another Adena form, this gorget has very excurvate sides which converge to form somewhat squared or even pointed ends. Some examples are quite long, up to six inches in length. Most specimen are made of glacial slate. This is a scarce Early Woodland artifact, especially in undamaged condition due to the size.

Expanded-center Adena
The most common Adena gorget form is the expanded-center, and there are a number of varieties. These are flat on the bottom, wide and thick at center, and taper to narrowed, thinner ends. A major type (the classic Adena form) is drilled with two holes to either side of the central expansion. On many of these (and other thick) gorgets, Adena-style drilling was done. Here, the drill-hole entered from one side only, the bottom. The emerging top drill-hole was thus kept quite small, though it is occasionally reamed out somewhat.

The alternate Adena form is very similar to the just-described gorget except that it lacks the drilling. Some persons tend to view such specimens as being incomplete or unfinished. However, they are indeed finished and polished, but evidently no drilling was ever contemplated.

Still another Adena expanded-center form may be drilled or undrilled, and has unusually narrow ends. Yet additional varieties may be flattened instead of rounded, and about ½ inch thick. Generally shorter than the classic specimen, this sub-type can also exist in drilled and undrilled versions. All expanded-center gorgets, like the entire class, are almost certainly *Atl-atl* stones.

Expanded-center Hopewell

This form is quite rare compared with the wide range of Adena expanded-center gorgets. The Hopewell form may be less long, with relatively wide ends, and these sometimes flare slightly before termination at the gently excurvate ends. Some specimen are also less thick at center. Variations of this Hopewell gorget may have the typical two holes, no hole, or rarest of all, a single hole in the center of the expansion.

Glacial Kame

A Late Archaic people of the Indiana-Michigan-Ohio region, the Gravel Knoll or Glacial Kame people buried their dead in the high, rounded kames left by glaciers. The gorget forms (*Atl-atl* stones) of these Indians are quite different and distinctive, this in three ways.

The gorgets are often thicker, or longer (or both) or have highly unusual configurations. Among the diagnostic types are the coffin, constricted, humped, oval, sandal, and spined or knobbed. Even though many of the types are highly different from the usual gorget forms, it is assumed they were attached to the lance-throwing stick in the same manner. This would be on the underside, with location averaging about halfway between handle and hook.

Indented-sides

This is a scarce type with wide rounded or squared ends, and ca. 1500 BC - AD 100. The mid-section on both sides is cut out in a shallow squared to rectangular opening. Forms with rounded ends then have eight distinct edges, while those with squared ends have twelve. Rounded-ends are more common. The surfaces of the indented-sides gorgets are flat to gently excurvate.

Quadriconcave

Also Adena, this type may be an elaboration of the biconcave form. Here, not only the sides are incurvate, but both of the ends as well. Some examples are fairly thick, and most are also quite wide. The majority of specimens are drilled with the usual two holes. Ultimate forms may have inspired the reel-type gorget.

Rectangular-plain

The classic rectangular-plain gorget form is usually from Late Archaic through Woodland times. This most common of all gorget forms has slightly excurvate sides, somewhat squared ends, flattish faces and two drill-holes. The most common materials are slate of many kinds, shale, siltstone and other semi-hard materials. This form may range from over two inches to over seven inches in length.

Rectangular-enhanced

This again is the common and basic gorget form, plus any major differences or additions. The difference may be extra-fine material, such as any of the colorful hardstones, or extreme thinness. The enhancement may be the addition of tally-marks on edges or incised markings of almost any kind on the faces. A few gorgets of this type are a bit convex on the top, a bit concave on the bottom.

Reel

Middle Woodland in origin, this is a rare type with deeply concave sides and ends. While the side indentations are usually larger or longer, all may at times be somewhat similar, giving the whole piece an ''X''-shaped configuration. Again two drill-holes are common for the type.

Salvaged Gorgets

Many gorgets seem to have been hard-used in prehistoric times, lending support to the theory that they were *Atl-atl* stones. Salvage took a number of forms. A broken half might be reground to form a smaller gorget or reshaped to become a one-holed pendant. Occasionally the original artifact was broken, and the pieces fastened together. This can be seen by the presence of smaller drill-holes along the line of the original break. Glue was likely also used, but few traces of such adhesive remain.

Semi-keeled

Early Woodland or Adena in origin, this is an unusual *Atl-atl* stone. The bottom or base is rectangular, the top convex from front to back. The sides were then faceted, ground off at an angle toward the top. The sides were then faceted, ground off at an angle toward the top. This gives the appearance of a short but thick artifact, the typical dimensions being about 2 x 3⅓ x 1½ inches thick. As with many other Adena artifacts, high-grade sandstone was sometimes used for the type. Two holes, drilled from the bottom, are standard.

While a distinction between gorgets and pendants has always been made – that gorgets have two or more holes, are long in comparison to width, and have similar ends – such is not always the case. Some gorgets have dissimilar ends and some are short and wide. Some have four or five holes, some none.

There are entire classes of undrilled gorgets and these may have no obvious signs of attachment, or may be grooved or notched or both. Most gorgets do not seem to be personal adornment as such, but decorated the owner's *Atl-atl* or lance-throwing board. Some examples certainly appear to be too large or too fragile even for such use, and may be more ceremonial than utilitarian.

Whatever these so-called gorgets once were, they are beautiful works of prehistoric art today.

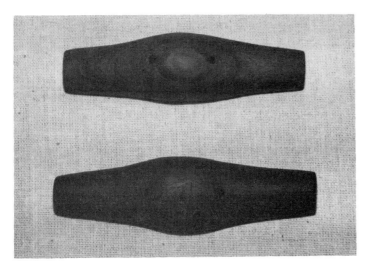

EXPANDED-CENTER GORGETS, Adena Indian (Early Woodland) in origin.
Top, grey banded slate, Miami County, Ohio; 1½ x 5¼ inches.
$450
Red slate, Clark County Ohio; size 1½ x 5⅜ inches. This piece also has four incised marks between the drill-holes. $600
Courtesy Gerald Bernacchi collection, Indiana

GRANITE TWO-HOLE GORGETS, left to right:
Size 1¾ x 3⅝ inches, from Saline County, Missouri. $350
Size 1⅝ x 3¼ inches, this piece is from Illinois. $325
Size 1⅞ x 4¼ inches, from Adams County, Illinois. $400
Courtesy Gerald Bernacchi collection, Indiana

HUMPED TWO-HOLE GORGET, black steatite, 1⅛ x 4¼ inches. From Montgomery County, Ohio $400
EXPANDED-CENTER TWO-HOLE GORGET, black steatite; there is a ridge between the holes. Size 1¼ x 3½ inches, from Montgomery County, Ohio. $325
Courtesy Gerald Bernacchi collection, Indiana

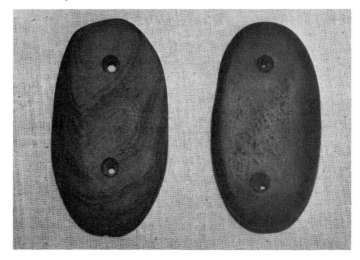

TWO-HOLE OVAL GORGET, left, green banded slate. From Logan County, Ohio, it is 2½ x 4½ inches. $225
TWO-HOLE OVAL GORGET, the material is red slate. Size, 2¼ x 4⅜ inches. From Posey County, Indiana, it is ex-coll. Cameron Parks. $225

Courtesy Gerald Bernacchi collection, Indiana

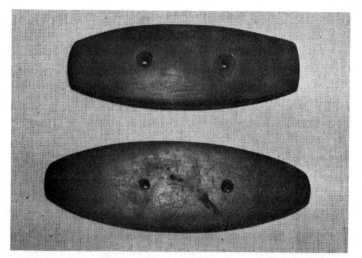

TWO-HOLE GORGET, top, made of unusual red slate. From Darke County, Ohio. Size, 1⅞ x 5¼ inches. This is a minority type of material for gorgets. $350
TWO-HOLE GORGET, bottom, made of black slate. From Monroe County, Ohio, it measures 1⅞ x 6 inches long. Gorgets of this size are not common. $350
Courtesy Gerald Bernacchi collection, Indiana

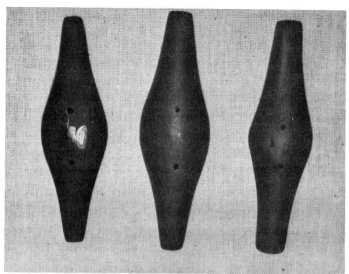

Expanded-center gorgets, Adena (Early Woodland) period, all l. to r.: Dark grey banded slate, Seneca County, Ohio; 1½ x 5 inches. $450
Grey banded slate, Allen County, Indiana; 1⅝ x 5¼ inches. $550
Grey banded slate, from Indiana; size, 1½ x 5¼ inches. $375
Courtesy Gerald Bernacchi collection, Indiana

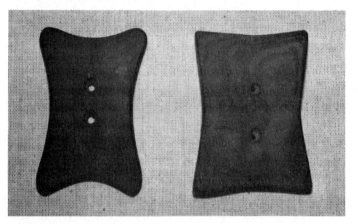

QUADRICONCAVE GORGETS, Adena Indian (Early Woodland) period; l. to r.: Brown banded slate, Paulding County, Ohio; 2 x 3½ inches. $350
Green banded slate, St. Joseph County, Michigan; 2¼ x 3¼ inches.
Courtesy Gerald Bernacchi collection, Indiana $350

RECTANGULAR HOPEWELL GORGET, hardstone, made of pink and grey speckled granite with an inclusion of black hornblende. From Will County, Illinois, size is 2 x 4⅝ inches. The material and colors combine to make this a very attractive artifact. $450-650
Private collection, Ohio

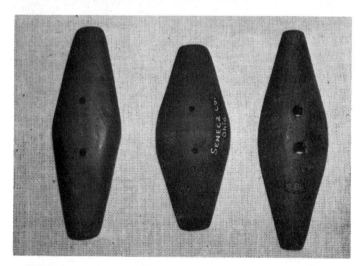

EXPANDED-CENTER GORGETS, all Adena (Early Woodland), l. to r.: Green banded slate, Floyd County, Indiana, 1½ x 4½ inches.$375
Center, Seneca Co., Ohio $300
Blue banded slate, Montgomery Co., Indiana, 1½ x 4⅞ inches.$425
Courtesy Gerald Bernacchi collection, Indiana

CONVEX-SIDED RECTANGULAR ADENA GORGET, made from a rare material, speckled granite in rose, pink, cream and black. From Ross County, Ohio, size is 2⅞ x 4½ inches. Adena gorgets are rarely seen in such fine hardstone material. This is a very pleasing piece.
                                                                     $650-950
Private collection, Ohio

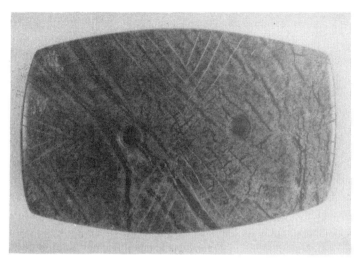

QUADRICONVEX RECTANGULAR GORGET, done in olive-green serpentine with black veining. It is 2⅜ x 3¹¹⁄₁₆ in. long, from Stark County, Ohio, and ex-coll. Max Shipley (#675). This is a very beautiful artifact and very interesting due to the engraved lines on all four face sides. Rare piece. $1500-2100
Private collection, Ohio

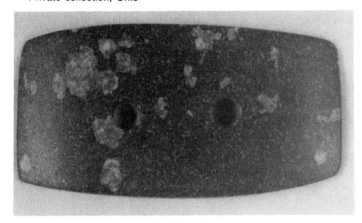

CONVEX-SIDED RECTANGULAR ADENA GORGET, made of porphyry, a rare material for the type. It is 1⁹⁄₁₆ x 3⅛ inches long, and from Licking County, Ohio. A very attractive and well-made item. $250-450
Private collection, Ohio

ELLIPTICAL TWO-HOLE GORGET, found in 1902 in Grant County, Indiana. It has an old inscription with this information. Material is pale green serpentine with black inclusions, and size is 1⅞ x 4¹¹⁄₁₆ in. long. This is a well-made piece with interesting colors. $450-700
Private collection, Ohio

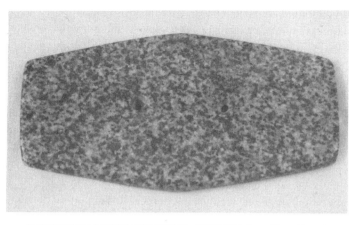

EXPANDED-CENTER HOPEWELL GORGET, from Ross County, Ohio. It is made of black, cream and pinkish-orange speckled granite and is 2⅞ x 4½ in. long. This is a highly polished and beautiful piece with the drilling done mainly from one face similar to the Adena-style. $750-1100
Private collection, Ohio

ADENA GORGET (Early Woodland) in a beautiful hardstone material which is a mottled black and cream. This two-hole example is ca. 300-400 BC and is from Holmes County, Ohio. Length of this fine specimen is 6 inches. $700
Courtesy Private Collection of Sam and Nancy Johnson, Murfreesboro, Arkansas

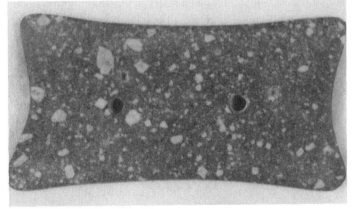

QUADRICONCAVE ADENA GORGET, Early Woodland time period, hardstone, made of grey and tan porphyry. Size is 1¹¹⁄₁₆ x 3¼ in. long, and artifact is from Warren County, Missouri. This is a well-made piece in rare material for type, and an attractive specimen. $450-700
Private collection, Ohio

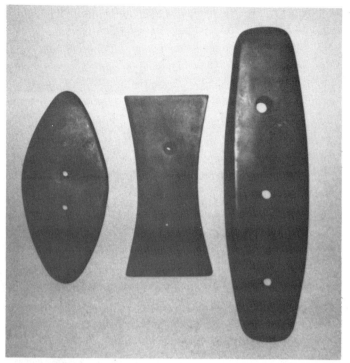

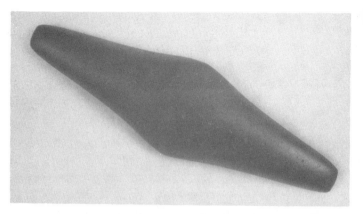

EXPANDED-CENTER ADENA GORGET, made of dark red jasper. Size is 1¹³⁄₁₆ x 6⅛ in. long. It is from Ohio and ex-coll. Phil Kientz. While undrilled, this is a fine, large, well-finished artifact in a very rare material for the type. $500-750
Private collection, Ohio

GORGETS, all left to right:
Black slate, Little River, Trigg Co., KY, 2 x 4¾ inches. $200-300
Banded green and black slate, Scioto Co., Ohio, 2¼ x 4½ inches, from Early Woodland (Adena). $300-400
Hematite three-hole, well-polished, from Brown Co., IL, 2⅛ x 7½ inches. Unusual form. $400-500
Courtesy Marguerite L. Kernaghan collection;
photographers Marguerite L. & Stewart W. Kernaghan

GORGETS, all from Tennessee. Left, Monroe County, grey siltstone, unfinished, ¼ x 2¼ x 2¾ in. $35
Middle, oblong type, Sevier County, steatite, ¾ x 1½ x 3 in. $135
Right, unfinished bar-type, Monroe County. Material is light and dark green banded slate, size ¼ x 1½ x 3 inches. $25
Photo courtesy Blake Gahagan, Tennessee

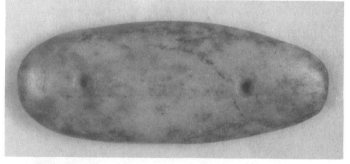

BOAT-SHAPED HOPEWELL GORGET, Middle Woodland period, in tan-cream quartzite with brown mottling. It is 1⁹⁄₁₆ x 4⅛ in. long, from Marion County, Ohio. Ex-coll. Dr. Gordon Meuser, it has the hole-drilling started but not completed. A fine piece in a scarce material. $300-450
Private collection, Ohio

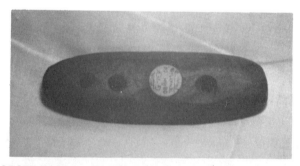

GORGET, 3-hole example, from Obion County, TN. Material is a red ferruginous shale. This artifact may have once been longer and was reworked or salvaged. The gorget is covered with tiny incised lines. Ex-coll. Edward Payne and John Waggoner. Size, ¼ x 1⅜ x 4¼ inches. $200
Photo courtesy Blake Gahagan, Tennessee

HOPEWELL TWO-HOLE GORGET, Middle Woodland period, made of quartz-jasper conglomerate hardstone. It is 1¹¹⁄₁₆ x 4⅝ in. long, Hancock County, Illinois, and ex-coll. Piedritt. This piece has very fine coloring and the material is rare. $950-1300
Private collection, Ohio

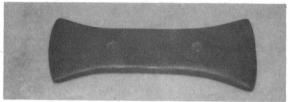

BICONCAVE GORGET, well-developed form, Adena (Early Woodland) in origin. It is made of grey mottled slate and came from the bank of the Tennessee River in Lauderdale County, Alabama. Size is 2 x 5 inches. $400-450
Courtesy Lawson Corley collection, Alabama

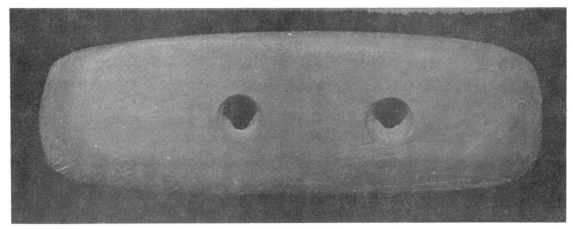

RECTANGULAR GORGET, from Indiana. This is a well-made and well-finished piece, in top condition. $300-375
Courtesy Larry Carter collection, Illinois;
photo by Philip Huntwork, Elgin, Illinois

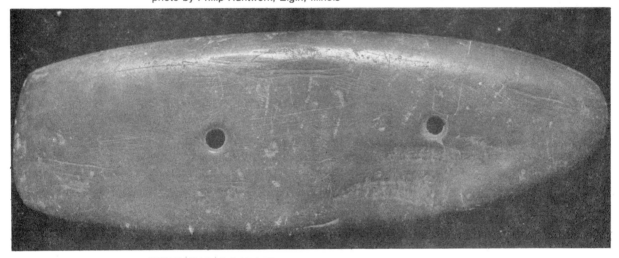

RECTANGULAR GORGET, from Indiana, one end is slightly wider than the opposite end. This is a nicely drilled example with good patina and large size. $225-325
Courtesy Larry Carter collection, Illinois;
photo by Philip Huntwork, Elgin, Illinois

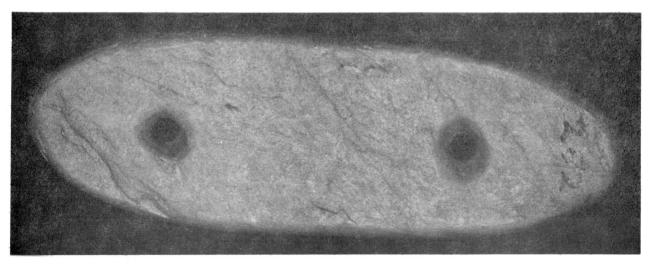

ELLIPTICAL GORGET, probably Early Woodland, found near Tazewell, Claiborne County, Tennessee. Ex-coll. Hughes (VA), this is a fine, large specimen made of a dark grey-green slate.
                    $250-350
Courtesy Larry Carter collection, Illinois;
photo by Philip Huntwork, Elgin, Illinois

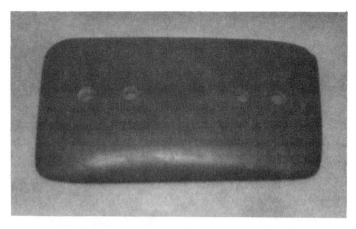

FOUR-HOLE GORGET, an unusual type, made of brown banded slate. It measures 2¼ x 4 inches and is from Ohio County, Kentucky. This may be a Woodland-era piece, with very high polish.
$400-500

Courtesy Lawson Corley collection, Alabama

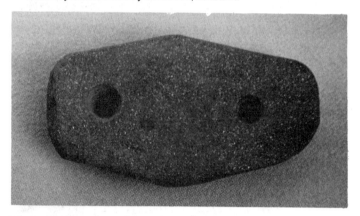

GORGET, made of gneiss (a hardstone that is granite-like, with layered minerals) and found on a campsite in Holt County, MO. The gorget's ends have been damaged and reworked in prehistoric times. Size, ⅜ x 2 x 4½ inches.
$45

Photo courtesy Mike George, Missouri

GORGET, quadriconcave type, probably Woodland period. It is made of quartzite and was a surface find in Holt County, Missouri. One corner was damaged by farm machinery. Size, ½ x 3¼ x 6½ inches.
$225

Photo courtesy Mike George, Missouri

TWO-HOLE GORGET, dark hematite, highly polished. Possible Midwestern U.S., it measures 1¾ x 4 inches long. This is a nicely made and finished artifact.
$325

Photo courtesy Zell Adams collection, California

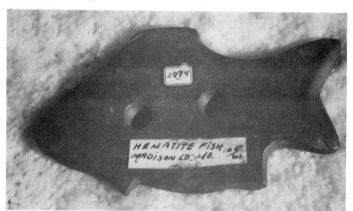

GORGET, fish effigy form, made of reddish-grey hematite. It is 2¾ x 5 inches long, from Madison County, Missouri. Ex-coll. Knoblock, effigy gorgets are scarce artifacts.
$400

Photo courtesy Zell Adams collection, California

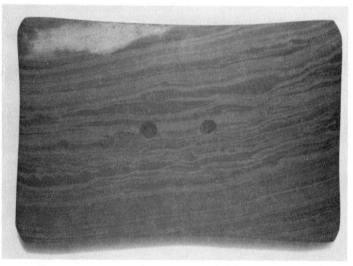

QUADRICONCAVE GORGET, Adena (Early Woodland) in origin. Note the very attractive banding and the light-colored incision. Blue and black banding, size 2⅞ x 4⁵⁄₁₆ inches. Ex-coll. John Berner, and from Anderson County, Kentucky. This is a superb example.
$1000-1500

Courtesy Dennis Bushey collection, Alabama

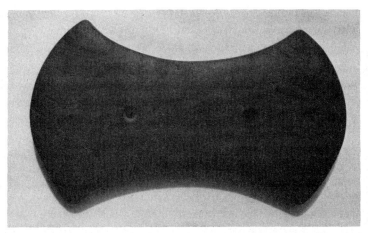

BICONCAVE GORGET, Adena (Early Woodland) period. This is a very fine, very symmetrical example made of purple and black banded slate, 2⁹⁄₁₆ x 4⁷⁄₁₆ inches. Holes are nicely matched and positioned; from Ohio, and ex-coll. Archie Diller. $750-1000
Courtesy Dennis Bushey collection, Alabama

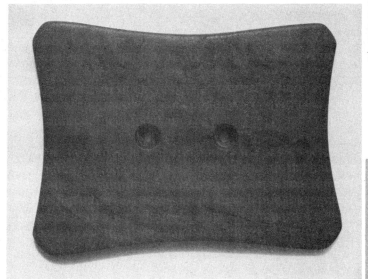

QUADRICONCAVE GORGET, Adena (Early Woodland) origin, a large and fine example. Size, 2⁷⁄₈ x 3⁷⁄₈ inches, ex-coll. Copeland. It is from Franklin County, Ohio. Note the classic touch at the corners, which are also very slightly straightened. A fine piece, and pictured in *Ohio Slate Types*. $750-1000
Courtesy Dennis Bushey collection, Alabama

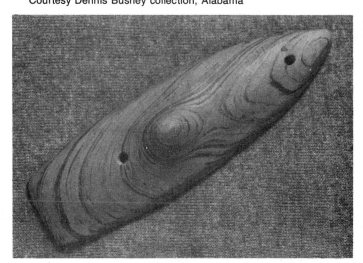

HUMPED GORGET, Glacial Kame Indian (Late Archaic) in origin, green and black banded slate. This has fine size and shape with excellent banding that focuses on the centered protrusion or hump. Size 1¾ x 5⁹⁄₁₆ inches, Ohio, ex-coll. Copeland. $2000-3000
Courtesy Dennis Bushey collection, Alabama

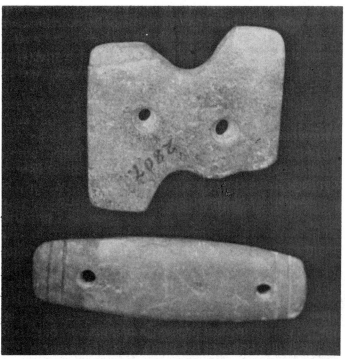

TWO-HOLE GORGETS.
Top, diorite material, rare form, 3 x 3 inches. It is drilled from both faces and is from Randolph County, Arkansas. $35-50
Bottom, red jasper, from Lawrence County, Arkansas, near Hardy. It is 1⅜ x 4½ inches; note the parallel decorative lines near each end. It is drilled from one face only. $250-$325
Photo courtesy James M. Dethrow collection, Arkansas

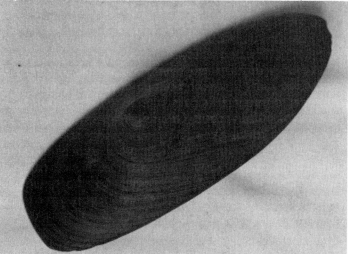

HUMPED GORGET, Glacial Kame Indian (Late Archaic) artifact. Material is a green and black banded slate, with bands that converge in the humped area. Size 1¾ x 4¾ inches, from Seneca County, Ohio, and ex-coll. Dr. Meuser. Good size, condition and shape, with fine banding. $2000-3000
Courtesy Dennis Bushey collection, Alabama

41

Chapter 9
PENDANTS – STONE

With the possible exceptions of face-painting, scar designs and tatooing, the pendant is certainly one of the oldest forms of human body decoration. All that was required was a suitable object and a way to secure that object around the neck. A few pendants were notched or grooved, but the cord could stretch and the pendant could slip and be lost or damaged. So, the majority were drilled to provide a single (rarely, two or more) suspension hole.

Stone pendants are found in one form or another all across North America (plus Central and South America), and from the earliest times (Paleo) to the coming of European trade goods (Contact). The pendants range from simple pebble forms to the large and elaborate and beautifully made pendants of Woodland times. The widest range of pendant types in terms of easily discernible classes appears to have been made in the 1000 BC - AD 1000 time frame..

Many different kinds of materials were used for stone pendants. Slate in a great variety of colors, monochrome to varigated to striped, was a favorite material. Hardstone was also employed, as was hematite, quartzite, and much else. No matter the stone, somewhere, sometime, a pendant probably exists made of that substance.

Though the pendant family is huge in terms of numbers, there are a relatively few basic types that can easily be recognized. This is because the pendant form itself in stone tends to be a fairly simple one. Most are small to medium-size (one to four or five inches long) and have one hole near one end. Other known pendant forms have two side-by-side holes, or one above the other. Even three or more holes are known, but by far the most common type is the one-hole, almost always above the center of gravity for that particular specimen.

In terms of design change over the thousands of years, the Archaic pendants seem to have a wider range, and are in a bewildering number of styles, often with only minor differences. They also tend to be smaller and thinner than in later times, and some do not exhibit the time and care lavished on some later pendants.

The golden age of Eastern U.S. pendants certainly arrived with Woodland times, ca. 1000 BC - AD 1000. Then, pendants tended to become large, very well-made and in approximately a dozen styles that are quite distinctive. For most of the Woodland examples it is possible to separate the types into Early Woodland (Adena) and Middle Woodland (Hopewell). Some Late Woodland forms existed, but in many cases they are less well defined.

And while Woodland pendants command the most collector attention, it is well to remember that the average pendant is not necessarily one of the large and fine ''named'' Woodland types or varieties. Instead, it is average in size and workstyle, and from an uncertain time-period which is likely to be either pre-Woodland or post-Woodland.

Another difference is that while Woodland pendants tend to be made of select grades of glacial slate, Archaic pendants (though many indeed are of glacial slate) are often made of lesser grades. A possible reason for all this is that Archaic people seem to have concentrated their skills more on the *Atl-atl* stones and less on pendants. In short, pendants simply seem to have become more important in Woodland times, this possibly relating to the practice of widespread agriculture. There were certainly more people and probably a greater emphasis on personal appearance relating to status.

Adena Pendants

Bell – With a squared top, the sides expand gradually to a considerably wider base. The base line is straight to slightly excurvate. Some examples of the type are quite large.

Biconcave – No doubt related in design to the biconcave gorget or weight, also Adena, this pendant form has a nearly equal top and base. Both sides are incurvate to the same degree, and there is one hole near one end.

Flared – This form has a smaller top (where the hole is positioned) and a wider base, itself nearly straight or excurvate. The sides flare out, the degree ranging from slight to dramatic.

Keyhole – One of the more attractive pendants, the top is squared and the form's sides straighten to create rounded base-corners. The combination gives rise to many different varieties, but the squared top and rounded base remain.

Hopewell Pendants

Shield – With slightly excurvate topline, the sides are incurvate but expand. These terminate at opposite side-points and thereafter drop in excurvate lines to meet at the base center. Some better forms have one slightly excurvate obverse and a slightly incurvate reverse; that is, the front is slightly rounded.

Shovel – There is a narrow, rectangular top and approximately two-thirds the distance toward the base the sides are abruptly expanded and/or hooked. The edges thereafter drop to a squared baseline, usually the widest pendant part. There are many sub-varieties.

Adena and Hopewell – Similar Pendant Types

Anchor – With a squared or rounded top, this form expands near the base, which becomes the widest part. This in turn forms the baseline, pointed or at least well-rounded.

Convex-sided – Tops and bases are about the same width, and the corresponding edges are straight to slightly excurvate. The pendant sides are convex, excurvate, and the size range is from small to medium.

Additional Pendants

One of the classic pendants for the Mississippian period Fort Ancient culture is the fringed pendant. This is a small triangular form with deeply cut notches on the baseline. Probably, this is a stylized form of the "weeping eye" motif found so frequently in Mississippian-related cultures.

Still another popular form in most of prehistoric America is the triangular pendant. It is a simple design and there are many variations. The top is so narrow as to be almost pointed, and the base is quite wide. Some examples are extremely well-made, while others are less so.

So-called pebble pendants are found all across North America. For the most part, they are not true pebble pendants, for the stone was usually modified to some extent before drilling. This might be flattened somewhat on both faces or edge-modification or contour-changing.

For most pendants, the actual drilling seems to have been the last step, as some otherwise finished examples lack only the suspension hole. The cord itself may have been braided grasses or twined inner bark from certain trees, examples of just such cordage having survived in dry rock shelters. Also available were thin strips of leather thongs and sinews.

Once stone pendants were made, a very small percentage of them were further decorated. A great favorite was the addition of the so-called tally marks. They were named this from the belief that the marks must represent a count or score. More likely it was simply decorative. The marks are usually small, regular edge-marks or notches, and they range from very light to very deep. Something in favor of the marks-as-decoration theory is that often the marks balance on a piece, being either around the entire side or emphasizing a certain portion (as, base) of it. One would assume that true counts in many cases would be unbalanced and partial.

Incising or the cutting of thin lines into the pendant face was done occasionally. Usually the lines are somewhat geometric, whether regular or meandering. The rare forms may suggest animals or birds, while the rarest incising depicts humans; sometimes, the latter are merely stick-like figures.

The size and style range of stone pendants is great. As a rough comparison, early forms were small to medium-sized and fairly crude, while examples from Woodland times were large and comparatively ornate. At least for some of the later periods and specimens, some examples are so large, thick and heavy that it is difficult to accept that they were anything but special-occasion decorations. It is certainly impossible to prove that they were ceremonial items, but it is just as impossible to consider them as day-to-day wear.

Stone pendants also included other materials. Examples are pipestone (Catlinite from Minnesota, various shades of pipestone from Ohio's lower Scioto Valley and from Erie County, and from other areas), steatite or soapstone and turquoise. Whatever purpose pendants served in whatever prehistoric time-period, their range and beauty attracts collectors today.

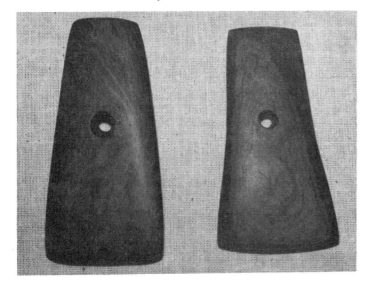

TRAPEZOIDAL PENDANT, left, Woodland or Mississippian time frame. Green banded slate, 2½ x 5 inches, Kent County, Michigan, ex-coll. Cameron Parks. $500
BELL-SHAPED PENDANT, right, Adena (Early Woodland) period. Size, 2½ x 4⅝ inches, from Noble County, Indiana, and made in a green banded slate. $350
Courtesy Gerald Bernacchi collection, Indiana

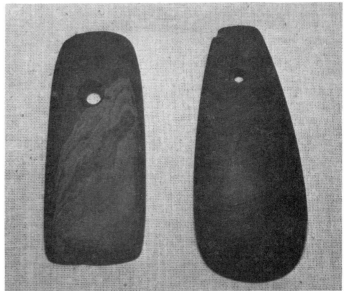

SLATE PENDANT, left, green banded material, size 2⅛ x 4⅞ inches. This artifact is from Michigan. $200
SLATE PENDANT, right, brown banded material. Size 2⅜ x 5⅜ inches, and from Kalamazoo County, Michigan. $150
Courtesy Gerald Bernacchi collection, Indiana

PENDANTS, all left to right:
Black slate, 1¾ x 2¼ inches, from Missouri. $30
Brown hardstone, 1½ x 2½ inches, from Trigg County, KY. $75
Brown hardstone 1⅝ in. high, from LaPorte County, Indiana. $15
Black slate, 1¾ x 2⅝ inches, from Missouri. $25
Courtesy Gerald Bernacchi collection, Indiana

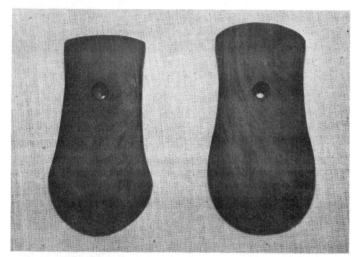

KEYHOLE PENDANT, left, Adena (Early Woodland), made of brown banded slate. Size, 2 x 4 inches, from Crawford County, Indiana.$325
KEYHOLE PENDANT, Adena (right), Early Woodland period, made of green banded slate. This is an extra-large and fine specimen. Size 2¼ x 4¼ inches, from Randolph County, Indiana. $475
Courtesy Gerald Bernacchi collection, Indiana

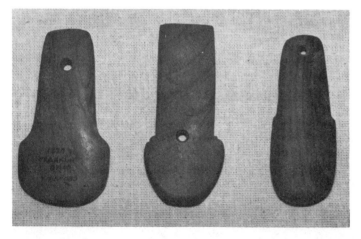

SHOVEL-SHAPE PENDANTS, (Hopewell Indian), Middle Woodland, all l. to r.:
Grey banded slate, Franklin County, Ohio; 2 x 3¾ inches. $175
Grey banded slate, Beaver County, Pennsylvania and ex-coll. Cameron Parks. Size, 1⅝ x 3¾ inches. $275
Grey banded slate, Seneca County, Ohio, 1⅜ x 3½ inches. $150
Courtesy Gerald Bernacchi collection, Indiana

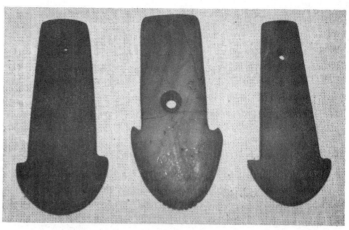

ANCHOR PENDANTS, Woodland period, all left to right:
Grey banded slate, from Indiana, 2 x 4½ inches. $325
Green banded slate, from Ohio, 2⅛ x 4½ inches. $275
Brown banded slate, from Indiana, 1⅞ x 4⅛ inches. $275
Courtesy Gerald Bernacchi collection, Indiana

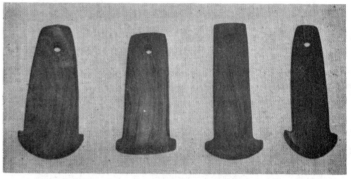

ANCHOR PENDANTS, Woodland, all l. to r.:
Brown banded slate, from Indiana and ex-coll. Warner, 1⅝ x 3½ inches. $350
Grey banded slate, Parke County, Indiana, ex-coll. Parks; size is 1½ x 3⅛ inches. $300
Grey banded slate, Rush County, Indiana, 1½ x 3⅝ inches. $300
Brown slate, from Michigan, ex-coll. Warner, 1½ x 3½ inches. $225
Courtesy Gerald Bernacchi collection, Indiana

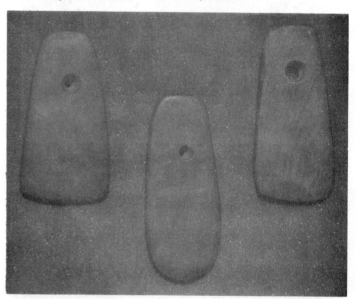

PENDANTS, three fine examples in slate. Large examples with well-done drill-holes are top collector items. Provenance, left to right: Kentucky, Indiana and Indiana. Each, $200-350
Courtesy Larry Carter collection, Illinois;
photo by Philip Huntwork, Elgin, Illinois

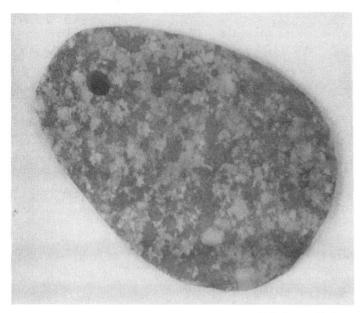

TRAPEZOIDAL PENDANT, in cream, orange and black speckled granite. From Delaware County, Ohio, size is 2⁵/₁₆ x 3³/₁₆ inches high. This pendant is very well made in hardstone and is nicely finished in a quality material. $300-500
Private collection, Ohio

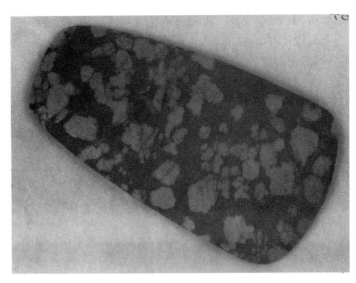

TRAPEZOIDAL PENDANT, rare hardstone example in beautifully marked porphyry. It is 2⅛ x 3 ¹⁵/₁₆ in. long, and from Union County, Illinois. This is a well-made and very attractive piece. $550-850
Private collection, Ohio

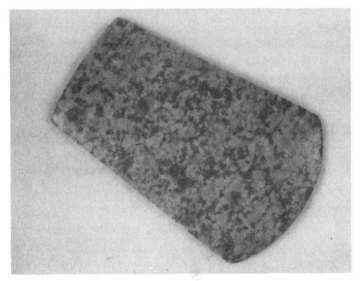

CONVEX-BASE BELL-SHAPED PENDANT, of black, cream and tan speckled granite. From Knox County, Kentucky, it is 2⁹/₁₆ x 4¹/₁₆ in. long. This fine hardstone ornament is well made and very highly polished, overall a rare artifact. $650-900
Private collection, Ohio

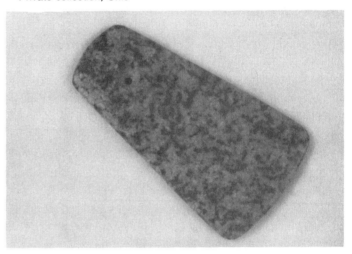

TRAPEZOIDAL PENDANT, in black, pink, cream and tan speckled granite. From Richland County, Ohio, it measures 2¹/₁₆ x 3¹¹/₁₆ inches long or high. This is a very well-formed piece with crisp, clean lines and fine finish. Very attractive artifact. $500-850
Private collection, Ohio

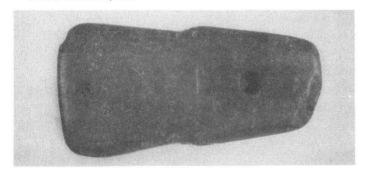

PENDANT, brownish slate, from the Eastern Midwest. Size is ¼ x 2 x 3⅞ inches, and there is slight damage to areas of the side and top. This artifact is probably late in prehistory. $75
Private collection

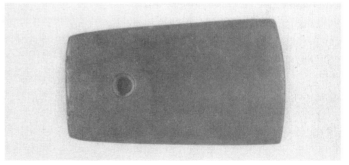

SLATE PENDANT, central Ohio, made in the Woodland period. It has a well-made centrally positioned drill-hole. Ex-coll. Wehrle, size 1¾ x 3¼ inches long. $195
Hothem collection, Ohio

45

TRAPEZOIDAL HOPEWELL PENDANT, in tan, black, rose and grey speckled granite. From Ross County, Ohio, it is 2½ x 6¹¹/₁₆ in. high. This was found in 1928 and is ex-coll. C.T. Love. It is extremely large for a hardstone pendant, which adds both to appearance and value. Fine piece. $950-1500
Private collection, Ohio

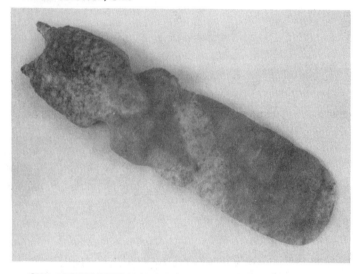

OWL EFFIGY PENDANT, material a black, grey and tan chlorite. It is 1¹/₁₆ x 3¹⁶/₁₆ in. high, and came from southcentral Kentucky. Somewhat of a mystery, this piece has definite characteristics from Costa Rica, Central America, where similar designs were made. Very unusual for area found, and a fine piece. $850-1100
Private collection, Ohio

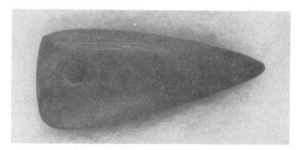

PENDANT, one-hole, compact brown slate material. Size, ⅞ x 2¼ inches with light coating of red ochre (powdered hematite) on top and one side edge. $30
Private collection, Ohio

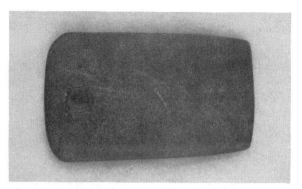

RECTANGULAR PENDANT, black hardstone, ¼ x 1¼ x 2¼ inches. This small but well-made piece is from Coshocton County, Ohio. $40
Private collection

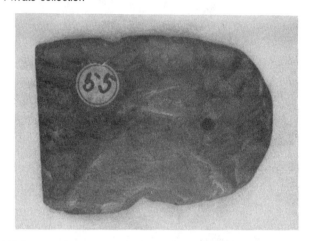

PENDANT, grey banded slate, from the Eastern Midwest. Size, 1⅝ x 2⅞ inches, ground off straight across the base. While polished, this piece is not particularly well finished and has some edge damage. Unknown old collection or museum number. $20
Private collection

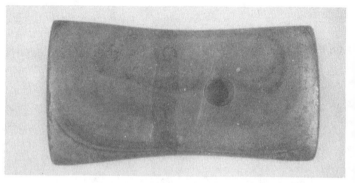

BICONCAVE PENDANT, probably Adena (Early Woodland) in green banded slate. This piece, ⅜ x 2⅛ x 4⅛ is from Crawford County, Ohio, and ex-coll. Max Shipley (Garth's No. 81). A fine piece$275
Private collection, Ohio

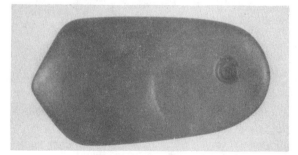

PENDANT, dark green slate with reverse inclusions of cream and black. Size, ¼ x 1¾ x 3½ inches. It is from Richland County, Ohio, and is possibly Woodland in origin. This is an unusual pendant form.
Private collection, Ohio $100

BICONCAVE PENDANT, probably Adena (Early Woodland) from Auglaize County, Ohio. It is ½ x 2 x 4⅛ inches, unusually heavy for size. This is a well-made and highly polished piece in mottled grey slate.   Courtesy private collection $225

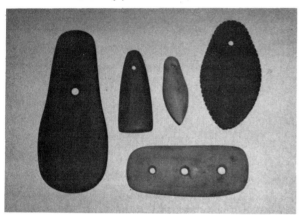

PREHISTORIC DECORATIVE ARTIFACTS.
Left to right, top row: Pendant, cannel coal, Little River, KY, 2⅜ x 5¾ inches. $250
Slate pendant, OH, 1⅛ x 2¾. $100
Drilled plummet, ¾ x 2¼ in. $175
Edge-tallied pendant, Marshall County, Kentucky, 2⅛ x 3¾ inches.
                                                     $250
Bot. right, 3-hole gorget, stone, Omaha Co., Nebraska, 2⅝ x 4⅛ in.
                                                     $200
Courtesy Marguerite L. Kernaghan collection;
photographers Marguerite L. & Stewart W. Kernaghan

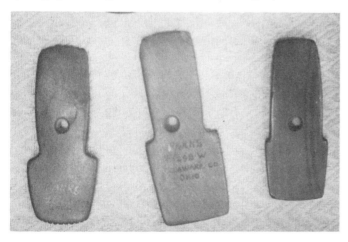

SHOVEL-SHAPE PENDANTS, center, also called spade-shaped. Middle Woodland or Hopewell in origin, these are a scarce ornament type. The off-center hole in central piece is not unusual for prehistoric drilling. All Eastern Midwest, and ex-coll. Cameron Parks, Indiana.
                                                     Unlisted

Lar Hothem photo

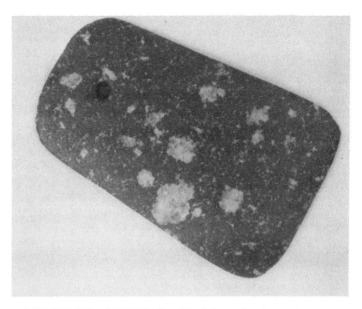

BELL-SHAPED HARDSTONE PENDANT, made of speckled porphyry, light on dark. It is 2⁵⁄₁₆ x 3⅝ inches, and from northwestern Kentucky. This piece has clean, dramatic lines and is a very well-made artifact. $500-750
Private collection, Ohio

ENGRAVED PENDANT, from Bucks County, Pennsylvania. Engraving on a drilled pebble pendant is very unusual, and this is a rare piece. Size, 1 x 1½ inches. $150
Courtesy Lee Fisher collection, Pennsylvania
Anthony Lang, photographer

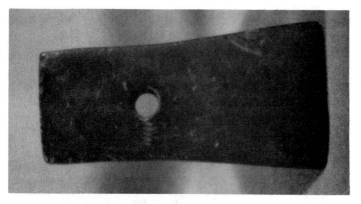

BELL-SHAPED PENDANT, red slate, one large hole. This piece is Adena, Early Woodland period, and from Allen County, Indiana. Length for this well-finished pendant is 4 inches. $250
Courtesy Lee Fisher collection, Pennsylvania
Anthony Lang, photographer

PENDANT, made of diorite. It is a surface-find from Holt County, MO. Size is ¼ x ¾ x 1½ inches long. $50
Photo courtesy Mike George, Missouri

PENDANT, turtle-effigy form, from Holt County, Missouri, campsite. It is ½ in. thick and slightly larger than a silver dollar. It is made of Catlinite, or red pipestone from Minnesota. Catlinite was widely traded by Indians both in historic and prehistoric times. $225
Photo courtesy Mike George, Missouri

PENDANT, found on a campsite in Holt County, Missouri. This hard-stone piece is made from granite and is ⅜ x 1¾ x 4 inches long. $65
Photo courtesy Mike George, Missouri

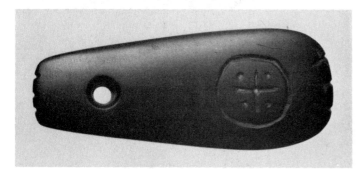

ENGRAVED PENDANT, ca. 4000 - 1000 BC. Material is a compact black hardstone that took a high polish, and size is 39 x 98 mm. Engraved pendants are quite rare and this piece is from Hardin County, Tennessee. Ex-colls. Furr (MS) and Callaway (LA). $1200
Photo courtesy Chris Callaway collection

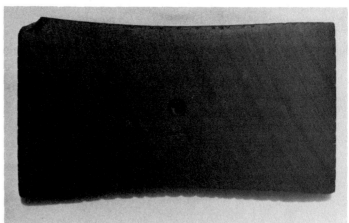

BELL PENDANT VARIANT, unusual form with hole about centered instead of being nearer one short side (top). Note the tally-marks on edges. Size, 2¹¹/₁₆ x 5⅛ inches; one corner was damaged and was smoothed in prehistoric times. From Ross County, Ohio, good large size. $600-1000
Courtesy Dennis Bushey collection, Alabama.

48

SHOVEL-SHAPED PENDANT, Hopewell Indian (Middle Woodland) period. Good size, 1½ x 4⅞ inches, compact glacial slate. This piece is rare for several reasons; one is the material, red slate, and the example has two holes instead of the typical one. From Athens County, Ohio, and ex-coll. Cameron Parks. $750-1000
Courtesy Dennis Bushey collection, Alabama.

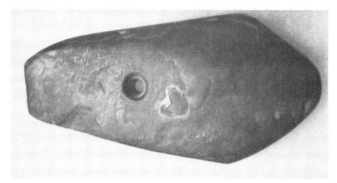

PENDANT, greenstone, from Berks County, Pennsylvania. This is a well-drilled nicely polished piece with good patina. Bower collection.
          $75

Photo courtesy Lee Hallman, Pennsylvania

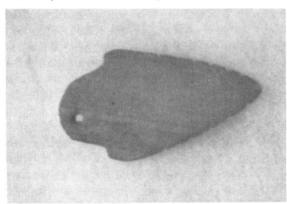

PENDANT, made of river pebble material, drilled for suspension. It is from a site on the Little Tennessee River, Loudon County, TN. Tallymarks on sides may represent serrations found on some chipped knives and points. Size, ⅛ x 1 x ⅞ inches. $60-90
Photo courtesy Blake Gahagan, Tennessee

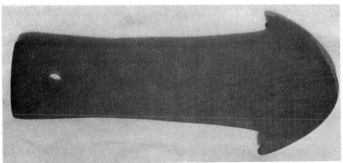

ANCHOR PENDANT, Early and Middle Woodland periods, good size and shape on this piece. Size 1⁵⁄₁₆ x 4⅞ inches, green, blue and black banded glacial slate. Ex-coll. C.C. Smith, from Ohio. Attractive banding form, top condition. $750-1500
Courtesy Dennis Bushey collection, Alabama.

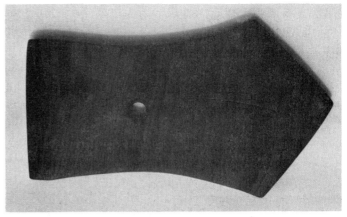

PENTAGONAL PENDANT, (also called shield-shaped) from Late Hopewell times; size is 2⁷⁄₁₆ x 4⁵⁄₁₆ inches. Material is a green and black banded slate, well-polished. Ex-coll. Zuber, from Butler County, Ohio. Excellent banding patterns, clean shape and top condition make this a superior piece. $750-1500
Courtesy Dennis Bushey collection, Alabama.

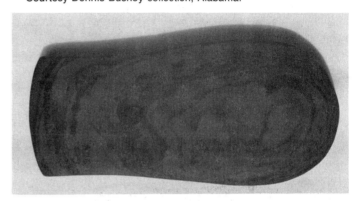

KEYHOLE PENDANT, Adena (Early Woodland) in origin. This piece measures 2¹⁄₁₆ x 4½ inches and is typically thick for type and very well made. Blue and black banded slate, with an unusual pattern; ex-coll. John Berner, and from Montgomery County, Ohio. $500-1000
Courtesy Dennis Bushey collection, Alabama.

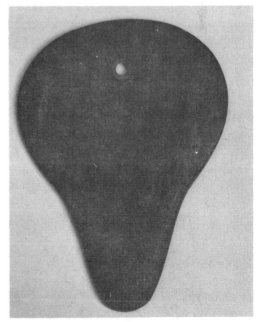

PENDANT, hardstone, found by Dale Guy in Mississippi County, Arkansas, in 1974. This piece not only has an unusual shape, but the hole is drilled in the end opposite where it normally would be positioned. Size, 2¼ x 2⅞ inches. $200
Courtesy Guy Brother's collection, Pinckneyville, Illinois

49

Chapter 10
PENDANTS – OTHER MATERIALS

As one of the major prehistoric decorative artifacts, pendants were made of many materials other than hardstone and glacial slate. Almost anything attractive and durable could be, and was, worked into pendant forms.

Antler was sometimes used, but this ultra-durable substance was more often reserved for tools – wedges, projectile tips, handles and flaking rods. Not so with bone, and many pendants were made of this material. Bone pendants had three suspension methods, notching, grooving and holing. One or more of these attachment methods might be used with any one piece, but the most common by far was perforation with a drilled or reamed hole.

Cannel coal (sometimes incorrectly referred to as ''canal'') is a soft, black bituminous coal. It got the name for an original use, ''candle'' coal, as it burns readily. This jet-like material is lightweight, somewhat fragile, worked easily, and took a very glossy polish. Beads were sometimes made from cannel coal and some thin discs of unknown purpose.

Claws (from animals) and talons (from birds) were often used for necklaces, necklace elements and pendants. Large carnivorous animals and birds of prey were the favored material types when such goods could be obtained.

Copper was occasionally used for decorative pendants, but this was another material (depending on the prehistoric culture) that might more often be reserved for either tools or other ornamental objects. In some areas (Eastern Mound Builders) it is difficult to determine if smaller, holed artifacts were suspended as pendants or sewn to clothing or other objects. Clothing-decoration is suspected in many cases. Copper, sometimes in combination with other metals, was much-used in Central America for pectorals or pendants and was often melted and cast into shape. Perhaps because of the green color of oxidized (patinated) copper, small frog-pendants were a favorite Meso-American design form.

Gold was another Central and South American material, and it was highly valued because of the color and the number of ways it could be worked. Some decorative artifacts were cold-hammered into shape, but gold (sometimes alloyed with other metals) could also be melted and molded into shape. Some sophisticated gold-working methods were developed, including beading and filigree.

Hematite (iron ore) exists in a number of shades and grades. Reds and yellows were closer to paint grades, while steel-blue, greys and blacks were often used for tools. Pendants seem to have been made of various grades, and tend to be mainly of the materials available. Since the hematite (''blood-like stone'') is very heavy, most pendants are not large.

Jade was much-used in prehistoric times, but mainly in limited geographic areas. One was the Pacific Northwest, where it was mainly relegated to tool use (often for adz blades) though some ornaments were made. Central America was an entirely different story. There jade had a valued and honored role, but mainly for ornaments. Jade is an ultra-hard material, difficult to work, but very attractive and capable of taking a very high, long-lasting polish.

Jade exists in a number of colors, many of them green. Jade also tends to be translucent, allowing the passage of light. This translucent quality ranges from near-transparent to a jade artifact that is translucent only at a thin edge. Colors may be solid, mottled or swirled. The ancients had many names to describe the colors of jade, among them the green of parrot feathers, young corn leaves and the deep-water sea. The Olmecs, when they could find the material in mountain streams, used a rare blue-green jade.

Pendants in many different styles and sizes were made throughout Central America. Even then, jade was scarce (at least the best grades) and so pendants were made from almost any stone that was green or had traces of green. But jade was also used in almost any form, including raw nuggets. Then, only two steps were required to complete the pendant. One end was drilled with a small hole, and the surface was polished.

One of the favorite pendant forms in the Costa Rican region was the Axe-god. Actually the blade form is that of an adz, and the features combine that of birds(?) (some say an owl) and humans. The adz blade forms the lower part of the pendant figure. Most have highly stylized features and a long beak above crossed or folded arms. The backs are flat to excurvate, and the suspension hole is drilled cross-wise in the neck area.

Jade was considered so precious that it was never wasted. A large jade pendant was sometimes cut in half longtitudinally, or even quartered. This was done with stone sawing (sandstone slab) or string-sawing (cord impregnated with sand). This last is a fascinating technique that could actually cut around corners.

Mica, also known as isinglass, is a mineral that divides easily into flat, semi-transparent sheets. It was favored by the Hopewell Indians who made some elaborate cut-out forms from it. Mica was imported into the Ohio Valley from the southern Appalachian region.

Pottery, a totally human-made material as opposed to a natural material, was also used for pendants. A few pendants were molded and baked in a pre-designed shape, sometimes with a design marked or painted on the surface. More common, especially in the Southwest, was to create a pendant from broken pottery shards. A hole was simply drilled near an edge, and the predecorated piece was ready to wear.

Rock crystal or clear quartzite was used to some degree. Mound Builders of the Midwest used it occasionally for rare, carved objects such as hemispheres or cones, and effigy boatstones. Less elaborate forms were made in

50

earlier times, and on small pendants the drill-holes can be so small that flint drills could not have made the holes. Probably drills of thorns with grit abrasive were used.

Shell was almost universally used for pendants, especially among Coastal groups. Freshwater shell was also often used. However, shell was widely traded in prehistoric times, and large seashell artifacts can turn up almost anywhere in North America. In terms of time, shell was most widely used in the period Late Archaic through the Mississippian period.

Glacial Kame Indians of the Eastern Midwest made large three-hole ''gorgets,'' actually very likely pendants, in a variety of sizes and shapes. One example is the ''sandal-sole,'' which may be up to 8 to 10 inches long. Drilled with the multiple in-line holes, the actual method of suspension is unknown. Some examples are incised or are carved with unknown patterns, though at least one has a bear in raised cut-out against a lower background. These shell gorgets were apparently so important that copies were actually made in glacial slate.

The Woodland-era Indians used shell for a number of pendant-like artifacts, though some were undoubtedly secured to leather or woven-fabric clothing. Mississippian-period Indians made thousands of shell ''gorgets,'' also probably pendants, in countless shapes. Usually the objects were carved in elaborate, stylized forms.

Silver, in prehistoric times in North America (it could be mined in South America) was found interspersed with Great Lakes copper, or was recovered from the glacial drift. Nuggest of silver seem to have been kept mainly as curiosities, and it was not widely used by itself. Silver was sometimes used to layer or coat other artifacts, especially wood or copper, and the Eastern Mound Builders were expert at this. In late historic times, much silver was worked by Southwestern artisans, and a number of techniques and styles developed.

Teeth, being small, bright and hard, were almost ready-made for pendants and necklace elements. These included the teeth of deer, elk, bison, fox, wolf, cougar and bear. The Hopewell Indians specialized in the use of imported (from the Plains and Rocky Mountains) grizzly bear canine teeth. Up to three inches long, these large tusks were worked in a number of ways, including cutting, sectioning, pinning and drilling.

A usual technique was to place freshwater pearls in large, counter-sunk holes in the teeth. Even shark teeth, both examples from extant sharks and fossil-finds, were drilled as pendants. Barracuda jaws and wolf mandibles were also cut, polished and made into pendants.

Turquoise was a favored Southwestern material for pendants, and was mined and worked from very early times. Turquoise, a semi-precious stone, was ground, shaped and drilled. Use included raw-nugget shapes and finely finished forms in various bird. animal and mythical-being representations.

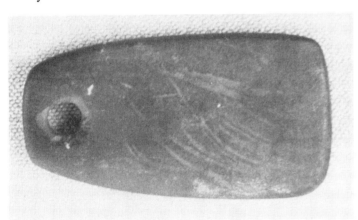

PENDANT, made of hematite (iron ore), found in Holt County, Missouri. It is 5/16 x 5/8 x 1 1/4 in. long. The single suspension hole shows considerable wear. $45
Photo courtesy Mike George, Missouri

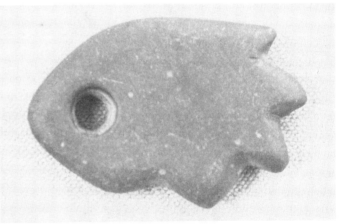

PENDANT, from Holt County, Missouri. It is made of Catlinite (red pipestone) and is 1/8 in. thick and a bit larger than a nickel. A similar piece is described by Gary Fogelman in the 1989 April-June issue of *Indian Artifact Magazine*. This is an unusual and scarce piece.$95
Photo courtesy Mike George, Missouri

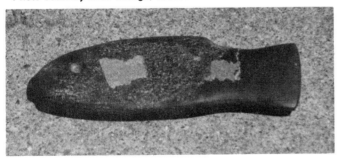

PENDANT, fish effigy form, made of dark hematite. This piece, possibly from the Midwestern U.S., measures 1 1/4 x 3 7/16 in. long. Note how the hematite has exfoliated on the body portion, a sign of age and environmental factors. $225
Photo courtesy Zell Adams collection, California

PENDANT, grey-black hematite, polished surface. This piece, possibly Midwestern U.S., is 1 7/16 x 3 3/8 inches. $150
Photo courtesy Zell Adams collection, California

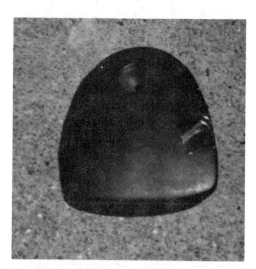

DRILLED PENDANT, black hematite, highly polished overall. Size is 1⅝ x 2 in. high; unusual pendant material, and a nice piece. Possibly Midwestern U.S. $125
Photo courtesy Zell Adams collection, California

DRILLED PENDANT, blackish-red hematite, with large suspension hole. It is 2 x 2⅝ inches, possibly Midwestern U.S. Hematite pendants are unusual. $85
Photo courtesy Zell Adams collection, California

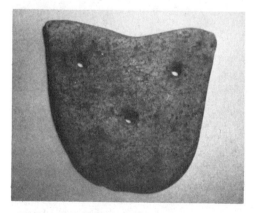

POTTERY GORGET OR PENDANT, three-hole, from Marshall County, Kentucky. Size is 2½ x 3 inches. This may or may not be a face effigy; unusual. $70-95
Courtesy Marguerite L. Kernaghan collection;
photographers Marguerite L. & Stewart W. Kernaghan

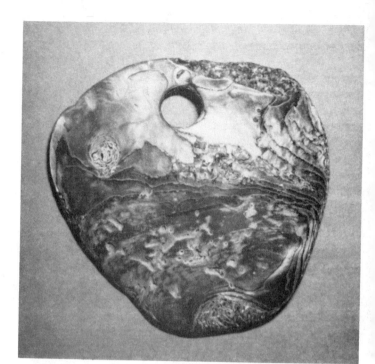

PENDANT, abalone shell (Haliotis species), from California. It is 3 x 3 inches, and multicolored. California Indians made many shell artifacts due to proximity to seashells of many kinds. An interesting piece. $50-100
Courtesy Marguerite L. Kernaghan collection;
photographers Marguerite L. & Stewart W. Kernaghan

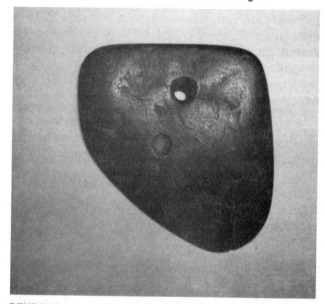

PENDANT, cannel coal, single suspension hole and with eye and mouth indicated on both sides. From Lyon County, Kentucky, it is 2½ x 3 inches. Pendants with animal features are very scarce. $125-175
Courtesy Marguerite L. Kernaghan collection;
photographers Marguerite L. & Stewart W. Kernaghan

PENDANTS OR ORNAMENTS, Tellico site, Monroe County, Tennessee. These were made from the cut-off ends of marine conch shell whorls and were then drilled for attachment or suspension. Average sizes, ⅝ x 1 x 1¾ inches.   Each, $15-30
Photo courtesy Blake Gahagan, Tennessee

Chapter 11
PERISHABLE PREHISTORY

While many ornaments were made of various stones, antler, shell, and bone, entire classes that were once common barely exist today. Only a few isolated examples have survived the centuries. Many items of personal adornment – bracelets, pendants, necklaces, earrings, etc. – were made of highly perishable materials in whole or in part. These are not normally found today; here are some examples of very rare decorative artifacts.

In 1935, when dry rock-shelters were excavated in Menifee County, Kentucky, some fragile artifacts were found. A deer-tooth was fastened to a short cord of bark fiber. It could have been a dangle or pendant, but was possibly associated with the remains of a nearby wooden cradleboard. If so, it may have been a decorative toy or a prehistoric pacifier. Another ornament was a well-polished piece of dried fungus, secured to a string, exact use unknown.

While not strictly a personal ornament but decorative nonetheless, a woven bag was found in an ''ash cave'' in Lee County, Kentucky, in 1929. The bag was ''. . . beautifully fashioned . . .'', had a top tie-string, and was 3 by 6 inches. It was filled with dried, shelled chinquapin nuts.

In Kentucky and Ohio dry rock-shelters, many woven fiber sandals or moccasins have been found. They are attractive, sturdy and well-made. Two manufacturing methods were used, one being a large rectangular fabric piece which was folded to foot shape and then sewn at front and back. Moss and grasses have been found inside sandals, probably a prehistoric sole-cushion. Another method of making footgear was the fastening together of three separate pre-woven fabric pieces, sometimes with a different fabric for the top and bottom.

Echo Cave, Jackson County, Ohio, produced a vest-like garment of woven rushes which had a deerskin front. Echo Cave, by the way, was a large shelter, being 108 feet wide, up to 55 feet deep, and about 50 feet high in places. Echo Cave also had a pouch-like woven container, 7 x 7 inches, which held seven split deer-bone awls.

Ohio's Kettle Hill Cave, just south of Lancaster in Fairfield County, protected a very unusual artifact until 1925, the year of discovery. This was a feathered neckpiece, with twisted attachment cords still in place. The neck ornament was made up of owl and wild turkey feathers, interwoven with fiber cords. Few other objects like this have ever come from early sites.

Large wooden objects, except for the occasional watercraft, are exceptionally scarce from prehistoric times. One however, was found in Florida, probably in 1921. This ''wooden idol'' was plowed up in an area where the waters of Lake Okeechobee had formerly been about 6 feet deep. Large-sized, the wood type was listed as Lignum vitae a tropical tree with heavy, durable, resinous wood. The figure was that of a squatting, long-haired human, with hands clasped over the knees. Such objects certainly had some sort of decorative clan or community function.

At least one nicely carved wooden bowl came from an Ohio mound, with an age of close to 2000 years. Freshwater pearls, used for many decorative purposes – including eyes for some rare effigy pipes – have been found in Midwestern mounds. The pearls may specifically have been sought for their own ornamental value, or were simply found during prehistoric clam-bakes.

Associated indirectly with decoration, a primitive paintbrush was found in an Ohio rock-shelter. It consisted of a five-inch length of wild grapevine with a leather-wrapped end. A trace of red pigment was still on the leather. Swallow Shelter, in Utah, produced what may have been another paintbrush. This consisted of an approximately seven-inch long thin bundle of grasses with a cordage wrap near one end. As a complement, Hogup Cave, Utah, had a paint container, made of the tip of a bison horn. The horn section was about 5 inches long, and still contained some powdered red hematite.

Swallow Shelter also produced a leather ball which was packed with bark and hair, possibly an early game piece. In Remnant Cave, Utah, was found a total of nine arrow sections, some of which were decorated with colored paint bands. The paint colors were black and red.

Hogup Cave, besides the container, held a number of ornament-related early objects. Among them was a patch of hide with five fringes; four fringes contained one tubular bone bead each, while the fifth had two. Rabbitskin robes were found, and moccasins made from the knee-joint area of deer were recovered. Small highly stylized figurines of wrapped plant fibers had horns at what is probably the top end, the horns consisting of splintered bone, wood or cactus spines. Their exact purpose or function is not known. Sections of Atl-atl dart-shafts were found and painted examples were in green or red.

Not only moisture-excluding dry rock-shelters have preserved materials that under normal conditions (average moisture) deteriorate and disappear within a century or so. Fabrics (woven fiber clothing, some with painted designs) have been preserved in mounds by contact with copper plates or plaques. The copper salts acted as a preservative. Closely woven fabric (some as early as 5000 BC) has been found in Florida swamps where large sections served as burial shrouds. The site water had a high mineral, and a low oxygen content.

In at least one prehistoric Northwest Coastal village (Ozette, the state of Washington) occasional mud slides covered houses. This sealed off oxygen and preserved the entire artifactual content of the area. Weavings were made of cedar bark, cattail and dog hair. Many wooden items, from combs to clubs, were preserved intact and found nearly in the same condition as when they were used.

Most of what we know about pottery is the vessel itself. However, at Wetherill Mesa, Colorado, normally perishable materials add a new dimension. Some large pottery vessels were apparently suspended (or at least enclosed) in yucca-fiber nets, and had a circular fiber base-rest also attached. In the general Southwestern area, fine woven-cotton clothing has been preserved, probably made of imported wild cotton. Basketry items, including a pillow, have been found in the Mesa Verde region. In Lovelock Cave, Nevada, reed duck decoys were found, very natural-looking and some were decorated with feathers.

Many wooden figurines were found when areas of Key Marco, southern Florida, were excavated many years ago. Among the fantastic finds were a deer-head mask with large ears that could be moved. A sitting cat-like figure was recovered, and a painting of a stylized bird, done on a wooden panel. Other decorative artifacts included a wolf's head, pelican head and animal-human masks. These artifacts and many others were preserved in salt-water bogs, some of which once served as ponds and canals.

When the Spiro Mounds in Oklahoma were excavated, some highly decorative complete axes were recovered. Effigy forms of the pilated woodpecker, the copper celtiform heads were, in several instances, still encased in long wooden handles. Elsewhere in North America, a rare few axes with original handles have been found, most of these being later prehistoric celt-types, with heavy, carved wooden handles.

These few examples at least give some idea of the perishable material culture of prehistoric America. Many of the items were decorative and/or ornamental, and they are extremely rare today. So much has been lost that surviving artifacts may be but a fraction of what once existed long ago.

ORNAMENTAL ARTIFACTS, Alabama. Top left, vertebra bone drilled for suspension, ¾ in. diameter. $20
Top right, finger ring made of bone cross-section, polished, ½ in. wide, 1 in. diameter. $40
Bottom, bone section cut at ends to make elongated bead. $10
Courtesy Cliff Markley collection, Alabama

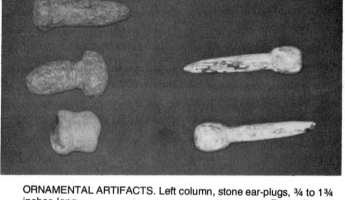

ORNAMENTAL ARTIFACTS. Left column, stone ear-plugs, ¾ to 1¾ inches long. Each, $15-40
Right column, matched pair of bone or ivory ear-plugs, 2 inches long. Pair, $95
Courtesy Cliff Markley collection, Alabama

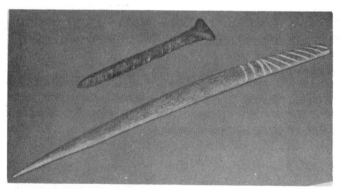

ORNAMENTAL ARTIFACTS. Top, flint hairpin or bodkin, 5 inches long, rare long size. $450
Bottom, bone hairpin or bodkin, incised-line decorations on end, 11 inches long. $125
Courtesy Cliff Markley collection, Alabama

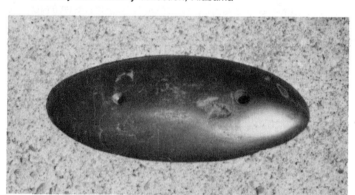

TWO-HOLED BOATSTONE, hematite, black high-grade material and well-polished. Possibly Midwestern U.S. $150
Photo courtesy Zell Adams collection, California

BOATSTONE, Late Archaic/Woodland period, drilled with the two typical conical holes. Size, 1⅛ x 3⅜ inches, material a green and black banded slate. From Ohio, this is a fine thin-walled and well-shaped specimen. $500-1000
Courtesy Dennis Bushey collection, Alabama

BOATSTONE, Late Archaic and Woodland period artifact, mottled granite. It is 1 x 3⅞ inches, and from Scioto County, Ohio. $500
BOATSTONE, grey banded slate, size 1⅛ x 4¼ inches. Found in Teagarden, Marshall County, Indiana. $475
Courtesy Gerald Bernacchi collection, Indiana

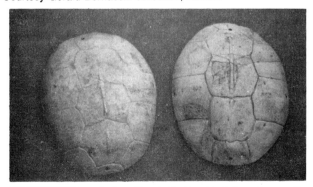

ORNAMENTS, made from the shell of land tortoises, from a site on the Clinch River in Anderson County, Tennessee. These were shaped and drilled at each end for attachment to the arms. Sizes, ¾ x 3 x 4 inches. Each, $60-100
Courtesy Blake Gahagan, Tennessee

ORNAMENTAL ARTIFACTS, both Texas. Top, boatstone of hematite, undrilled, Harrison County, size ⅝ x 1 x 2½ inches. $200
Bottom, Poverty Point type drilled bead, Bowie County, size 1 x 1½ inches. $50
Courtesy Willie Fields collection, Texas

CEREMONIAL BLADES from a Southwestern state, items found in 1959. The bottom blade is 7½ in. long. Large blades of this type and without use-marks are believed to have been ceremonial.
Courtesy private collection   Blades, ea. $800-1500

ORNAMENTAL ARTIFACTS. Top, pendant with three drilled holes on face, ⅛ x 2¼ x 3 inches. $40
Left, salvaged pendant. $15
Center, tally-stone grooved both faces, marked edges, unusual, from Cass County, Texas. $60
Right, salvaged pendant. $30
Courtesy Willie Fields collection, Texas

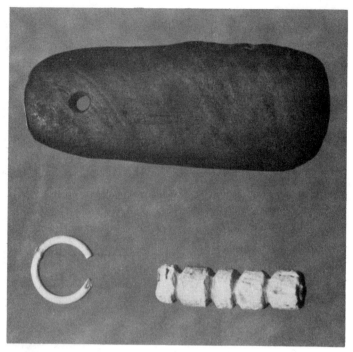

ORNAMENTAL ARTIFACTS. Bottom left, bone ring ⅞ in. diameter, Colorado, high polish. $25
Bot. right, carved bone, Colorado, 1½ x ⅜ inches. It is probably a preliminary stage of bead-making with beads ready to be cut off. $40
Top, pendant, Illinois, 1¼ x 3⅝ in., greenstone, polished. $50
Courtesy Larry Shaver collection, Oklahoma;
Larry Merriam, photographer

DECORATIVE ARTIFACTS, SOUTHCENTRAL U.S. Top, red cone, $5; loafstone, $30; brown cone, $8. 2nd row, undrilled pendant, $8; pendant, $20; gorget, $40. 3rd row, hematite, $15, incised stone, $30, preform gorget, $10. 4th row, sandstone cone, $4, polished cone, $35, greenstone cone, $4, discoidal, $25.
Courtesy Wilfred Dick collection, Mississippi

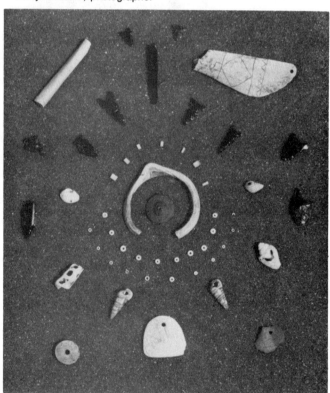

HEMATITE ARTIFACTS, all from Texas. Left and right, worked pieces that may be plummet preforms. Each, $35
Center, drilled plummet with break across the top above hole; size ⅞ x 1⅛ x 2¼ inches. $65
Courtesy Willie Fields collection, Texas

ORNAMENTS, a collage of Southwestern material including shell and bone beads, polished turquoise, shell bracelet and incised bone. Ca. AD 1200. Note the obsidian pendant at top center and ear-plug inside bracelet. Group, $150
Courtesy Larry Shaver collection, Oklahoma;
Larry Merriam, photographer

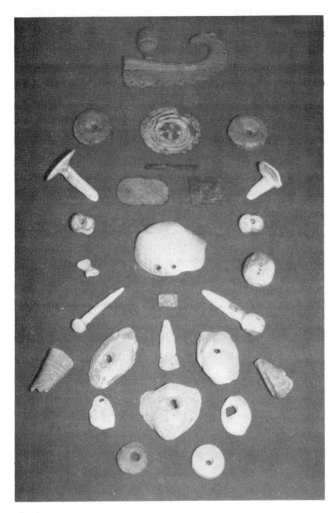

METAL AND SHELL DECORATIVE ARTIFACTS. The shell earplugs range, pair, to $175. Shell pins, $25. Top, brass trade-era pipe, Massachusetts, $200. Lower, copper ear-spools, pair, $175. Objects of copper and shell from prehistoric times are rare.
Courtesy Wilfred Dick collection, Mississippi

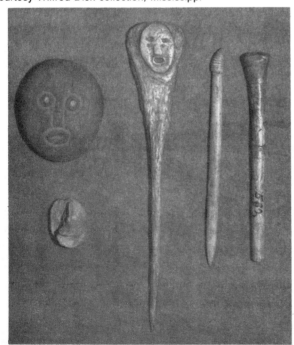

ORNAMENTAL AND DECORATIVE ARTIFACTS, from western New York state, Early Historic period. Antler effigy awl, $350-450; Stone face, $200-300; Small False Face head, $100-150; Bone awl, incised top, $50-200; Antler flint-faker, $50-75.
Courtesy private collection

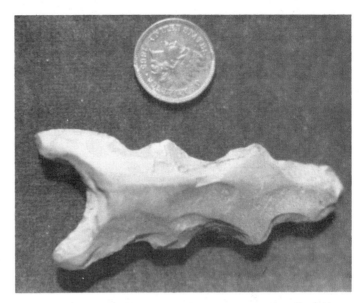

EFFIGY OR ECCENTRIC ARTIFACT, made of grey slate. Found by Darrell Thompson in Gregg County, Texas. It does not seem to be a weapon or tool, and the purpose or use is unknown. $50-75
Courtesy Darrell Thompson collection, Texas

PLUMMET, the name derived from a carpenter's look-alike plumb-bob. The provenance is unknown, but plummets are from the Archaic period and widely found. The piece illustrated is made of brown hard-stone and 1¼ x 3 inches high. There are many theories as to what these were, including use as a pendant. $100-150
Courtesy Lawson Corley collection, Alabama

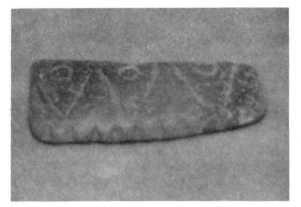

POTTERY OBJECT, with triangular lines and circles on top, notches on side. The use of such artifacts is not precisely known, but some were used as game counters or gambling tokens. Size, 2¾ inches long. $25-30
Courtesy Lawson Corley collection, Alabama

ENGRAVED DISC, Catlinite, from Missouri. It is a little larger than a silver dollar and edges are tally-marked. The surface has figures of a bird, fish and two mammals, dogs, foxes or wolves. From Holt County, MO. $150
Courtsy Mike George, Missouri

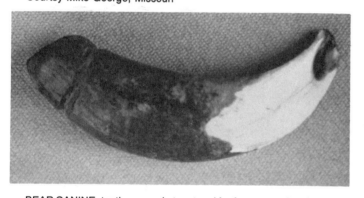

BEAR CANINE, tooth grooved at root end for for suspension. It was found in Holt County, Missouri, in a house floor. Bear-tooth necklace elements and pendants were favorite Indian ornaments of prehistoric times. $25
Photo courtesy Mike George, Missouri

DISCOIDAL, red hematite, barrel-type. Size is 2 x 2 inches, and the piece is from Illinois. There is a similar example on p. 82 of Moorehead's book on hematite artifacts. $350
Photo courtesy Zell Adams collection, California

FISH EFFIGY, black hematite, nicely carved and well-finished on both sizes. Size, 1⅝ x 4⁷⁄₁₆ inches, this may be a Midwestern U.S. piece. Ex-colls. Payne, Parks, Kirkley and Palmer. $425
Photo courtesy Zell Adams collection, California

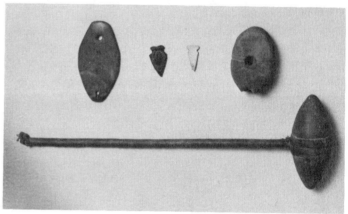

DECORATIVE ARTIFACTS, top, l. to r.: Two-hole gorget, tally-notched, 2 x 4 inches, Venango County, PA. $200
Hematite point, Clarion Co., PA $35
Point, clam-shell, Armstrong Co. $30
Pipe, drilled pebble, Clarion Co., PA $50
Bottom, "skull-cracker" club, 15 in. long, 4½ in. head, Seneca Indian, Warren County, PA. $300
Photo courtesy William E. Garis Sr. collection, Pennsylvania

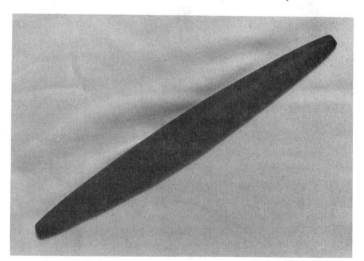

PICK CEREMONIAL, Intrusive Mound culture, Late Woodland period. These are very rare pieces, this example in purple and black banded slate. It is ¾ x 6⅝ inches, from Pickaway County, Ohio, and ex-coll. Seeley. A fine specimen, in top condition; it is pictured in *Ohio Slate Types*. $500-800
Courtesy Dennis Bushey collection, Alabama

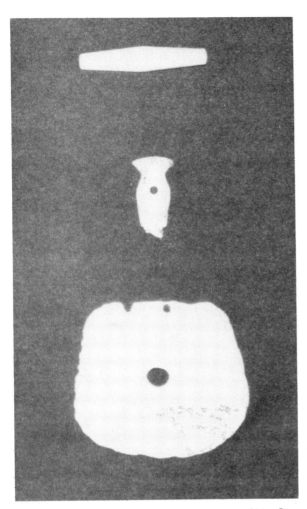

NECKLACE ELEMENTS (?) from a rockshelter, Ohio County, Kentucky. Top, bone polished bead, 2 inches long. $35-50; Middle, bone effigy, 1¼ inches, $50-75; Bottom, shell gorget with two suspension holes and decorative center hole, 3 in. diameter, $150-250
Photo courtesy Steven R. Dowell collection, Kentucky

LATIN AMERICAN DECORATIVE OBJECTS. Left and right, hard-stone effigies with features partially string-sawn. Each, $100
Center, necklace element, bronze, ax motif, Chimu, Peru, ca. AD 1300. $100
Courtesy Lawson Corley collection, Alabama

HEARTSTONE, a rare artifact believed to have been carried in a leather pouch around the neck. See p. 69 of *Indian Relics of North-east Arkansas and Southeast Missouri.* $100
Photo courtesy James M. Dethrow collection, Arkansas

EASTERN U.S. DECORATIVE ARTIFACTS, the upper pendant shown elsewhere in the book. Left, long and slender plummet, Virginia, $125. Right, incised object (phallic?) in sandstone, from western New York state, $50
Photo courtesy Lee Hallman, Pennsylvania

59

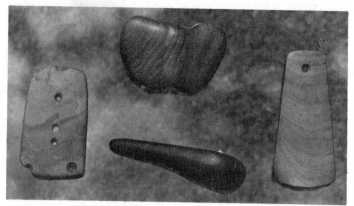

DECORATIVE ARTIFACTS, clockwise, top. Winged banner, Illinois, $350. Pendant, banded slate, 4 in. $250. Rattlesnake effigy, tail marked with circles, head with eyes and mouth. Unusual, gift to Chris Merriam from J.J. Culbertsen, Jr., $300. Gorget, Illinois, multiple holes, $90
Courtesy the Merriam collection

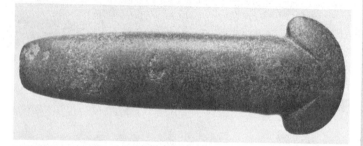

CEREMOIAL SPUD, collector identification no. 3123. From Greene County, Illinois, the piece measures 55 x 156 mm. Mississippian period, dark green hardstone, well polished, Ex-colls. Waters (IL), Thompson (MO), Morast (GA) and Callaway (LA). This is a superb ceremonial/ornamental piece. $2000-plus
Photo courtesy Chris Callaway, Louisiana

BOATSTONE, top view, from Crawford County, Ohio. This piece is unusual in that it is made of fine-grained sandstone and has a connecting cord-channel between the two holes. Ex-coll. Stanley Copeland. $300-500
Courtesy Larry Carter collection, Illinois;
photo by Philip Huntwork, Elgin, Illinois

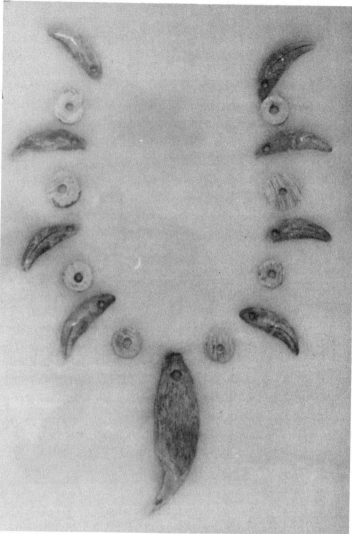

BEAR-TOOTH AND SHELL NECKLACE, from Lima, New York state area. It is believed to be historic, Seneca Indian and ca. AD 1640-1660.
The elongated objects are bear canines. This is a scarce set of necklace elements. $350-450
Courtesy Larry Carter collection, Illinois
photo by Philip Huntwork, Elgin, Illinois

Chapter 12
BEADS – PREHISTORIC

The earliest known American stone beads were undoubtedly drilled pebbles. These, with a minimum of work, could be strung on a sinew or thong cord. While stone bead use in Paleo (earliest) times probably occurred, so few sites have been thoroughly excavated that widespread use is somewhat conjectural.

Stone beads have been found on many Archaic-period sites, so their use certainly goes back at least 8000 years in the Americas. As with many artifact forms, the early beads were sometimes crude, somewhat tentative in form. Many specimen were little more than rounded river or glacial pebbles of the desired sizes, drilled through the center. But even these very old examples show that often colorful (attractive) and dense (durable) materials were purposely selected.

Some of these early beads were chosen as to size to form a complete necklace, and these tended to be of two kinds. One was uniform-size, with all beads about the same in diameter. The other type was the graduated-size, with small beads at the top, medium-sized beads at the sides, and large beads at the bottom center. This was not only a pleasing bead arrangement, but the extra weight toward the bottom ensured that the necklace hung properly.

Shell (both freshwater and marine) was also used from very early times. Some shells were used whole and merely drilled, while others were carefully sized and shaped after drilling. Here, uniform sizes were the common designs, but graduated sizes were also widely used. From finds on inland and coastal sites all across the country, it is evident that there was a thriving trade in raw shell material in prehistoric times.

Copper was another material widely used when it was available as a native ore and in regions where it could be traded. The usual manufacture method was to cold-pound copper into thin strips of various widths, and work them into spheres, discs or cylinders. In general, if much copper was available (Old Copper Culture) it was used for tools and implements, common artifacts made from plentiful material. If comparatively little copper was available, it was often reserved for decorative and ornamental objects (Adena and Hopewell lifeways).

Here is a random sampling of bead types and usage in prehistoric America.

In the late BC centuries, steatite or soapstone vessels were made in or near the quarries of the Eastern United States. These stone pots were carefully treated, but when they were in fact broken, the pieces were often salvaged. Sections were cut into thick beads, and often the edges were notched as a further decoration. (Ritchie, *The Archaeology Of New York State*, 1980, p. 151.)

Whole, small shells were used for some beads while others were made from durable sections of shell from abalone, clam, mussel and scallop. Basically, and with variations, there are three types of shell beads: Discoidal or flat disc-shaped, spherical or round, and tubular or cylindrical. (Martin, Quimby & Collier, *Indians Before Columbus*, 1949, pp 48-49).

West Virginia's Cresap Mound contained a large number of copper beads, all these from the Early Woodland Adena culture. These totalled 380, and were usually of a uniform size when found together. Find-positions suggested usage as bracelets, necklaces, a sash and a very long strand. All were made by rolling thin strips of copper together and pounding the copper into the final form, which in some cases was barrel-shaped. The bead-surfaces were smoothed and sharp edges had been ground dull. (Dragoo, *Mounds For The Dead*, 1963, pp 121-123).

The McKees Rock Mound, of probable Adena origin, is located in southwestern Pennsylvania. It was very large, 16 feet high and 85 feet in diameter before its 1896 excavation. A variety of beads was found. These included small, whole marginella (shells with distinctive borders or edges) beads, pearl beads and both disc and tubular shell beads. Another interesting decorative object was a copy of a bear claw, made from native copper. (Dragoo, *Mounds For The Dead*, 1963, pp 153-156).

A very unusual glimpse of early bead-making was found at the Late Archaic site of Indian Knoll, Ohio County, Kentucky. Large marine shells were imported and the shells cut into narrow strips. These in turn were cut into small squares, which were next drilled. The four corners were then ground off carefully. The importance of beads is indicated by the finding of a single necklace that had approximately 2000 beads. An interesting aspect of other necklaces that were made up of a few large disc-shaped shell beads is that they often had one or more stone beads at the bottom center. This not only provided visual impact but the added weight helped keep the necklace in the correct wearing position. (Webb, *Indian Knoll*, 1946, pp 205-207).

Necklaces made up of individual beads of all types were the principal Early Anasazi ornaments in the Southwest. The beads were made of bone, colored stones, lignite or coal, seeds, shell and wood. Ear-dangles were used, so also hair ornaments of several long bones fastened together, with feathers. (Martin, Quimby & Collier, *Indians Before Columbus*, 1949, p 110).

Beads were drilled with narrow flint tips, and both the bow and pump drills were employed for this task. For small beads, a bead-vise was sometimes used. This was a split stick, the open end which held the bead securely. The stick near the opening was fastened tightly with cord, and the bead could then be manipulated with the large handle. (Heizer, *Handbook Of North American Indians*, Vol. 8, 1978, p. 292)

Dallas Indians of the Mississippian lifeway in the Tennessee area made extensive use of many kinds of shell beads. River and marine shells were used, as well as pearls up to half an inch in diameter. In addition to the usual necklaces, beads were fastened to garments. Headbands, belts, legbands and wristlets were also made. Bead sizes ranged from very small pearls to beads as large as walnuts. (Lewis & Kneberg, *Tribes That Slumber*, 1973, pp 110-112)

Of interest are shell beads found during the excavation of the Archaic-period Carlson Annis Mound in Butler County, Kentucky. The work was begun in 1939. A major shell deposit, it measured 300 x 350 feet and was about 6 feet above the ground surface. Large shell disc beads were recovered in strands, and the four strings (20 beads found) averaged 5 beads each. Medium-sized shell disc beads (15 and 1606) averaged 107 beads. Small shell disc beads (22 and 2748) averaged 125 beads. Long tubular beads (3 and 17) averaged nearly 6 beads, while short tubular shell beads (16 and 1196) averaged 75 beads per strand. (Webb, *The Carlson Annis Mound*, 1950, p 304).

Some 23 bone artifacts in some degree of preservation were found in the Cresap Mound, West Virginia, an Adena earthwork. Among the items were four tubular bone beads, and others had been present. Three box-tortoise cups were also found. Two worked antler sections, probably knife handles, were also recovered. The most elaborate item was an elk-antler headdress. Similar headdresses were used earlier in the Archaic and later with the Hopewell Indians. (Dragoo, *Mounds For The Dead*, 1963, pp 123-126)

A lovely example of a Pueblo necklace (ca. AD 900) was found in the Whitewater District of Arizona. It consisted of six strands with well over 1300 beads. The finely shaped and highly polished disc beads were made of dark shale and light-colored gypsum. Of choker or collar length and form, the necklace was styled so that the darker beads were at the sides and back of the neck, and alternately spaced on the front. One strand alternated color in groups of three beads, while four strands had a different color every other bead. The remaining strand retained all dark beads. (Roberts, *Archaeological Remains In The Whitewater District / Eastern Arizona*, 1940, pp 128-129, Plate 50)

Shells most used by California Coastal Indians included in northern areas dentalium shells from Vancouver Island plus haliotis and olivella shells. In central and southern California, disc-shaped clam-shell beads were favored. Haliotis (abalone) shell was traded far into the American Southwest. Also, steatite from the Channel Islands was made into beads and pendants. (Martin, Quimby & Collier, *Indians Before Columbus*, 1949, p 74)

Modified Basket-Maker (Anasazi) peoples in the American Southwest had the usual range of personal adornment items, plus beads of turquoise, some large and saucer-shaped. Turquoise pendants were made and turquoise and shell were sometimes placed together in mosaics. Bracelets and necklaces might include beads of crystal. (Martin, Quimby & Collier, *Indians Before Columbus*, 1949, p 119)

The late prehistoric Indians that followed the Mississippian lifeway in the Lower Midwest made large numbers of beads from a material known as fluorite. Also called fluorspar, it is translucent and ranges in color from light shades of brown to blue, green, violet and yellow, to colorless. It is no. 4 on the Moh hardness scale, somewhat medium in hardness. In addition to beads of many sizes and shapes, other small decorative objects were also made. (Chapman, *Indians And Archaeology Of Missouri*, 1972, p 72)

One method of making bone beads is documented from the Garoga Site, AD 1500-1575 (late prehistoric Iroquois) in eastern New York state. There, the metatarsal bone of a bear was found already worked for bead-making. The bone was deeply cut or grooved in two areas; upon completion, the beads would have been snapped off one by one. (Trigger, *Handbook Of North American Indians*, Vol. 15, 1978, pp 322-323, 331)

The only prehistoric turquoise artifacts known to have been found east of the Mississippi River came from Edwards Mound near Clarksdale, Mississippi. It is a child-sized bracelet of dozens of disc-shaped turquoise beads, with a drilled pendant-like turquoise dangle. (NGS, *Clues To America's Past*, 1976, p 95)

BEADS, found by Darrell and Joyce Thompson at Lake Cherokee, Rusk County, Texas. Material is white with black inclusions and two also have a turquoise color. Similar beads have come from Coles Creek and Poverty Point cultures.   Each, $10-20
Courtesy Darrell Thompson collection, Texas

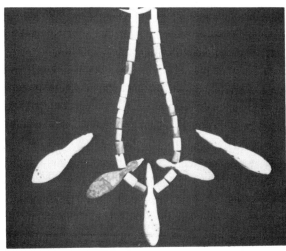

ORNAMENTAL NECKLACE. Lower objects are called "ducks" and are strung along with European style wampum. The ducks are often inscribed with designs or patterns. Rare examples.
Artifacts are from the state of New York and Pennsylvania
Wampum, per inch $25
Ducks, each $75-200
Courtesy Gary Fogelman collection, Pennsylvania

SHELL BEAD NECKLACE, from a mound in San Francisco County, California. Found in 1928, the secured strand is 23 inches long. Such beads in the shape of the natural shell are often rather early in prehistory. Olivella beads, as here, were commonly used. $100-175
Courtesy Marguerite L. Kernaghan collection
photographers Marguerite L. & Stewart W. Kernaghan

BEADS, from the Tellico site, Monroe County, TN. Small central beads are made of pottery, each, $2-4. Outside beads are made of pebbles, each drilled and the top example has two holes and other indentations. Average size, 1 inch. Each, $5-35
Photo courtesy Blake Gahagan, Tennessee

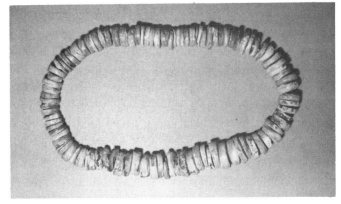

BONE DISC BEADS, this necklace from the Cree Indians, Canada. Secured, this strand is 6½ inches long. Due to the amount of work involved – cutting, shaping, sizing, drilling – preformed trade beads became quite welcome. $200-300
Courtesy Marguerite L. Kernaghan collection
photographers Marguerite L. & Stewart W. Kernaghan

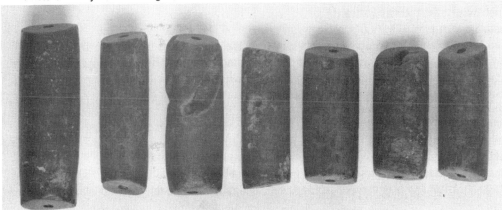

JASPER BEADS, the material an opaque variety of quartz. These are red in color and length ranges from 39 to 55 mm. They are from the Archaic period, and from Lowndes County, Mississippi; found as a set, each bead is perforated for stringing. Ex-colls. Furr (MS) and Callaway (LA) Set $800
Photo courtesy Chris Callaway, Louisiana

Chapter 13
BEADS – HISTORIC

When Columbus and his men brought beads to trade in the New World, they were carrying on an old tradition. Europeans had much earlier taken beads to Africa. Beginning around 1492, astronomical numbers of beads were brought to the new lands known as America. Many beads were from the great glass-houses of Venice, Italy, which contributed the largest share. However, beads were also manufactured in half a dozen other European countries.

Most of the trade beads came into North America during the fur-trade period, from the AD 1500's into the late 1800's. Thus, there were nearly four centuries during which glass beads were a major trade item. Beads were made in hundreds of sizes, styles and colors. While Venice remained the primary supplier for traders, Amsterdam became a major competitor in the AD 1600's and 1700's, at the height of the fur trade. (See Shumway, *Trade Bead Catalog*, 1973, p 2)

The first beads were generally large and fragile and relatively few survived. They were mainly used by Indians for necklaces and earrings due to their size and scarcity. Later, when smaller beads were available in uniform sizes, shapes and colors, they were more suitable for decorations on clothing. Beads were one trade item that never declined in popularity.

While basic trade beads were always welcome, some Indian groups had a decided preference for certain types. Some of the European traders in the Pacific Northwest complained that the appeal of certain kinds of beads might change from trading season to trading season and types that were once highly valuable no longer elicited much interest from the Indians.

Beads were occasionally traded by weight, but more often by strand. And the length of a strand varied from that of a spread hand to outstretched arms. For some less valuable beads, and in areas frequented by sea-traders, the lengths were measured by the fathom or in units of six feet.

Here are some facts about historic glass trade beads.

Among the many colors of beads used by Indians, two colors generally received preference. One was medium-blue, acceptance of which may have been keyed on the use, or knowledge, of turquoise. White was also popular, as the color was similar to some pearls and some shells. (Hothem, various sources)

Beads were very readily accepted by Indians in the historic trade period because the beads were similar to decorations they already had. And of all the artifacts likely to be found on an historic Indian site, the greatest quantity and variety is likely to be glass beads. (Good, *Guebert Site*, 1972, p 92)

In the Americas, gold beads were made only in Central and South America. Gold was mined from native deposits and the extent of trade in the finished product is uncertain. The country of Ecuador (through which runs the Equator) has produced pottery beads that had been coated or gilded with a thin layer of gold. (Van der Sleen, *A Handbook On Beads*, undated, p 119)

In portions of the Eastern U.S., after the fur trade declined in the region and trade goods became scarce, there was an apparent shortage of decorative beads. Beads in the earlier AD 1630-1690 period had been plentiful and many had been placed in graves of that period. There is some evidence that earlier graves were uncovered by later Indians, who removed only shell wampum (Indian-made) and glass beads (European-made). At such sites, 25% to 90% of the graves were "mined" by later Indians for the specialized contents. (Fridley, *Aspects Of The Fur Trade*, 1967, p 61)

Indians were greatly attracted to trade beads for a number of reasons. The material was novel (glass, porcelain, metal) and the colors were vivid, sometimes with several colors in the same bead. Shapes were varied as well, and faceted beads or those with multiple faces or planes were much-admired. One of the biggest advantages, however, is that the beads were ready to use. They did not require drilling, formerly a painstaking, time-consuming task. (Hothem, various sources)

Upon the arrival of European trade beads, even some decorations on native weapons changed. Two fighting clubs from the East, perhaps Iroquoian, in the AD 1600's reflect the change. While one has a huge double-ended pick-like blade of stone, the other has a steel blade. The curved wooden handles, inlaid (set in gum) with shell beads, also have some glass beads incorporated in the design. For such use, sometimes the glass trade beads were split before being set with the now-flat side down. (Trigger *Handbook Of North American Indians*, Vol. 15, 1978, p 87)

Even if the exact place or time of manufacture for glass beads is not known, their presence can help date a site as being proto- or post-contact. A complete absence of glass beads on a late prehistoric site means either that it is pre-contact, or if actually historic, trade beads did not reach that particular place for some reason. Or, beads did not reach that place in quantities or circumstances that left at least some behind to be found today. The story can become even more complicated. Sometimes, for various reasons, historic trade beads can be intrusive on a late prehistoric site, coming onto the scene dozens or scores of years later, thus making the entire site appear to be later. The location and stratification, plus the absence or presence of other trade goods, should clarify the time period. (Hothem, various sources)

In the trade-era period, beads of copper and shell were considered as units of value and objects of wealth; lengths of shell beads measured by an arm served as money in Virginia in AD 1650. Tubular beads and dark shell beads were more valuable than disc-shaped lighter colored beads. (Trigger, *Handbook Of North American Indians*, Vol. 15, 1978, p 259)

Of all glass bead types and varieties, there are only two basic manufacturing methods. The first is the hollow-cane method, in which a large mass of molten glass with an air pocket is drawn out into a thin cylinder. The second method is the wire-wound, and beads are individually formed and shaped by wrapping softened glass around a thick wire which is later withdrawn. Faceted beads were further shaped by being pressed in a mold while still hot. (Good, *Guebert Site*, 1972, pp 95-97)

Beginning ca. 1590, the Eastern middlemen for most trade goods were the Cherokee, Huron, Iroquois, Powhatan and Susquehanna tribal organizations. They controlled both the supply of furs leaving interior regions for the Coast, and the trade goods coming from coastal disembarkment sites. Inter-tribal skirmishes occurred due to this economic situation. (Fridley, *Aspects Of The Fur Trade*, 1967, p 57)

SCUBA divers, working Minnesota white water below rapids and falls for traces of fur trade materials, found many artifacts. In addition to axes, chisels, musket balls, brass kettles and tin plates, many beads were found. In one instance, hundreds of trade beads were picked up that had spilled from some sort of container. In all, many thousand glass beads of over two dozen types were recovered. (Fridley, *Voices From The Rapids*, 1975, pp 16, 95-99)

Eskimos also made use of historic trade beads when such were available. In addition to sets strung in strands on bars or spacers, for earrings and decorations for hair, an unusual necklace was worn. These were strands with small hooks at each end which attached to the earlobes. The strand was then worn under the chin in choker fashion. (Thiry, *Eskimo Artifacts – Designed For Use*, 1977, pp 66-67)

Some Indians learned to work glass, though in a rather makeshift fashion. At the Guebert (Kaskaskian) Site in Illinois and among the Arikara of South Dakota, glass pendants or other decorations were made. The raw material used was pulverized trade beads. These were shaped in the desired form or design and heated in a fire after being placed on a piece of metal, such as the detached butt-plate of a trade gun. The glass melted and fused in the new form. (Good, *Guebert Site*, 1972, p 83)

The Missouri Indians, based on the Oneota culture, made extensive use of French trade goods when they became available in the Missouri region. Such goods included blue glass beads of Venetian origin, brass and copper rings, bracelets, cylindrical beads and small metal cones or tinklers. (Chapman, *Indians And Archaeology Of Missouri*, 1972, pp 91, 93)

The Pomo Indians of California made fine utilitarian feather-decorated baskets for special occasions, such as gifts. One example, with feathers in five colors, has a rim of large disc beads. Another, with woodpecker and quail feathers, has blue trade beads attached to dyed splints. (Heizer, *Handbook Of North American Indians*, Vol. 8, 1978, p 291)

Collectors and students have various ''generic'' names for beads. Hudson's Bay Company beads traded in western North America, especially those that were red and white, are referred to as HBC beads. Star or chevron beads are made of colored glass in layers, the ends which formed 12-pointed stars. Early bugle beads were long and slender glass tubes and in later years these became shorter. Seed beads are very small, and were used for ornamental designs on clothing and footgear. Pound beads are slightly larger than the tiny seed beads, and were sold by that weight. Pony beads are so-called from being packed on the trader's ponies, and are larger and opaque. Cut beads were faceted and reflect light from the individual faces, while others had the facets pressed or molded onto the bead. There are other types of beads with general names, and these sometimes refer to slightly different beads in various parts of North America. (Woodward, *Indian Trade Goods*, 1967, pp 9-15)

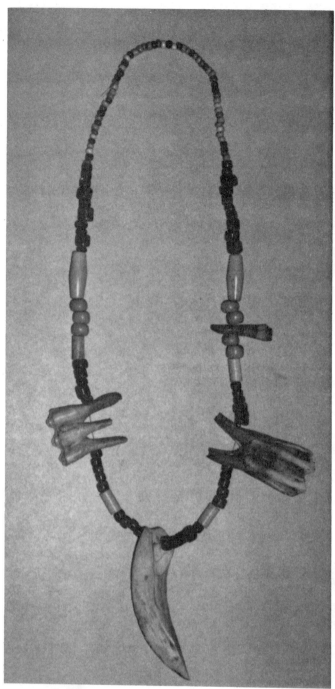

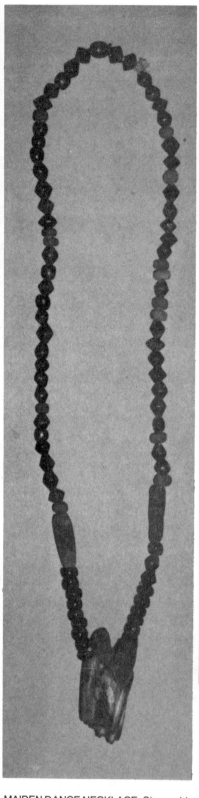

CHIEF'S NECKLACE, Comanche, quite old. It contains a boar tusk, two horse teeth, large seed beads and bone beads. It also has yellow and red rounded Corneline d'Aleppo and tubular red with white center beads. A nice combination for this outstanding piece. $275-375
Courtesy Marguerite L. Kernaghan collection
photographers Marguerite L. & Stewart W. Kernaghan

MAIDEN DANCE NECKLACE, Sioux, old, with bison-tooth dangle. It featured blue and red transparent pony beads, various shaped brass beads and pottery beads. These beads are rarely found with bison teeth. Yankton Sioux from the Sioux reservation, South Dakota, and 15 inches long. A fine, authentic specimen.
$300-400

WEST COAST NECKLACE with red, white and blue Chevron beads and tubular Corneline d'Aleppo orange frosted with white interior beads. Secured length is 12 inches for this unusual arrangement. $200-300

Courtesy Marguerite L. Kernaghan collection
photographers Marguerite L. & Stewart W. Kernaghan

Courtesy Marguerite L. Kernaghan collection
photographers Marguerite L. & Stewart W. Kernaghan

66

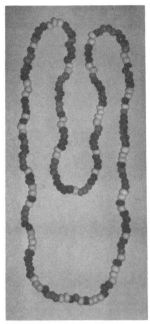

HUDSON BAY COMPANY TRADE BEADS, opaque light blue, dark blue, white, light green, orange and black. These were traded to West Coast Canadian and American Indians. Beads average about ¼ x ⅜ inches and sizes vary somewhat. Secured length, 19 inches long.
$200-300

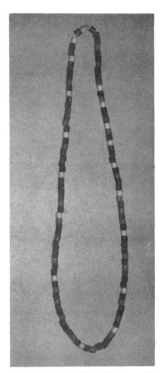

TILE BEAD NECKLACE found in Iowa and doubled length 12 inches long. Bead colors are red, light blue, dark blue, black and white. Such beads were fairly widely traded with the Indians. $125-175

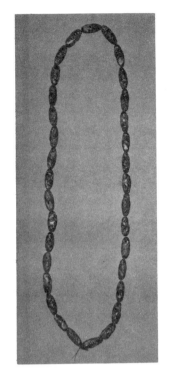

OVERLAY BEADS, multicolored, found near Old Gallup, New Mexico. Strand, 11 inches long, is the type widely traded to the Pueblo Indians. $350-475

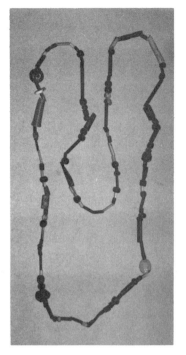

ASSORTED BEADS, Oklahoma, including: Corneline, faceted blue, Catlinite ring, striped black on white, blue, grey and white tube beads, flat blue with embossed star, copper cone, white ring, bone beads and red tube with diagonal blue stripes. Strand is 21 inches long and represents many bead types.
$325-450

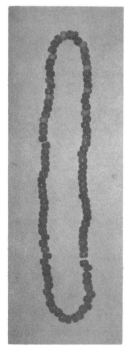

MONTANA NECKLACE, beads traded to the Crow Indians, Crow Agency, Montana. It has red, yellow, light and dark blue beads, some shiny, some frosted. Sizes range from ⅜ to ½ inch and strand is 12 inches long when strung. An attractive piece. $175-225

PONY BEAD NECKLACE, striped beads in many different color combinations. It is from the Crow Agency, Montana, and is, secured, 12 inches long. This is an attractive necklace of beads that were used for many decorative purposes. $275-350

PONY BEAD NECKLACE, beads striped in a variety of colors, with five elk-tooth extensions. This piece was traded to the Sioux Indians, Old Rosebud Reservation, South Dakota. Secured, this necklace is 12 inches long.
$350-500

This page
Courtesy Marguerite L. Kernaghan collection; photographers Marguerite L. & Stewart W. Kernaghan

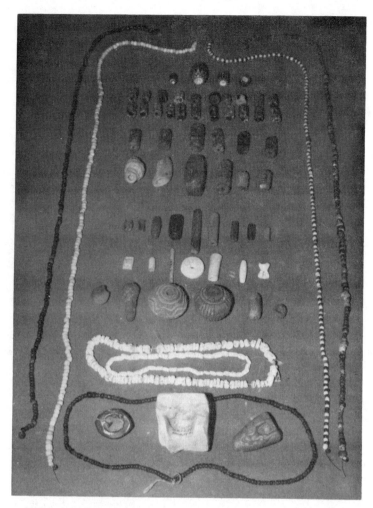

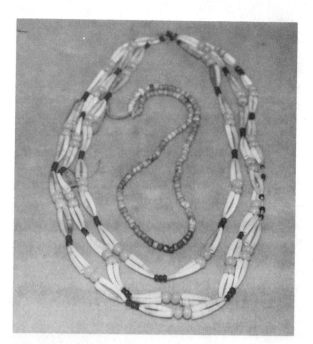

NECKLACES, outer three strands of red, white and blue beads with connecting dentalium shells. Tlingit, Alaska. $250-300
Central strand, first provenance a museum in 1898, another in 1947. Bone, Tlingit, Alaska. $100-150
Courtesy Lawson Corley collection, Alabama

BEADS, HISTORIC AND PREHISTORIC, U.S. and Mexico. Single prehistoric beads range, each, to $50. Historic beads, glass, each, range to $35. Shell bead strands, white, lower, $20 and $35. The outside strands are Hudson Bay white and red types, per strand value (HBC) $65-95. This is a fine display of early bead types.
Courtesy Wilfred Dick collection, Mississippi

BRACELET, jade beads, once belonged to a Dakota's chief's wife. Ca. AD 1870's, fine quality. $200-300
Courtesy Lawson Corley collection, Alabama

Chapter 14
TRADE ORNAMENTS

Collecting trade-era ornaments has long been a somewhat little known field, if only because there have been far fewer available artifacts. This is a relative comparison, in that while there are billions of prehistoric Indian artifacts of all kinds, there are only millions of historic trade-era pieces. And of the historic artifacts, trade ornaments are much fewer in number, not counting the almost unlimited quantity of glass beads scattered across thousands of old Indian villages and campsites.

Again excepting the glass items, trade ornaments of iron, steel and silver have suffered from only a few hundred years of contact with the earth. While some pieces were collected long ago and protected from the elements, much iron and silver has been plowed up or spotted by surface-hunting collectors. Often the iron and steel are pitted and rusted, the silver badly corroded.

The single largest class of trade ornaments are those made of silver or other metals. Individual forms include brooches, gorgets, rings, pendants and armbands and bracelets. And of these forms, brooches exist in the highest numbers. Brooches were used in ways that might seem unusual, but to Indians they were ornaments and decorations and personal wealth made visible. So brooches might be worn as pins or hair decorations or be fastened to clothing or wearing blankets in large numbers. Several dozen brooches worn at one time was fairly common in some places where trading was active.

Brooches themselves could be in any of many forms and designs, hearts and circles, Masonic emblems and much else. Plain forms sometimes were further decorated by punched holes or designs engraved in the metal. Most brooches had a pin or tongue across the center for easy and solid attachment. Canadian and U.S. silversmiths turned out huge numbers of silver ornaments. Many were made of thin sheet-silver; the Indians liked the lighter weights so many brooches could easily be worn.

Some very early examples were occasionally made of silver coins. This practice was prohibited because it brought about local coin shortages, and raw silver metal was used thereafter.

For special ornaments, cast-silver ornaments were made, small to medium-large and in the form of beavers, though turtles and otters were also popular. The heavier objects when made with silver were expensive to make, so a compromise of sorts was reached with some forms made by hollow-casting. This gave a much thicker exterior than sheet silver, but the main body portions were hollowed or empty. This decreased both weights and the amount of silver used, and larger objects could be made.

Normally, a trading company would place an order with a silversmith based on the market preferences of the trading region. A certain number of ornaments of a certain size were specified, based on a given amount of silver. Sheet silver was often used, as it was preformed and easier to work, and a large number of ornaments could be made from a given weight of silver. Often the mark of the smith or his shop (the "hallmark") was die-stamped somewhere on the silver. Some pieces made for Hudson's Bay Company were also marked with this designation, a conjoined "H" and "B".

Throughout the trade period, in addition to silver, ornaments were also made of copper, brass, pewter and German silver. The last actually had no silver, though it looked like the precious metal. It was an alloy of copper, nickel and zinc and more durable than silver.

For a thorough, factual account of these trade ornaments, the author recommends the book *North American Indian Trade Silver*, by W. H. Carter of Canada.

Beyond the standard trade items exchanged with Indians, the U.S. government sometimes presented special gifts to prominent Indian leaders. Such presentations included gorgets, peace medals, pipes and high-grade pipe-tomahawks. One such of the latter was given to the Seneca chieftain Red Jacket. It was silver-mounted, with a silver mouthpiece and silver heart-shaped inlay on the blade with the figure of an American eagle. Overall length of the rare specimen is just under 17 inches. (Sturtevant & Washburn, *Handbook Of North American Indians*, Vol. 4, 1988, p 31)

Some of the most popular trade items were brass thimbles, but not necessarily for use with needle and thread. Indians made a small hole in the center of the top and suspended a bead from a sinew or cord. This made an attractive and musical jingler or tinkler, which was used to decorate clothing. (Woodward, *Indian Trade Goods*, 1967, p 23)

Trade in the largely Canadian region covered by Hudson's Bay Company was managed by a standard economic unit until at least 1810. This was the "Made Beaver" system, with the measure being the prime winter pelt of a large beaver. This in turn was related to other furs and all trade goods; Made Beaver was of two kinds. Coat beaver might be worn by Indians a season or two, then traded. Parchment beaver meant fresh skins obtained solely to be traded. Both lightly used and fresh new pelts were considered of equal value. (Sturtevant & Washburn, *Handbook Of North American Indians*, Vol. 4, 1988, p 340)

Buttons designed for European fashions were also used by Indians, but not as clothing fasteners. Instead, they became ornaments for blankets, robes and necklaces. (Woodward, *Indian Trade Goods*, 1967, p 24)

One of the favorite trade pieces was the pipe-tomahawk, combining the features of a hatchet and long-stemmed pipe. Once these decorative/status objects reached the Indians, the handles were further ornamented to enhance their appeal. Examples of such additions include beaded flaps with or without fringes at the handle end, feathered attachments of several kinds and beaded handle or hand-grip wraps. Plain handle ornamentation included file-branding, some carving, and patterns of brass tacks. Fancier work consisted of pewter or silver inlays of many kinds. At times, metal mouthpieces were attached to the handle end. (Peterson, *American Indian Tomahawks*, 1971, various plates)

The fur-trade period included many kinds of pelts from fur-bearing animals plus hides. In the early days, the best furs went to Europe for hat-making and to China for trimming clothing; few Americans could afford such luxuries. Two important hides, in general, were buffalo (bison) and deerskins, though elk was a major product in the North and raccoons in the Great Lakes region. Furs came from animals ranging in size from weasels to bears. Three major furs, however, were beaver from the North American interior, fur seals from far northern waters and sea otters from coastal waters of the Pacific Northwest. Of all pelts, the most valuable were large, prime sea otter furs; in some places, ten beaver were required in trade for one otter pelt. Note that these are not the smaller pelts of otters from inland waterways; sea otter pelts were prime year-round in the far north, and a large example could be 3 x 6 feet in size. (Hothem, various sources)

The trade silver cross is a common artifact in collections, but not all are marked (or intended) for religious use. While some Christianized Indians may have worn crosses as a symbol of belief, many other examples were simply an attractive pendant form with a crossed-sticks design. The crosses were made in both single- and double-armed forms. (Hothem, various sources)

Trade goods in some areas of North America increased in quality due to competition. Chief factors (heads of "factories" or trading posts) of the Hudson's Bay Company dealt mainly in English goods. They were encouraged to please their Indian customers, and (in an early form of consumer surveying) asked them what they liked or disliked about specific trade items. Chief factors also puchased examples of superior trade goods of French (the main competition) manufacture in order to upgrade similar English items. Suppliers were then given instructions for changes so that better trade goods could be offered for furs. (Sturtevant & Washburn, *Handbook of North American Indians*, Vol. 4, 1988, p 338)

In very early trading years, the possession of a trade musket was as much a status symbol and ornament as it was a weapon or hunting tool. In fact, native-made bows and arrows had many advantages and some Indians carried them in addition to the firearms. Drawbacks of early muskets included failure to operate in very wet weather, lack of repair knowledge and parts, dependence on traders for supplies of powder and shot, and loud noise which frightened game and betrayed position. For the trade gun to be effective, conditions had to be just right. (Hothem, various sources)

TRADE BRACELET, made of twisted copper wire, found in Holt County, Missouri. It is 4¼ inches in diameter. $25
Photo courtesy Mike George, Missouri

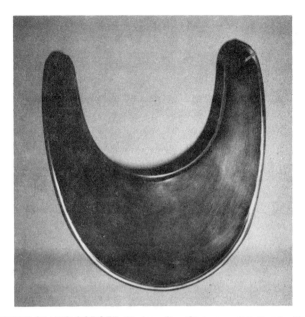

TRADE-SILVER GORGET, Hudson Bay Company. It is lined with red wool, and stamped H.B. Weight is over 3 ounces; this is a trade item, ca 1850, Canada. Size is 5½ x 6 inches. Trade silver pieces this large and fine are rare. $700-1200
Courtesy Marguerite L. Kernaghan collection;
photographers Marguerite L. & Stewart W. Kernaghan

TRADE-SILVER ARTIFACTS, from various New York state sites.
Items include crosses, different brooch types and "kissing" otters.
Museum quality

Courtesy private collection

71

Chapter 15
BEADWORK AND QUILLWORK

One of the traditional American Indian ways of decorating clothing and other personal items has been to use beads and/or quills. While it is generally true that quilling is older than beading (in terms of trade-supplied European beads), such is not always the case. For example, portions of a beaded blanket were found in Ohio's Ater Mound, in Ross County (see chapter listings). Fragments of beadwork have been found elsewhere, just enough to suggest that beadwork is at least 1500 years old in the American Midwest.

Quillwork as collectors are familiar with the term has several aspects. One is the Eastern Woodlands work, which involved some clothing including moccasins, and many small birch-bark baskets with quilled designs. Another is the Northcentral area, where quilling was done on much clothing, pipestems, moccasins and containers of many kinds. Quilling was usually done in panels or strips.

Quillwork involved a number of steps, beginning with plucking the quills from a recently living porcupine (the names means "little pig"). The quills or sharp spines were boiled in water to soften them and if dyed, this step then took place. Natural colors of the quills might be used, since the hard surface of quills made them difficult to dye. While still pliable, the quills were flattened and then dried somewhat. In use, both ends of quills were sewn and tucked beneath the surface fabric or material, leaving only the flat shaft exposed. Natural quill colors are whitish and yellow-brown, with some darker.

After Contact times, many pieces were decorated with a combination of seed beads and quills, since the beads gave new colors and a different appearance. They were also precolored and required no extensive preparation. Eventually, mainly beads were used, and most old Indian items in collections are beaded or beaded/quilled instead of being fully quilled. The exceptions are small quilled Micmac or Micmac-style boxes from the northern woodlands, partially or fully quilled on lid and sides. Quillwork of this sort is still being done today.

See Chapter 20 for other examples of later Indian beadwork.

One of the few truly new trade items readily accepted by Indians of northern areas was the quill-flattener. These were made of steel, and had flat, angled spatula-like surfaces at each end of a short rod. They were used for pressing and flattening porcupine quills prior to decorative use. Previously, Indians had no similar tool or at least tools that were not as efficient. (Hothem, various sources)

The Mojave Indian women of the Southwest, in the late 1900's, wore large and elaborate beaded collars. These covered the shoulders nearly to the breasts and elbows. One example had a network construction of blue and white seed beads and fringes that terminated in large white beads. The designs were often thick geometric lines. (Ortiz, *Handbook Of North American Indians*, Vol. 10, 1983, p 68)

Beaded moccasins were done in somewhat abstract designs in the Kansas-Nebraska border area. One example pair has floral designs on the inner ankle flap and elongated designs on the outer ankle flap, with rounded toe designs. Ca. 1860 and 10¾ inches long, the beading was done in eight different colors. (Feder, *American Indian Art*, 1982, pp 36-37)

What remained of a beaded blanket or covering came from the Ater Mound, near Frankfort, Ohio. Recovered sometime prior to 1900, the covering had some 1500 conch shell beads in an elongated diamond pattern. The original size of the 100 BC - AD 500 creation was 1.83 x 2.50 feet. (Hothem, *Treasures Of The Mound Builders*, 1989, p 101)

An example of fine decorative beadwork and quillwork on clothing is a set of Kutchin garments, including shirt, trousers, moccasins, mittens and hood. The shirt has a quilled shoulder band and quilled fringe. The trousers have quilled strips running up the legs and both mittens and hood have quilled strips. The base material is well-tanned caribou hide. (Helm, *Handbook Of North American Indians*, Vol. 6, 1981, p 521)

In terms of quillwork, some Plains Indians used split bird quills rather than porcupine quills. Such work was done up until about 1900 and was mainly used to decorate garments. In using porcupine quills, Plains artisans often used maidenhair fern stems in place of black quills, at least in the pre-1850 period. (Fedor, *American Indian Art*, 1982, p 64)

The longest known surviving Iroquis belt of wampum is the Washington Covenant Belt. It contains approximately 10,000 beads in purple and white, with 13 human figures representing the 13 original colonies. The belt, ca. 1775-1789, is a little over 5 inches wide and about 76 inches long. (Triger, *Handbook Of North American Indians*, Vol. 15, 1978, p 423)

One of the best extant early historic wampum belts represents the 1670 defeat by the Iroquois of the Algonquian Indians. Made of purple and white quahag shell beads, a trade war-hatchet is depicted in white. The belt ranges in width from 4⅛ - 4½ inches and is 43⅛ inches long. The framework materials are wild hemp and deerskin. (Peterson, *American Indian Tomahawks*, 1971, p 89, Plate 24)

A few beaded charms were made by the Ojibwa and they were connected to the Grand Medicine Society. These were rectangular sections of dark cloth with white seed-bead borders. Within were outlined human and mythical figures in white beads; they were worn as talismans for good health. (Feder, *American Indian Art*, 1982, Plate 219)

Subartic Indians did masterful beadwork on clothing, and techniques reached a peak ca. 1880-1920. The work was overlaid (spot stitching) whereby strands of seed beads were sewn to garments with a stitch every few beads. Seed beads in many colors (Venetian and Czechoslovakian, in diameter from $\frac{1}{16}$ to $\frac{3}{32}$ inches) were used. (Helm, *Handbook Of North American Indians*, Vol. 6, 1981, pp 722-723)

Large items were usually partially beaded, and these included leggings, shirts, skirts, pipe bags, bandoleer bags, dresses, breechclouts, lance cases, bow cases, arrow cases, saddle blankets or pads and collars. Smaller items that were partially to wholly beaded included moccasins, peyote fans, awl cases, strike-a-light bags, tobacco bags, umbilical fetishes and ration cases. (Hothem, various sources)

A fine example of Western beadwork is in the Denver Art Museum. It is a beaded storage bag, made by the Arapaho about 1890, and is 15 x 22½ inches. It has beaded sides and flap, and a pictorial side panel depicts two birds and a horse and rider with feathered bonnet. (Feder, *American Indian Art*, 1982, pp 30-31)

Indians of the Northern Plains region used porcupine quills to decorate a wide range of objects. Examples include a bison-horn spoon with quilled handle, a parfleche container with quilled carrying strap, and a pipe (with bowl of Wind River pipestone) with quilled wooden handle. Quillwork was done well into historic times in the area. (D'Azevedo, *Handbook Of North American Indians*, Vol. 11, 1986, p 323)

Somewhat related to quillwork in the northern regions was the decorating of objects with moosehair. This was used as a sort of colored thread (and trade thread was common as early as 1850) which could be employed both in natural and dyed colors. Much moosehair decoration was done in the 17th and 18th centuries. The normally brown hair might be dyed black, white or orange-red. (Hothem, various sources)

An excellent example of a beaded cradle-cover is in the Peabody Museum, Massachusetts. It is Eastern Sioux, ca. 1830, and the reconstructed wooden backboard is 15 x 34 inches. The cover consists of hanging beaded panels on the front and on each side; the carrying strap is fully beaded. (Feder, *American Indian Art*, 1982, Plate 9)

One of the reasons black trade cloth of medium weight and velvety texture was so popular with Indians is that any colored decorations were boldly accented. The other reason is that the cloth took the place of black dyed buckskin, the making of which was difficult and time consuming. The preparation of black buckskin may now be a lost art. (Hothem, various sources)

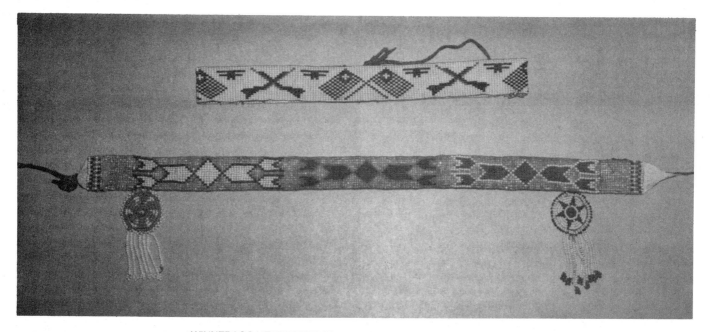

WINNEBAGO HEADBANDS. Top, seed-beaded in white with crossed flags and crossed guns, loomed 1¼ x 20½ inches. A very nice piece.
$300-500
Bottom, clear bead background with geometric designs and two round drops, loomed. Loomed portion 1 x 18½ in. drops 1½ inches, with bead fringe, 1 x 1½ inches. Fine.
$425-600
Courtesy Marguerite L. Kernaghan collection
photographers Marguerite L. & Stewart W. Kernaghan

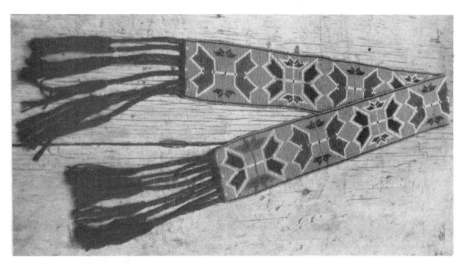

BEADED SASH, origin unknown, with design in five colors on a blue background. Sash ends are red yarn. Piece is 3 inches wide and 34½ in. long. This item is in perfect condition and a well-made sash.
$300
Courtesy Jon and Bonnie Mau collection, Wisconsin

LOOMED SASH, Potawatomi, seed-bead leaf-like designs on white in alternating yellow and red, yellow and black. Fine condition, ex-coll. Killy, ca. 1910. Size is 1 x 24½ inches. $200-300
Courtesy Marguerite L. Kernaghan collection; photographers Marguerite L. & Stewart W. Kernaghan

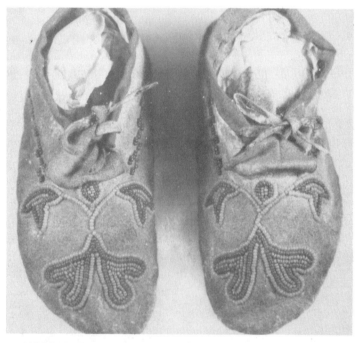

MOCCASINS, child-size, Eastern Woodlands, 6 inches long. Top border is red trade-cloth, while material is white-tanned doeskin. Toe and side decorations are in seed-beads, blue, yellow and green. Excellent condition. $175
Lar Hothem collection, Ohio

BEADED COIN PURSE, Flathead-Kutenai, Montana, ca. 1950. Geometric design and trim are in eight seed-bead colors. Backing is leather, zipper closure, and lining is cloth. In perfect condition, size is 2½ x 3 inches. $175-225
Courtesy Marguerite L. Kernaghan collection; photographers Marguerite L. & Stewart W. Kernaghan

HEADBAND, Prairie Tribes, loom-woven ca. 1900. It is done in red and black seed-beads on a white and silver-colored ground, all attached to deerskin. Beaded area is 1¾ x 14 inches. In very good condition, this piece shows use. $300-400
Courtesy Margaruerite L. Kernaghan collection photographers Marguerite L. & Stewart W. Kernaghan

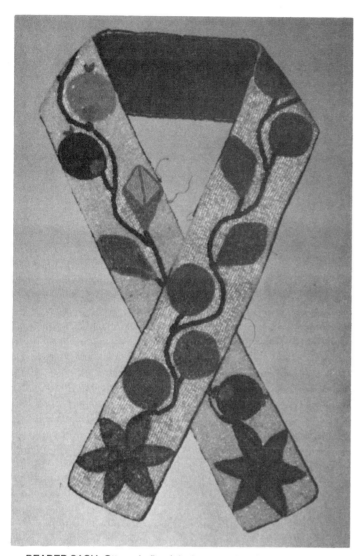

SHOULDER AND BREAST ORNAMENT, Winnebago, women's and ca. 1920. Leather-mounted, it is trimmed with trade beads, seed-beads, maribou feathers and metal tinklers. Size is 6½ x 18 inches, and the decoration is well-worn. $400-500
Courtesy Marguerite L. Kernaghan collection;
photographers Marguerite L. & Stewart W. Kernaghan

BEADED SASH, Ottawa in floral design, ca. 1915. It is 3 x 40 inches, mounted on cloth, with beads in ten colors. In good condition, it is ex-coll. Julie Williamson, Santa Fe, New Mexico. $500-750
Courtesy Marguerite L. Kernaghan collection;
photographers Marguerite L. & Stewart W. Kernaghan

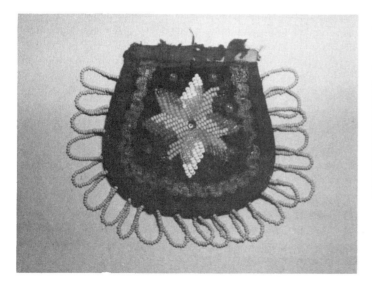

HATBAND, Ponca Indian, early period and ca. 1870. It has a beaded design in five colors and is in perfect condition. Size, 1⅛ x 22½ inches. $150-225
Courtesy Marguerite L. Kernaghan collection;
photographers Marguerite L. & Stewart W. Kernaghan

BEADED POUCH, Mohawk Indian, New York State ca. AD 1890. It is decorated with sequins, seed-beads, metallic braid, red trade-cloth and red silk. Size is 4½ x 5 inches including the beaded loops. A well-made, attractive Eastern Woodlands piece. $300-500
Courtesy Marguerite L. Kernaghan collection;
photographers Marguerite L. & Stewart W. Kernaghan

BEADED POUCHES, Athabaskan (northern Canada), quite old. Left, seed beads on leather, some beads missing, 2½ x 4½ inches.
$125-175
Right, seed beads on leather, some beads missing, size 3 x 3½ inches.
$125-175
Courtesy Marguerite L. Kernaghan collection;
photographers Marguerite L. & Stewart W. Kernaghan

YAKIMA BEADED BAG, old, 9 x 10 inches. Beaded design is outlined in black, with yellowish elk, reddish log and foliage in two colors. Border is red trade-cloth. An attractive Indian-done design, cloth is worn but beading is perfect. $700-1100
Courtesy Marguerite L. Kernaghan collection;
photographers Marguerite L. & Stewart W. Kernaghan

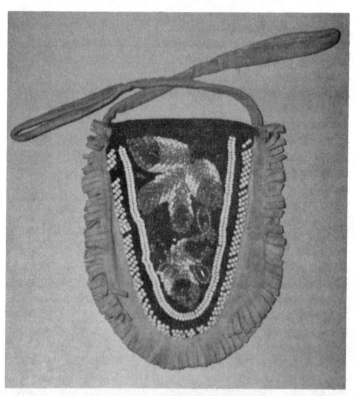

IROQUOIS POUCH, decorated with black velvet, made of deerskin. Floral design with eight bead colors plus seven pony beads. Size exclusive of handles is 5¾ x 6¾ inches. An old piece, it is in perfect condition. $300-500
Courtesy Marguerite L. Kernaghan collection;
photographers Marguerite L. & Stewart W. Kernaghan

COLLAR AND NECKDROP, Sioux, fully loom-beaded in red, white and blue seed-beads. Designs are American flag and eagles, overall size is 7½ x 14 inches. This was collected at Pine Ridge, South Dakota. Item was made ca. AD 1920. In perfect condition, this is an excellent Indian-worn piece. $700-1100
Courtesy Marguerite L. Kernaghan collection;
photographers Marguerite L. & Stewart W. Kernaghan

Chapter 16
PLAINS INDIAN

When one considers the Plains Indians, the visuality is one of dash and excitement, of sound and color. This way of life was fairly correct after horses were acquired and the Plains groups became mounted hunters and warriors. However, before about the AD 1700's, the lifeway was mainly hunting various animals and the gathering of wild foods.

Plains Indian artifacts command much respect today, partly because of the artistry involved, partly because of rarity. While such items as hide-scrapers and skull-crusher clubs are still fairly common, most other pieces such as decorated objects and Indian-made, Indian-used weapons are quite scarce. There are a number of reasons for this.

A semi-nomadic seasonal pattern meant that not many objects could be carried along during movements. Compared to some other Indian groups, the Plains people were limited in numbers, and the best traditional pieces were made only for a couple of centuries. Inter-tribal warfare accounted for some destruction. Later, expeditions of soldiers caused much elimination of the Plains Indian material culture when camps (and goods) were regularly destroyed.

Old and authentic Plains Indian items are thus quite rare, and many of the best pieces went into museums as early as the mid-1800's. During the late 1800's and early 1900's, as Indians settled into a reservation lifeway, huge numbers of artifacts and artworks were collected by individuals and institutions.

Around AD 1640, Indians of the southern Great Plains had some knowledge of horses. By 1730-40, several large groups (Comanche and Shoshone) of the northern areas were using horses for hunting and raids, though they had earlier used horses mainly as pack animals. By 1830, all Great Plains areas and peoples had horses, and relied on them as a way of life. Hunting, skirmishing and trade were enhanced, and many decorative accoutrements were carried by the horse. These included bridles, saddlery, stirrups (when used), single and double saddle-bags, saddle blankets or saddle cloths, cruppers and quirts. (Hothem, various sources)

Non-horse decorated items of the Plains Indians included: mirror cases, gun cases, quivers, bow cases, pipe bags, pipe tampers, tobacco containers, needle and awl cases or carriers, strike-a-light containers (boxes or bags), leggings, half-leggings, moccasins, pipe stems, spoon, dipper and ladle handles, dance wands (sometimes pipe stems as a second use), ration-ticket holders, rattle handles, charms of many sorts, drums and drumsticks, tipi covers and liners, dance and battle shields and much else. (Hothem, various sources)

Great Basin Indian clothing, in the Plains area, could be quite elaborate, especially the garments for special occasions. In addition to painting both face and hair, clothing was at the same time practical and decorative. Buckskin shirts could be both beaded and painted and have skins or furs attached. Robes were colorfully woven and might also have beaded strips. Medicine bags were common accessories. Shoulder or bandolier bags were first worn by men, later also by women, and were often highly decorated in many ways. Moccasins might have cuffs lined with red cloth and have beaded or quilled designs. Various other ornaments, depending on the user's fancy, might be worn. (D'Azevedo, *Handbook Of North American Indians*, Vol. 11, 1986, pp 344-345)

Plains Indians often used paint to decorate bison hides, tipis and shields. Before the early 1800's (when commercial dyes and paints became available) only natural colors were used. Red was made by heating yellow ochre, while charcoal made black. White came from clay. Blue was made from a certain kind of earth, and green was made from water plants. (Furst & Furst, *North American Indian Art*, 1982, p 168)

Dance wands were among the most ornate specialized artifacts used by American Indians. In the Great Basin, long wooden wands might be topped with crane's heads. Other examples included wands with feathered and quilled tops, often with dyed horsehair, beads and tinklers. Besides the wands, dance paraphernalia included fans, arm and ankle circlets, belts, aprons, bustles and whistles. (D'Azevedo, *Handbook Of North American Indians*, Vol. 11, 1986, pp 328-329)

To Plains Indians, pipe-smoking was mainly done for ritualistic reasons. The bowl, usualy of catlinite, was difficult to make and the long wooden stem required much careful labor. Stems were hollowed for the smoke-hole either by boring with a hot wire, or by being split, channeled and glued. In the late 1700's to early 1800's, two kinds of pipe-stems were popular. One was the ''puzzle'' stem, flat and so intricately carved that only the maker knew where the smoke-hole was. Spiral stems had twisted forms, which were carved into shape. (Furst & Furst, *North American Indian Art*, 1982, p 171)

Cradleboards, usually made by tribal women, ranged from relatively plain to quite decorative. All were sturdy and could be laid flat, propped, hung from a tree branch, or carried by way of a strong strap. Frame types are the oldest, followed by the board type. Examples can be fully or partially beaded, and with an awning and/or hood. Some examples laced up, and had beaded buckskin security straps for the baby. In later years, cradleboard tops might be heavily beaded. Children sometimes placed dolls in miniature cradleboards. (D'Azevedo, *Handbook Of North American Indians*, Vol. 11, 1986, p 347)

On the Great Plains, as much care was given in early days to decorating items for children as for adults. This is especially true in clothing, and for babies it was the cradleboard or infant-carriers. It was the custom for a pregnant woman's female relatives to decorate the cradleboard, and one or more might be made for the same person. (Furst & Furst, *North American Indian Art*, 1982, p 166)

Many Great Plains groups were vivid artists with paint, decorating numerous objects such as wide, shallow drum-heads and shields, both of stretched hide. The material used was generally cured and shrunken bison-hide. Many different naturalistic and mythical figures were used, including the human form, thunderbird, and bison. Some pictorials were done in dull earth-tone color, while others had splashes of bright paint from roots or berries. Another large surface frequently painted was the exterior of the portable, conical dwelling called the tipi. At first, these were of bison-hide, and later, of canvas. (Hothem, various sources)

Decorative miniature shields 3 to 6 or 7 inches in diameter were made by some of the Great Basin Indians. They may have been charms or toys, and were painted similarly to the full-size counterparts. Buckskin was the preferred leather. (D'Azevedo, *Handbook Of North American Indians*, Vol. 11, 1986, p 320)

There is somewhat of a problem in making precise identifications (as to true tribal origin) of some Plains Indian artifacts and artworks. Often gifts were exchanged or items were traded back and forth. Intermarriage or war booty might be involved. The beadwork of the Crow and Nez Perce groups is a case in point, with a confusing blending of styles. Further, certain European clothing styles were partially copied by some Plains groups, which accounted for many similarities. (Feder, *American Indian Art*, 1982, pp 28-30)

SIOUX DANCE BUSTLE, feather and seed bead decorations, 36 inches diameter. A large and fine piece, it is Pine Ridge Reservation, South Dakota. Feathers are pheasant and dyed maribou; this piece in very good condition, is undated but old. $400-600
Courtesy Marguerite L. Kernaghan collection;
photographers Marguerite L. & Stewart W. Kernaghan

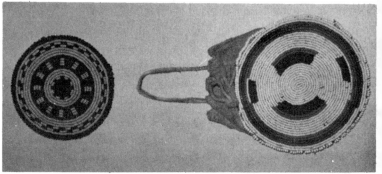

TARGET POUCH, Blackfoot, circular, ca. 1910. Designs in turquoise and red-brown seed beads. Size, 3¼ in. diameter, top condition. $175-225
TARGET POUCH, Blackfoot, ca. 1910. It has the overlay technique of seed beads on leather, six colors. Size 4¼ in. diameter, top condition. $200-250
Courtesy Marguerite L. Kernaghan collection;
photographers Marguerite L. & Stewart W. Kernaghan

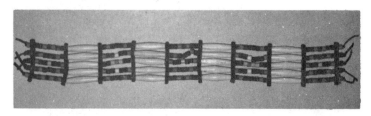

SIOUX CHOKER, with trade beads and hairpipe beads. The hair-pipes were made in New Jersey and the colored, smaller beads (in five colors) are tile trade beads. Restrung, from the Crow Agency, Montana. Size is 2 x 15½ inches. $275-400
Courtesy Marguerite L. Kernaghan collection;
photographers Marguerite L. & Stewart W. Kernaghan

APACHE BAG (side A). Size 7 x 14 inches, deerskin backing with fringes. Design is in six seed-bead colors. This is a well done, bright and attractive work, ca. 1950. $600-850
Courtesy Marguerite L. Kernaghan collection;
photographers Marguerite L. & Stewart W. Kernaghan

APACHE BAG (side B). Size 7 x 14 inches, deerskin backing with fringes. Design is six seed-bead colors. A very attractive piece, ca. 1950. $600-850
Courtesy Marguerite L. Kernaghan collection;
photographers Marguerite L. & Stewart W. Kernaghan

SIOUX BEADED BELTS, loomed. Top, 1¾ x 26 inches, white, green, pink, yellow, in geometric design. $300-500
Middle, 1¾ x 33 inches, white, blue, red and brown beads. $400-600
Bottom, 1¾ x 29 inches, green with rod, white and blue geometric designs and four American flags. $300-500
Courtesy Marguerite L. Kernaghan collection;
photographers Marguerite L. & Stewart W. Kernaghan

DANCE ANKLETS, Sioux, pair. Each has eight metal bells on leather and is ¾ x 9½ inches. From Pine Ridge Reservation, South Dakota, and ca. 1900. An old and unusual set in fine condition.

$200-350

Courtesy Marguerite L. Kernaghan collection;
photographers Marguerite L. & Stewart W. Kernaghan

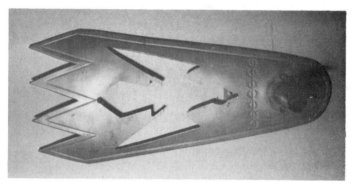

ROACH SPREADER, Kiowa, made of German silver. The tube is brass and a thunderbird design is cut from the base; edge-design is stamped. Size 2⅞ x 6⅛ inches. This is an interesting and unusual piece.

$175

Courtesy Marguerite L. Kernaghan collection;
photographers Marguerite L. & Stewart W. Kernaghan

SIOUX BEADED BAG, seed beads on deerskin and ca. 1890. The same design is on both sides but in different colors. The front has beads of red, blue and green. A fine old piece, in top condition, it is 2½ x 3¼ inches.

$250-375

Courtesy Marguerite L. Kernaghan collection;
photographers Marguerite L. & Stewart W. Kernaghan

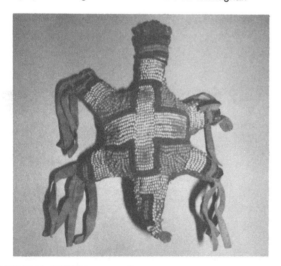

UMBILICAL FETISH, turtle, Sioux Indian, 2½ x 3¼ inches. It is decorated with seed beads in five colors, and has two trade beads for eyes.

$450-600

Courtesy Marguerite L. Kernaghan collection;
photographers Marguerite L. & Stewart W. Kernaghan

Chapter 17
ANTLER, BONE, IVORY, SHELL AND WOOD

Artifacts made of organic materials were widely and heavily used in all of North America. Rather than a long introduction to half a dozen large classes, a better overview can be obtained by reading a series of separate listings.

In westcentral California, shell artifacts were used in late prehistoric times. Clamshell was made into disc beads, and olivella was used for rectangular types. Haliotis shell was used for a wide variety of necklace elements and pendants, with some forms becoming quite elaborate. The drill-holes on some specimen suggest that instead of being suspended, they were sewn to garments. (Hothem, various sources)

Eskimos were undoubtedly the most careful workers in ivory and made numerous small objects from narwhale and walrus ivory, and the teeth of large sea mammals. These included buttons, toggles and fasteners, often carved as miniature animals or fish. Other ornate artifacts included kayak spear-rests, bag plugs, cord joiners, belt accoutrements and swivel blocks. Often such pieces were artistically made and/or further carved to be attractive. (Thiry, *Eskimo Artifacts – Designed For Use*, 1977, pp 74-77)

In the American Southwest, craftsmen not only carved *on* imported (Pacific Coast) shells, they carved *with it*. That is, they sculpted the shell to make finger rings or bracelets or animal and human carvings. The prehistoric Hohokam of southern Arizona were masters at this work, doing much design in relief so the figures were raised from the background for a three-dimensional effect. (Hothem, various sources)

Bone needles, some of them finely finished and decorated, are a common artifact across the country. One site that has produced a selection of early needles is Graham Cave in central Missouri. A true needle (slender, with eye) as opposed to awls and punches means sewn clothing, in itself decorative when compared with rough, loose-fitting clothing. Such needles are found in cold and temperate climates where the need for tailored clothing is vital. (Chapman, *Indians And Archaeology Of Missouri*, 1972, pp 31-32)

The Hopewell Indian Ogden-Fettie group of mounds in Illinois produced a fascinating decorative artifact made from a large bear canine tooth. Hopewell artisans worked these teeth in many different ways, cutting them with flint blades. This canine was cut two-fifths of the way down, and some of the interior was removed along with the top. The resulting object resembled a small knife and handle, with sheath. This is the only known instance of such an artifact being made. (Cole & Duel, *Rediscovering Illinois*, 1975, pp 10-11, Plate XXVI-B)

The Mississippian cultures of the southern Midwest and U.S. South were extensive users of shells for artifacts in an almost unbelievable array of types. These included beads of marginella and disc forms and pendants of whelk which were drilled through the small end. The central column was made into beads and pendants. (These people also made distinctive decorative pins with long shafts from bone.) Several kinds of shell ear-ornaments were made, as well as the ornate gorgets (probably pendants) of curved conch-shell. The whelk was so important to the culture that effigies were made in pottery. (Chapman *Indians And Archaeology Of Missouri*, 1972, pp 72-73)

Bone as a raw material to be exploited was a ready by-product of food animals, and in some areas was more available than quality hardwoods. Polished bone is both attractive to see and touch, factors that certainly made it very popular with Amerinds. Bone was used for pendants, gorgets, hairpins, wristlets, bracelets and necklaces. Related materials – claws, small bones and teeth – were used as ornaments in themselves. (Martin, Quimby & Collier, *Indians Before Columbus*, 1949 p 47)

Near interior rivers, freshwater mussel shells were often used for ornaments. Along the East Coast, oyster shells were common and along the West Coast, abalone shell was a favorite material. The Gulf Coast had numerous shell types, the most-used probably being shells of the conch family. (Hothem, various sources)

Ca. AD 1000 and later, the Plains Village peoples of the Middle Missouri region used considerable shell and bone for ornamental artifacts. There were clamshell disc beads, large circular objects with central holes and simple elongated pendants. Bone animal effigies were sometimes holed for suspension and there were thin bone or antler objects, sometimes incised, that may have been wristguards for the slap of a bowstring. Shell and bone bird effigies were fairly common, and may have been for decoration or ceremonialism. (Wedel, *Prehistoric Man On The Great Plains*, 1978, p 176)

The Archaic Lamoka phase of New York state produced tubular bone beads in many shapes and sizes. Some were up to 2 inches long, and cleanly cut off at each end. Perforated bear teeth and deer bones may have served as pendants or necklace elements and drilled bones from species as diverse as foxes and turtles are represented. (Hothem, various sources)

Paleo Indians (Folsom lifeway) were some of the first highly successful Indians in North America. Their sites have produced tubular bone beads, tabular bones (gaming tokens?) with simple incised marks, and line-decorated pieces of larger bone. (Martin, Quimby & Collier, *Indians Before Columbus*, 1949 p 85)

Of all the bone artifacts, both decorative and utilitarian, the most commonly used was that of the deer. This is true in most sections of the country and in most prehistoric time-periods. While certain regions relied more heavily on other animals – Plains, bison; Northern Woodland, elk – deer, overall, were still the major game animal. Besides meat, hide and antlers, deer bones were used for many other objects from awls to pendants, needles to gambling bones. It is thus not surprising that deer were often pictured or sculpted by Indians in one form or another. (Hothem, various sources)

An unusual bone hairpin was found at the Late Archaic Indian Knoll site in Ohio County, Kentucky. About 7 inches long and with a shaft diameter of about ⅜ inches, the head was formed by a shaped mass of asphaltum. (This is a mixture of bitumins from natural deposits, and is also known as mineral pitch.) Four large shell beads were attached to the top of the mass, and four small shell beads were set on the sides. (Webb, *Indian Knoll*, 1946, pp 214, 216)

The early Lamoka and Frontenac cultures of New York state and surrounding areas had antler pendants which were striped with red paint. Bone awl-like artifacts (hairpins?) were similarly treated, or had engraving. (Martin, Quimby & Collier, *Indians Before Columbus*, 1949 pp 239-242)

An almost endless array of decorative bone objects was used by Plains Indian groups. These included whistles both plain and incised, decorated tubes, snow-snake heads or tips (used for winter game), incised quill-flatteners, decorated combs and decorated knife handles. Gambling markers or incised chips were used by the Mandans, who also made bird(?) headed bone objects of unknown use. Bird-like ornaments and pendants were used by Middle Missouri peoples. (Wedel, *Prehistoric Man On The Great Plains*, 1978, Plates XIII, XIV and XV)

In the Sedentary period of the Hohokam in the Southwest, a unique way of creating ornamental shell objects was invented. It was actually a form of acid-etching. A seashell surface was covered with pine pitch or asphaltum in such a way that areas left free helped form the desired pattern or design. This surface was then repeatedly coated with fermented juice from the saguaro cactus. This acetic acid then dissolved the desired shell portions, leaving a raised design. (Martin, Quimby & Collier, *Indians Before Columbus*, 1949 pp 187-188)

As an example of the importance of antler, bone and shell in prehistoric times, over 55,000 total artifacts made of these material were recovered from Kentucky's Indian Knoll site. Of these, 4342 were of antler, 8427 were bone, and 25,125 were of shell. (Webb, *Indian Knoll*, 1946, p 229)

The Key Marco Indians of late prehistoric times lived on the southern Gulf Coast of Florida and had some unusual ornaments. These included the usual range of ornaments for the times, but with the addition of wooden brooches inlaid with turtleshell and ear ornaments inlaid with shell. Wooden discs with designs may have decorated the ears and turtleshell plates had dolphin-like creatures incised on them. (Martin, Quimby & Collier, *Indians Before Columbus*, 1949 pp 395-398)

The Late Archaic Indian Knoll site in Kentucky produced shell ornaments of a wide variety. Occasionally shell was worked to imitate, or at least follow the form of, canine teeth or claws of large carnivores. Such artifacts were often found in pairs, each with a suspension hole, suggesting use as ear-ornaments. (Webb, *Indian Knoll*, 1946, pp 212-213, 316)

In Northwest Coastal areas, copper was used for crescent-shaped pendants(?) and pendants were made of animal teeth and claws, bone, deer hoofs, horn, shell and stone. Lip labrets of bone, stone or wood were worn in the lower lip. (Martin, Quimby & Collier, *Indians Before Columbus*, 1949 pp 468-469)

Eskimos in a sense had a different decorative emphasis than did most other North American prehistoric peoples. Instead of purely ornamental personal objects (though some were made) the more common practice was to ornament tools and other utilitarian objects. Thus, kayak lance-holders, knife handles, awl-cases and the like were often beautifully crafted and carved or incised. This might be termed high accomplishment in the art of the everyday. (Hothem, various sources)

People of the prehistoric Thule culture, of Arctic Canada, had necklace beads of one of the most unusual materials in North America. This was amber, a durable, translucent fossil resin in colors of brown-yellow, orange or yellow. (Martin, Quimby & Collier, *Indians Before Columbus*, 1949 p 507)

In the early AD centuries, the Ipiutak peoples of Alaska did some of the finest work ever done in ivory. This included openwork carving of effigy tools and tool parts, line swivels, snow goggles with slit eyeholes, and much more. Their unique highly stylized masks made up of separate ivory parts have never been equaled. Some of the objects have no known use, other than being attractive in themselves, and many are unusual ornament forms. (Jennings, *Prehistory Of North America*, 1968, pp 316-317)

Nose ornaments were more common to Indians of certain South American cultures, but a few North American Indians wore them. The prehistoric Late Kachemak Bay people of Cook Inlet, Alaska, not only had bone finger rings but wore bone nose pins. (Martin, Quimby & Collier, *Indians Before Columbus*, 1949 p 501)

Shell "masks" or at least stylized representations of the human face made from sections of large marine shells are found throughout the Southeastern U.S. Usually there are drill-holes for eyes and mouth, and it is possible they were used as pendants. Most, however, show little wear or damage from such use in the eye-hole region where they would logically have had suspension cords. In addition to such "masks," circular pendants or gorgets incised with many different designs were made. Birds, spiders, snakes, circles and humans were depicted in many forms. On some, a strong influence from Mexican American cultures is obvious. (Hothem, various sources)

Bone hairpins were used by many Amerind groups. Most have a long shaft, a point and enlarged top decorated in some fashion. In some areas, the bone pin was augmented or followed by hairpins of wood, wood covered with copper and pins of copper only. Later prehistoric times may have produced more, and a wider range of, specimens. (Bell, *Oklahoma Indian Artifacts*, 1980, pp 82-83)

The Anasazi of Pueblo Bonito in the valley of the Chaco River, New Mexico, had some unusual decorative artifacts. These included figurines and finger rings of jet (a dense, black coal suitable for carving and taking a high polish), small copper bells and turquoise effigies and pendants. Two bone scrapers had inlays; one 5 inches long had inlaid turquoise, while a 6½ inch specimen had inlaid jet. (Jennings, *Prehistory Of North America*, 1968, p 273)

The Frontenac Phase of the New York state Archaic period used elk antler for various artifacts. A cup was made from the base of an antler that had been shed (seasonal dropoff). Elongated spoons were also carved from elk antler. An antler six-toothed comb topped with inward-facing birds was particularly well done and measured nearly 3½ inches high. This people also produced shaped wolf mandibles, which were found in pairs and may have been hair ornaments. (Hothem, various sources)

Late Woodland sites along the Maine coast have produced some attractive antler and bone artifacts. These include long, curved bone hairpins or bodkins, with incised chevron designs. Antler decorative combs had several long teeth and tops decorated by both carving into shape and surface incising. Still other antler large-headed pins may have been clothing fasteners. (Trigger, *Handbook Of North American Indians*, Vol. 15, 1978, p 67)

Small sections were used for inlays in mosaic work at the Hohokam settlement of Snaketown, Arizona. Marine shell was used and figures cut ranged from geometric to effigy to fanciful. Many inlays had beveled edges which fit closely together for a permanent placement. (Gladwin, et al., *Excavations At Snaketown*, 1975, Plates 69, 70)

Two of the artifacts often highly decorated by graceful styling and fine carving by California Indians were mush paddles and large cupped spoons or ladles. Wooden paddles had long handles that were both intricately carved from the sides and carved front and back in a variety of styles. Wood or horn spoons, often used only by men, were large enough to require two hands to eat or drink the contents. Some had openwork and scalloped or zigzag handles. Horn was more often used for spoons. (Heizer, *Handbook Of North American Indians*, Vol. 8, 1978, p 152)

Bone of many kinds was widely used for beads and other ornaments all across North America. A favorite style was the cylindrical or tubular bead form, in diameter from ⅛ to nearly one inch, and from ¼ to over 6 inches long. There are several reasons for this. Bone was already largely formed into the cylindrical shape, and was strong and light. It was readily available from food animals, larger forms were hollow or partially hollow, and bone polished well. Such ornaments were used in dozens of different ways. (Hothem, various sources)

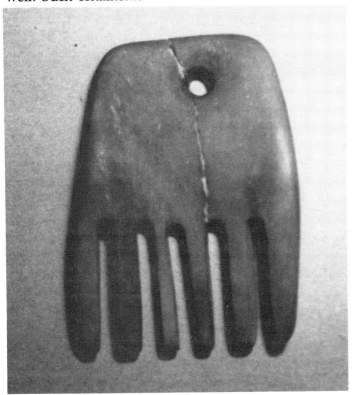

BONE COMB, drilled for suspension as a pendant. It was excavated from Cache River, a Union County, Illinois, Shawnee village site. Found in the early 1800's, it is mended at the breakline. Size, 1½ x 2¼ inches. A well-shaped and polished piece, probably proto-historic. $100-150
Courtesy Marguerite L. Kernaghan collection
photographers Marguerite L. & Stewart W. Kernaghan

ENGRAVED GORGET, three-holed, made of freshwater mussel shell with scalloped edges. Size 2 x 3 inches, from the Cumberland River, Livingston County, Kentucky. An interesting piece, in fine condition, possibly Fort Ancient in Weeping Eye form. $150-200
Courtesy Marguerite L. Kernaghan collection
photographers Marguerite L. & Stewart W. Kernaghan

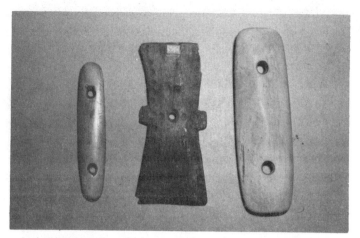

BONE ARTIFACTS, prehistoric period. Left, gorget, Trigg Co., Kentucky, cave find, ⅝ x 2¾ inches. $125
Center, pendant, flared and decorated, Umatilla, Oregon, 1½ x 3⅛ inches, heavy age patina. $150
Right, gorget, Trigg Co., Kentucky, cave recovery, 1½ x 3¾ inches. $225
Courtesy Marguerite L. Kernaghan collection
photographers Marguerite L. & Stewart W. Kernaghan

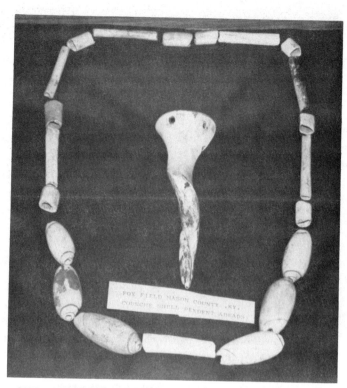

SHELL PENDANT AND BEADS, Fort Ancient culture, Mason County, Kentucky. The conch pendant is 5 inches long; ex-coll. Glass. $200
Courtesy Cliff Markley collection, Alabama

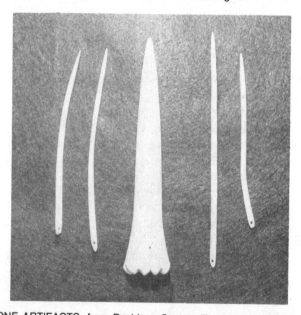

BONE ARTIFACTS, from Davidson County, Tennessee. Longest specimen is 5½ inches, and all are of very high quality. Large central bone awl, $125. Bone needles or pins, each, $75-125.
Courtesy Michael Darland, Kentucky

PENDANT OR GORGET, 1½ x 3 inches, ca. AD 1200. From a Southwestern state, it exhibits fine polishing and well-inscribed lines. $50
Courtesy Larry Shaver collection, Oklahoma
Larry Merriam, photographer

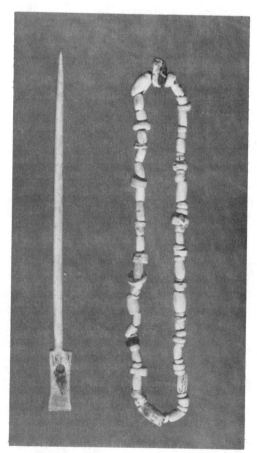

ORNAMENTAL ARTIFACTS, left, hairpin from the Arkansas River Valley, ½ in. wide at base, 7 in. long, heavily polished overall. Made of bone, it has a ⅛ in. tassle (?) hole. $150. Right, shell beads, Arkansas River Valley, strand 16 in. long including a drilled stone bead. $50
Courtesy Larry Shaver collection, Oklahoma
Larry Merriam, photographer

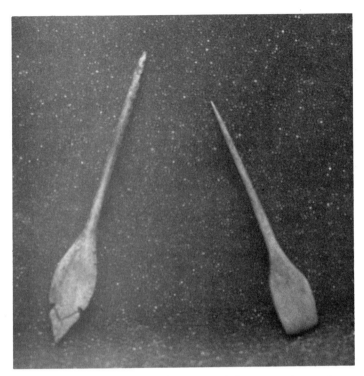

BONE HAIRPINS, both from Tennessee. Left, engraved example, from a site on the Clinch River, Roane County. It is ½ x 3½ inches, $75-100. Right, paddle-shaped pin, Davis Creek area, Clairborne County. It is ½ x 2¾ inches, $50-75
Photo courtesy Blake Gahagan, Tennessee

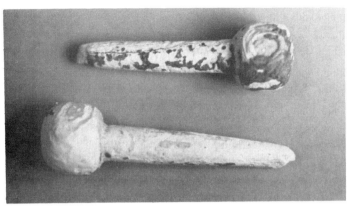

EAR-PINS, conch shell collumella, from Washington County, Virginia. The surface on one of the artifacts has patination. Sizes, 3¾ inches long. A nice matching set of a scarce artifact type.   Pair, $125
Courtesy James E. Maus collection, North Carolina

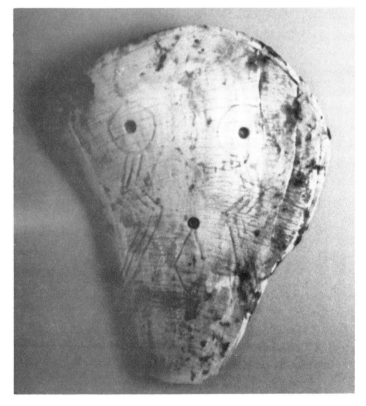

HUMAN FACE GORGET, late prehistoric, shell with Weeping Eye motif. From Lauderdale County, Alabama, this engraved piece is 3½ in. wide and 4½ in. high. This is a rare artifact in fine condition. $1000
Courtesy James E. Maus collection, North Carolina

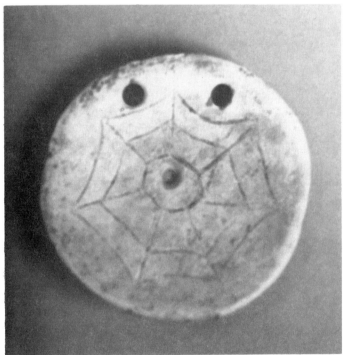

SHELL GORGET, engraved with the Spider Web design, from Smyth County, Virginia. Well-made piece with good design; it is 1¾ in. in diameter. $400
Courtesy James E. Maus collection, North Carolina

ENGRAVED SHELL GORGET, Saltville Rattlesnake design, from Stokes County, North Carolina. Note the different suspension (?) holes for this fine piece. Size, 2½ inches in diameter. $600
Courtesy James E. Maus collection, North Carolina

SHELL GORGET, Saltville Rattlesnake design, nicely engraved. It is from Stokes County, North Carolina and is 3¼ inches in diameter. The meaning, if any, of some gorget/pendants is unclear. $800
Courtesy James E. Maus collection, North Carolina

ORNAMENTAL ARTIFACTS. Top center, shell bracelet from Mason County, KY, 3½ in. diameter. $35
Left and right, 4 shell pendants, Largest 2½ x 4 inches, Each, $8-30
Bottom center, shell-bead bracelet, one pearl bead at top, largest bead ¾ x ⅝ inches.   Bracelet, $125
Courtesy Cliff Markley collection, Alabama

SHELL GORGET, engraved with Citico Rattlesnake motif, piece 4¾ inches in diameter. This artifact is drilled with two holes and also fenestrated with small enlongated, window-like openings. These were shaped by starting with a drill-hole, then by cord-sawing. This is a very rare and attractive example. $1500
Courtesy James E. Maus collection, North Carolina

SHELL GORGET, with Citico Rattlesnake motif, excellent engraving. It is from Smyth County, Virginia and measures 3⅝ inches in diameter. Many shell gorgets have twin suspension (?) holes near what is probably the top. $900
Courtesy James E. Maus collection, North Carolina

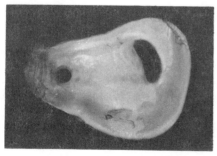

PENDANT made of a nearly complete oyster shell and found on a village site in Humboldt County, California. It measures 2 x 3½ inches. $50
Courtesy Lee Fisher collection, Pennsylvania
Anthony Lang, photographer

BONE EFFIGY human face carved on a broken needle or hair-pin. From Rogers, Arkansas. Depictions of humans are scarce in most prehistoric cultures in the U.S. and this is a rare little piece. $135
Courtesy D.W. Austin collection

SHELL BEAD NECKLACE, marginella beads spaced with curved and tube-shaped beads. The strands are 11 and 12 inches, respectively. From Fairfax County, Virginia. $50
Courtesy Lee Fisher collection, Pennsylvania
Anthony Lang, photographer

BEAR-EFFIGY GORGET or pendant, Lower Brule, South Dakota. This is a fine bone object. $135
Courtesy D.W. Austin collection

CONCH-SHELL DECORATIVE PIECE, from the Arkansas River Valley, 6 inches long. Note the two drill-holes for probable suspension. $150
Courtesy private collection

SHELL PENDANT OR DECORATION, engraved across the entire face, 3 inches in diameter. This piece, probably late prehistoric, is from Fairfax County, Virginia. $50
Courtesy Lee Fisher collection, Pennsylvania
Anthony Lang, photographer

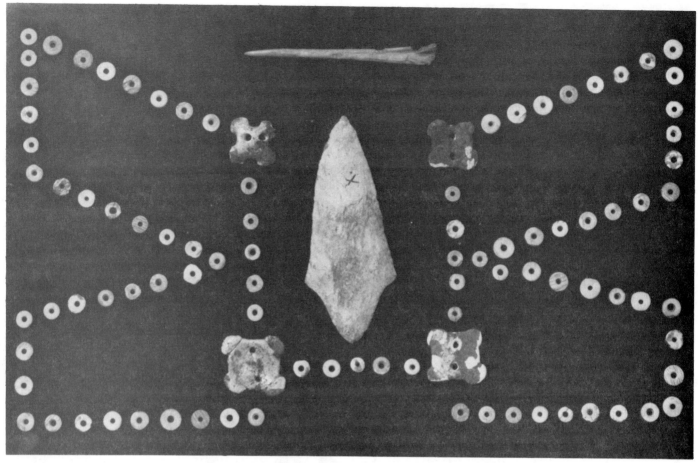

DECORATIVE ARTIFACTS, all from Arkansas. These include shell
beads and shell turtle effigies, a fine flint blade, and a bone awl or
pin. Shell material is not common because it easily deteriorates under
moist conditions.   Frame, $350
Courtesy Larry G. Merriam collection, Oklahoma

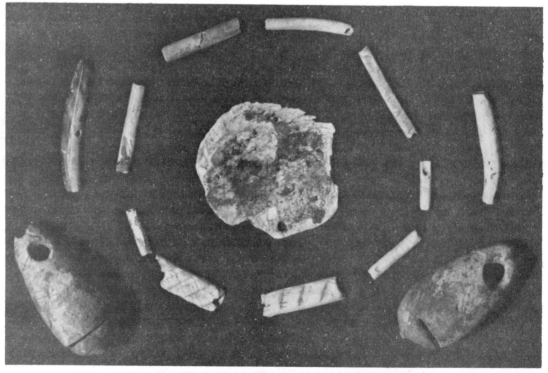

SHELL AND BONE ARTIFACTS, all from Leon, Texas. The large
shells are 3 inches long and may be plummets. The center gorget
has a spider effigy.   Frame, $150
Courtesy D. W. Austin collection

Chapter 18
PIPES

The use of pipes in North America goes back into Archaic times in the Midwest, when simple tubular ''cloud-blower'' forms were made. Many were carefully formed from glacial slate and a variety of the softer hardstones. There is some confusion among collectors as to whether some specimens are tubular bannerstones or tubular pipes. The pipes may have a tapering hole and are usually larger at one end, and are typically longer. Banners often have one side somewhat flattened for the length of the piece, are rarely over about 4 inches long and have a uniform-diameter center hole.

Adena Indians of the Early Woodland period had a number of tubular forms, some with a smaller mouthpiece hole. At times this was partially blocked with a pebble so that the smoking material could not enter. Adena pipes were undoubtedly derived from Archaic examples, and their early forms are quite similar in shape. Fine-grained sandstones and limestone were often used for the tubular forms. A very few rare tubular effigy forms were made, sometimes of pipestone.

The finest pipe-makers in prehistoric North America were the Middle Woodland Hopewell Indians, who crafted a range of flat- and curved-base platform types. Most were of the plain variety, but many hundred effigy pipes were made, mainly in the form of birds and animals.

Some effigy pipes were so finely detailed – the effigy usually surrounding the short bowl – that the exact species can be determined. A few, for added realism, had inset pearls for eyes. In a few cases, ancient breaks were repaired with a copper sheath or strip. For material, colored Ohio pipestone from the Lower Scioto River Valley and possibly from Erie County, was used almost exclusively.

Some ''great pipes'' were made, largely in the South, and these massive animal or bird forms were done in the favored material, steatite. By far the greatest variety of pipes developed in Mississippian (late prehistoric) times, so many it is difficult to classify them. Forms were plain, incised and effigy. Styles included elbow, rounded-bowl, straight and curved trumpet-shaped, angular and many more. At this time also, pipes were made of pottery as well as stone, a pipe material also used somewhat in the earlier Woodland period.

The Plains pipes in rounded form with round bowl set at right angles was widely popular, and a few effigy forms were made. The material was usually redstone or Catlinite. In the Southeast and Northeast, steatite was a favored material. In the Northwest, the delicate ''wineglass'' tubular pipes were widely used, and were made of several close-grained stones. Many different stones were selected for pipes in North America, but baked clay was also widely used.

A number of materials were used for smoking and leaves, stems, grasses and bark might be mixed (at least in historic times) with tobacco on special tobacco boards. Eventually the inexpensive mold-produced clay pipes made by Europeans became the fashion and were used in much of North America. True tobacco was usually smoked in such pipes, though Indians sometimes mixed other substances with the tobacco.

Historic Huron pottery pipes from southern Ontario, Canada, were versions of the upswept trumpet form. Many effigies were created, including one well-made example depicting an owl. The pipe bowl is the body, with the opening behind the head. (Griffin, *Archaeology Of The Eastern United States*, 1952, Figure 27)

Among the rarest of the large platform pipes from late prehistory is a large frog-effigy pipe exhibited at the 1893 World's Fair at Chicago. One of its unusual characteristics is that it seems to have been made of Catlinite. All features of this large effigy form were faithfully rendered. The use of Minnesota redstone is highly unusual, if the material indeed was correctly identified. (Editor, *The Archaeologist*, November 1893, p 209)

The Hupa of California had carefully made tubular pipes made of wood and stone. One example, over 4 inches long, had a wooden stem that flares at each end. The larger flared end has a round steatite bowl in it, the bowl exterior flush with the wood. (Heizer, *Handbook Of North American Indians*, Vol. 8, 1978, p 167)

Especially in pipe-making, some Indians did a surprising amount of work with metal. Eastern Algonquians and Iroquis, as early as the mid-1600's, made entire pipes from brass, lead and pewter. The Eastern Sioux and Ojibway were experts at inlaying lead and pewter (largely tin) into grooves or channels of pipes made of Catlinite or steatite. This work was done mainly in the early 1800's. By the late 1600's, the Fox and Sauk Indians of Illinois and Wisconsin were mining lead ore deposits and smelting the metal into rough ingots. (Furst & Furst, *North American Indian Art*, 1982, p 195)

Contrary to popular belief, not all Catlinite Plains-style pipes have been made by Indians. Machine-turned Catlinite pipes were provided to Indians of the Upper Missouri by such groups as the Northwest Fur Company. The Company traded nearly 2000 such pipes between the years 1865-1868. (Sturtevant & Washburn, *Handbook Of North American Indians*, Vol. 4, 1988, pp 401-402)

The proto-historic Susquehanna Focus of the Northeast U.S., about the time grade goods arrived, had several forms of the curved trumpet-shaped pipe. Both had long, slender stems which upturn for a considerable distance before enlarging to form the pipe bowl. One version was plain, the other effigy. (Griffin, *Archaeology Of The Eastern United States*, 1952, Figure 25)

An original source of pipe material for much of the eastern Midwest was the rock known as Ohio pipestone. Called "fireclay" by early mound explorers, this is a dense, colorful material in shades of red, grey, pink, yellow, brown and more. The ancient quarries are on the east side of the Lower Scioto River Valley in southern Ohio. This material was heavily favored, and was also used for other decorative objects, such as pendants, gorgets, bar amulets and a small, special-type birdstone. (Hothem, various sources)

One of the great *caches* of prehistoric Hopewell pipes was uncovered by the early explorers, Squier and Davis, in the year 1846. This was Mound No. 8, Mound City Group, 5 miles north of Chillicothe, Ohio, the overall site now a National Monument. Nearly 200 stone pipes, mainly Ohio pipestone in different colors were found; most had been ceremonially broken or damaged by fire. Among the rare forms were those of an otter with fish in mouth, heron with fish, and a hawk with bird. (Hothem, *Treasures Of The Mound Builders*, 1989, pp 108-109)

Eskimos made a wide variety of pipes, most with a long, upcurved stem and a small, rounded flared or lipped bowl. The bowl itself was made of lead, brass, bone or ivory. The stems were wood, often lead-inlaid or even reinforced with wrapped cord. All-ivory pipes are rare and some were beautifully etched or carved with animals, fishing or hunting scenes. (Thiry, *Eskimo Artifacts – Designed For Use*, 1977, pp 96-99)

One of the interesting things about pottery pipes for Indian peoples in the late ceramic period is the matter of shaping pipe bowls. In some instances, the pipe bowls copied to some extent the shape of pottery cooking vessels for the area. (Hothem, various sources)

The Kipp Island people of the Woodland period in the Northeast U.S. made four kinds of pipes. There were two varieties of platform pipes, plus an obtuse-angle elbow pipe in baked clay. There was also a right-angle elbow type in both baked clay and stone. (Hothem, various sources)

The Mogollon (beginning around 200 BC) of the Arizona and New Mexico Southwest had several smoking devices. One was a reed cigarette. Another was a tubular pipe which was made of baked clay or stone. (Snow, *The Archaeology Of North America*, 1980, p 112)

Smoking-tobacco as we know it was not generally used by Indians, at least as the sole smoking substance. A widely used word for such substances was *Kinnikinnick*, which has a meaning similar to "mixture." Many kinds of leaves and stems were blended with tobacco, which economized and provided different flavors and aromas. (Pipestone Indian Shrine Association, *Pipes On The Plains*, 1975, p 13)

Adena (Early Woodland) Indians of the Ohio River Valley had six major pipe types: Tubular (cigar-shaped); normal tubular; constricted (mouthpiece) tubular; modified tubular (tall bowl on tube near one end); flared (mouthpiece) tubular; and effigy-form tubular (such as the famous Adena pipe from the original Adena Mound). Also a possible elbow-type may have been used. (Dragoo, *Mounds For The Dead*, 1963, pp 180-181, 183-184)

A large stone pipe was found in Coahoma County, Mississippi in 1893, plowed from the ground. A discoidal or chunkey gamestone was found a dozen feet away. The figure is that of a crouching man, his upper arms bound across his back. Such figures are known from elsewhere, and are called bound prisoner or captive pipes. They are generally quite late in prehistory. This pipe was said to be very well made. (Clark, *The Archaeologist*, March 1894, pp 84-85)

The Early Woodland Middlesex Phase in the Northeast U.S. used a plain elbow pipe. The bowl-set was at an obtuse angle. It is almost as if the end of a tubular pipe had been enlarged and bent upward. These fairly simple pipe forms were made both in pottery and stone. (Hothem, various sources)

Many styles of pipes in stone and pottery were made in the Central Plains region. These included the early tubular ("cloud-blower") types, and variations that had a small, right-angle bowl at one end. Human and animal effigy pipes were fairly common in later centuries. Some pipe forms had multiple drilled holes in some portion, probably for decorative fringes of yarn or feathers. Others had a single hole, probably to accommodate a cord to prevent breakage or loss. (Wedel, *Prehistoric Man On The Great Plains*, 1978, Plates XII, XIV lower)

About the time the Cherokee Indians began receiving trade goods from Europeans, they had several kinds of original-design stone pipes. Both were modified elbow-type pipes. One had a thick, rectangular stem with rounded bowl set at an obtuse angle. The other had a thinner, rounded stem and conical bowl set at right angles. (Griffin, *Archaeology Of The Eastern United States*, Figure 111)

One of the pipe forms used by the Late Archaic Meadowood peoples of the Northeast U.S. was a tubular form. These were made of baked clay (pottery) and were up to 6 or more inches long. In the eastern Midwest, this pipe form may have continued into Early Woodland times, inherited from the Red Ochre people who made the tubular pipe in stone. As yet, the transfer of pipe designs in prehistoric times is imperfectly understood. (Hothem, various sources)

In the Middle Columbia area of the Northwestern Plateau, the elbow pipe replaced tubular pipes in historic times. In addition, the disc-bowl or discoidal pipe was introduced in late prehistoric times in the Yakima Valley. The disc forms the pipe body, with the bowl set in one edge, the stem hole entering at about 90 degrees to it. (Martin, Quimby & Collier, *Indians Before Columbus*, 1949, p 457)

The Anasazi of Pueblo Bonito, New Mexico, had several pipe styles. One example is a stone elbow pipe with stem, 3½ inches long. Another is made of pottery with a painted stem, also 3½ inches long. The last example somewhat resembles the Anasazi dippers. (Jennings, *Prehistory Of North America*, 1968, pp 272-273)

The Plateau region of the Northwestern U.S., much of the region drained by the Columbia and Fraser rivers, was noted for tubular pipe forms. These were often made of talc schist, which is similar to steatite. Some pipes had a flared end, also a flared bowl, and there where many variations. In the AD 1800's, following influence from Plains examples, the primary pipe form became elbow types. (Martin, Quimby & Collier, *Indians Before Columbus*, 1949, p 450)

Proto-historic Indians of the Northeast U.S. – such as the Onondaga-Oneida and Seneca – had various versions of the trumpet-shaped pipe in baked clay. All were one-piece, had a long, tapered pottery stem and upturned, enlarged bowl. The bowl area in turn might be fairly plain, ringed with incised lines to give a tightly coiled appearance, flared or effigy. (Griffin, *Archaeology Of The Eastern United States*, 1952, Figure 19)

In the U.S. Midwest, Late Archaic - Early Woodland tubular pipes range from about 3 to 9 or more inches long. From cigar-shaped early in the period to carefully-made cylindrical types in Adena times, the form remained essentially the same. The drilling of the large central hole was accomplished with wand or reed drillsticks and such holes had four different configurations as seen in side-section. One was a more-or-less uniform diameter. More common was the tapered hole, larger at one end. Less common was the double-taper, larger at each end and becoming smaller within the tube toward the center. The final form was the blocked-end Adena pipe, with the large hole being met by a very small hole at the mouthpiece end. (Board Managers, *Ohio Centennial Report*, 1877, pp 124-126, Plate 10)

Tube pipes are certainly one of the oldest known styles and they were made of stone or bone in the prehistoric Great Plains country. Pipes having an ''L'' shaped bowl and a long wooden stem were used on the Plains in historic times; here, the bowl is at the end of the pipe. ''T'' shaped or Sioux-style pipes have the bowl about midway on the pipe. Elaborate, highly carved (often effigy motifs) pipes of whatever fanciful design were usually made by Plains Indians after they acquired metal tools from European traders. Some, after ca. 1864, were made by non-Indians. (Pipestone Indian Shrine Association, *Pipes On The Plains*, 1975, pp 6-10)

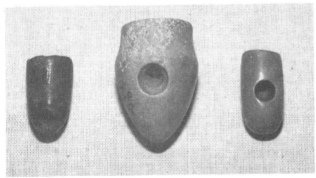

OHIO PIPE FORMS, all left to right: Black steatite, extremely thin bowl sides, ⅞ x 1½ inches, from Pickaway County, OH. $145
Yellow quartz, 1¾ x 2⅜ inches, from Warren County, OH. Ex-coll. Dr. Meuser, his number 1612 over 5. $350
YELLOW-TAN OHIO PIPESTONE, ⅞ x 1¾ inches, from Adams County, OH. $235
Courtesy Gerald Bernacchi collection, Indiana

EFFIGY GREAT PIPE, from Stewart County, Tennessee and found near the Cumberland River. This is a highly polished artifact and extremely rare. It is 10 inches long. $6000
Courtesy Dr. Gary Meek collection, Arkansas

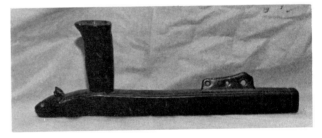

STONE EFFIGY PIPE, from Madison County, North Carolina. This is a well-made piece and the small holed crest may have had decorative dangles at one time. Size, 3½ in. high, 10 in. long. $1500

Courtesy Dr. Gary Meek collection, Arkansas

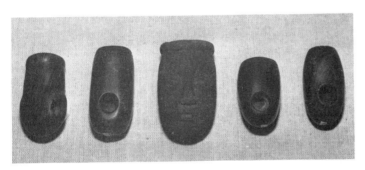

BOWL-TYPE PIPES, all left to right: Green banded slate, 1⅜ x 2⅛ inches, DeKalb, IN, ex-Parks. $325
Brown slate, 1¼ 2⅜ inches, two rings around bowl-top, Indiana, $175.
Red fine-grained sandstone, human face, 1½ x 2½ inches, from Ohio, $175. Brown banded slate, 1⅛ x 1⅞ in., tally-marks by stem hole, Indiana, $200. Green banded slate, 1 x 2⅛ inches, from Indiana. There are 18 tally marks around the stem-hole, $200
Courtesy Gerald Bernacchi collection, Indiana

ELBOW-TYPE PIPE, late prehistoric period, made of dark honey-colored chlorite. Size is 1⅞ x 3⅝ in. long and origin is Mahoning County, Ohio. The pipe rim is tally-marked completely around the bowl. This is a very attractive piece in an unusual and rare material.
$1700-2550
Private collection, Ohio

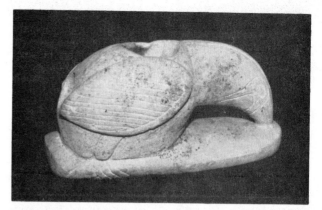

EFFIGY PIPE, platform type of a feeding bird, probably a hawk or eagle. Size is 3¾ in. high and 7½ in. long; material is a grey-white limestone. Ex-coll. Durham. This piece is from Southcentral U.S. and a fine example of stone carving. It is probably late prehistoric.
Museum quality
Courtesy private collection

FROG EFFIGY PIPE, late prehistoric, unknown provenance. This is a large, well-made piece, size 2 x 4 x 6 inches.
$1200
Courtesy Dr. Gary Meek collection, Arkansas

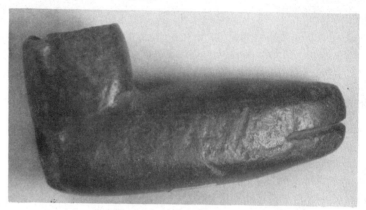

"GREAT PIPE" SNAKE EFFIGY, steatite, 2½ x 5½ in. long. From Wyoming County, Pennsylvania, it is ex-coll. Dr. Johnson. Pipe is very unusual in that the stem hole does not enter from the smaller, effigy end but through the terminal elbow end below the bowl.
$1200-1800
Courtesy Len & Janie Weidner collection, Ohio

EFFIGY PIPE, pottery, Southcentral U.S. Size, 3¼ in. high, 2½ x 5½ inches. This may symbolize the three worlds, being a kingfisher(?) with a turtle on the neck. The turtle would be Middle World, while the bird is Upper (in air) and Lower World (diving in water after fish). A very interesting effigy.
Museum quality
Courtesy private collection

WALKING-BEAR EFFIGY PIPE, in yellow quartzite, 4 x 6 in. long. This was originally collected from a Kentucky farm family and was found at the turn of the century. A fine piece with good detail, executed in a very hard material.
$2500-3000
Courtesy Len & Janie Weidner collection, Ohio

EFFIGY PIPES, both in steatite. Left, North Carolina, excellent three-dimensional effigy of a squirrel. Right, Wisconsin, 1¾ x 3⅛ inches, fine engraving on this piece. Ex-colls. Edmundson and Neil, the pipes are both exceptional type specimen. $850-1500
Courtesy Len & Janie Weidner collection, Ohio

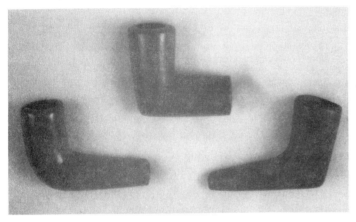

OHIO VALLEY ELBOW PIPES, materials pipestone or slate. Left example is 1¾ x 2¾ inches; all Ohio, and ex-colls. Shipley, Wehrle and Neil. These little pipes are found over a wide area of OH, IN, KY, IL and WV. Material and workmanship is above average on these. The value depends on material and workstyle more than size.
$225-650
Courtesy Len & Janie Weidner collection, Ohio

PLAINS-TYPE PIPES, Catlinite, large example 4 x 7 inches. Smaller piece is from the Dr. Johnson (PA) collection and is from Shawnee County, Kansas. Larger pipe is from Buffalo Co., South Dakota. These have good mellow color with some yellowish-orange spots. Value depends on size, color and design. Smaller, about $175; larger, about $450.
Courtesy Len & Janie Weidner collection, Ohio

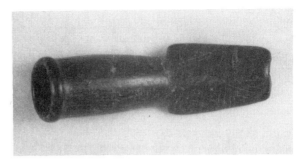

OBTUSE-ANGLE PIPE, steatite, 1¾ x 5 inches long, originally collected by Billy Lea, ex-coll. Dr. Goldberg, this piece is from Virginia. This is a highly engraved well-made example; authentic examples from the area are difficult to acquire. $2000-2500
Courtesy Len & Janie Weidner collection, Ohio

DEER-HEAD EFFIGY PIPE (small Great Pipe). Made of steatite, it is 2¼ x 3 inches, originally collected by Steve Olenick, northern Ohio. Very fine three-dimensional effigy forms are very rare; this is a top-of-the-line example of prehistoric art, in superb condition. $2000-2500
Courtesy Len & Janie Weidner collection, Ohio

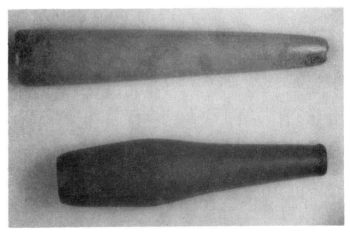

ADENA-CULTURE TUBULAR PIPES. Top, 1 x 6 in. long, from Gallipolis, Ohio and ex-coll. Dr. John F. Neil. Ohio pipestone is a rare material. Bottom, slate, from Ohio River area, this is a rare and highly developed tubular form. $800-1500
Courtesy Len & Janie Weidner collection, Ohio

TURTLE-EFFIGY GREAT PIPE made of steatite, 2 x 5 in. long. From Ross County, Ohio, it is ex-coll. Shipley. A turtlehead rendition is a rare effigy form, and this is an excellent example.

$1500-2000

Courtesy Len & Janie Weidner collection, Ohio

OWL PIPE, two holes drilled in the back, weight 19 pounds. From Kay County, Oklahoma, the material is tan-buff, close-grained. This piece is Mound-builder period. Size, 8½ x 8½ x 9½ inches.

Museum quality

Courtesy Marguerite L. Kernaghan collection
photographers Marguerite L. & Stewart W. Kernaghan

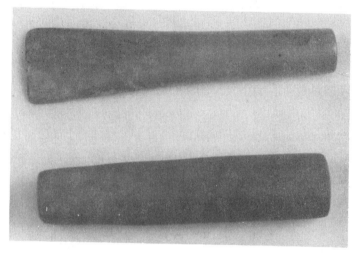

ADENA-CULTURE TUBULAR PIPES. Top, pipestone, 1¼ x 5½ in. long. This is ex-coll. Dr. John F. Neil and is from Gallipolis, Ohio. The flattened mouthpiece is a rare feature. Bottom, compact sandstone, from Pickaway County, Ohio, excellent form. $800-1500
Courtesy Len & Janie Weidner collection, Ohio

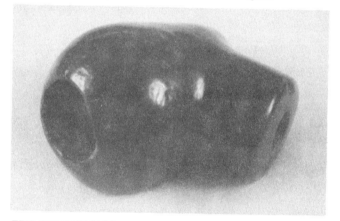

ERIE CULTURE ELBOW-TYPE PIPE, late prehistoric, made of dark green nephrite jade. It is 2¹⁄₁₆ x 2³⁄₁₆ inches and from northestern New York state. The pipe has fine color and is very highly polished and quite attractive; the gem material adds to both interest and value.

$1700-2500

Private collection, Ohio

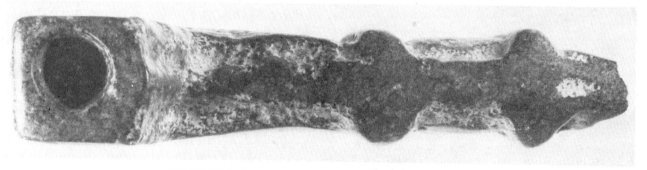

EFFIGY PIPE, elbow type, with image of lizard-like animal along the stem top. Possibly from Missouri, it is 1¼ in. wide and 6½ in. long; mouth-end was broken off and pipe originally was longer. Material is a charcoal grey hardstone with some dark green. $400
Courtesy Jon and Bonnie Mau collection, Wisconsin

Chapter 19
OTHER DECORATIVE OBJECTS

It is uncertain when basketry developed in North America, but the presence of mortars in Western sites that have been dated reach back to at least 5000 BC. Mortars are generalized seed-grinding tools, and containers were needed to gather seeds and nuts. Possibly the earliest forms were carrying baskets, though storage baskets may well have also been present. Very ancient basketry sandals have been found that may even predate the baskets themselves.

Basketry has been decorated in many ways. The usual method is to use different colors of the same material (dyed) or different materials to form patterns or designs in contrasting color and/or textures. Feathers from small birds, or beads were used to decorate special baskets intended as gifts rather than for everyday use. Basket forms are limited only by the capability or physical properties of the natural materials used.

Pottery in North America is not nearly as old as basketry, and was widely made only by 2500 BC or so. Due to the plasticity of the medium, pottery has an extra dimension in that it can be shaped into decorative forms before firing. The ''final touch'' decoration is applied in several ways. Pottery can be enhanced by the way it is coiled, and with the addition of parts such as lugs or handles or spouts. Pottery can have designs incised or punched or rolled into the surface and hundreds of combinations are possible.

Color, however, is the main way Indian pottery is decorated, at least in the last several thousand years. The colors of clay can create the colors of pots. Firing itself can be done in a reducing atmosphere to make a black pot and this can be further worked to produce a glossy or a matte finish. The most common method of pottery decoration is painting, usually over a thin slip or slurry that prepares the surface. The range of designs or figures on pottery is nearly endless.

Weavings, probably wearing blankets or cloaks at first, are also very old in North America. Fine samples of fabric have come from mounds several thousand years old, and caves and rock-shelters have produced fabrics that are probably even earlier. Florida swamps contained finely woven shrouds that may be 9000 years or more old.

While there is evidence that some of the Mound Builder's weavings had painted designs, most blankets or clothing if decorated had woven-in designs or patterns. This was accomplished with dyes or with different materials. It is thought that Woodland-era Indians also had sewn-on decorations made of mica and sheet copper cut-outs. And in historic times, wearing blankets and other clothing were often decorated with trade silver ornaments, mainly brooches.

In addition to these broad classes just mentioned, and thick books have been written about each, there are other, largely stone artifacts that are partly or entirely decorative.

Charmstones from the California region are elongated, rounded objects, usually heavier on one end and with an attachment means at the other. Many were made of beautiful gem-like stones, while others are of various grades of hardstone. Many theories have been advanced as to what purpose these served, including use as pendants and magical charms. Whatever, they are decorative in their own right. Charmstones are probably related to the plummets found elsewhere in the United States.

Cones are another enigma, and while a dozen theories exist as to their real use, purpose or function, that remains somewhat of a mystery. Once called ''hemispheres,'' cones are from Woodland (Mound Builder) times. Some are wide and flat-based, others higher and narrow. All do have a flattish base, and some have a hollowed-out center. A few are incised or have a tally-notched basal edge.

A very wide range of materials was used, including hematite and hardstones of all kinds. The very rarest forms were made of rock crystal and very few such examples exist. If there is a common factor, most cones were made of durable material that took a high polish. Strangely, most cones do not have signs of use or wear.

Discoidals are artistic circles in stone, 1 to 6 inches in diameter, and there are perhaps a dozen types or variations. Somewhat similar objects from California have been referred to as club-heads and digging-stick weights. However, the discoidals or disc-shaped artifacts from the Southcentral and Eastern U.S. do have a known function.

These objects are common from the late-prehistoric Mississippian lifeway and were used into historic times. Discoidals (also called ''chunkey-stones'') were used in a game called ''chunkey,'' and there are many different spellings of the word. Too, there are a number of different historic accounts of how the game was actually played and these often vary a great deal in detail. It is known for certain that a special, flat playing field was involved. The discoidals were rolled around the ground and spear-like sticks were thrown by standing or running players. Some early accounts state that players and/or spectators often wagered large amounts on the outcome of the game.

Some discoidals do show signs of rough usage, being chipped and battered. Others may be made of beautiful materials and are finely formed and highly polished. Such specimen usually do not have use or wear signs. Different forms (biscuit, barrel, Jersey Bluff, etc.) are all rounded, but have varying treatment of the sides or faces. This ranges from excurvate to flat to incurvate. Many examples are ''dimpled'' with smaller concave indentations, or have a central hole through the midsection, face-to-face.

Discoidals were made from sandstone and other softer materials, but many were shaped from quality hardstone. This includes speckled and dark diorite, spotted porphyry and conglomerates known as "puddingstone." In some cases, the large discoidals seem to have been more carefully made, but there are exceptions. The Fort Ancient people of the eastern Midwest often decorated their discoidals with shallow drill-holes in patterns, and incised lines that often radiated out from the center of the faces.

Effigies (other than the "lizard" forms of Chapter 4) are rare artifacts, though they turn up across the country from most time periods. Often the original function is obscure, but use as magical charms, for ceremonies, as decoration, or even toys or playthings may be supposed. Effigies are usually of animals and birds, less often of humans. Stone, bone, antler and wood were often used.

Pestles or elongated stones for grinding seeds, nuts and dried meat are found in most of North America. Mortars, or the receptacle holding material for the pestle, are usually large slabs or cups of stone. Some mortars were decorated with paint, or carved into an artistic form, but these are unusual.

Pestles were sometimes decorative in themselves and two examples are given here. In the Wisconsin region, some elongated spud-like pestles had pecked eyes, giving the appearance of a short, wide snake. Some pestles from the Northwest Coast are beautiful works of art, with the handle end opposite the grinding base being artistically carved, or in the image of animals or humans. For the finer examples, use was probably restricted to important occasions.

Plummets, also found across much of the U.S., have simple, elongated shapes. Again, there are types and varieties. Plummets (named after the carpenter's plumb-bob, which they somewhat resemble) average perhaps 2½ inches long. They tend to be heavier at the bottom end, while the top end usually has some method of attachment or suspension. This may be either a thin groove or a drill-hole.

Some plummets, though obviously finished, show no attachment method at all. While it is thought that plummets may be tools – weights for *bolas* sets, or for the edges of small, thrown nets – there are other examples that show no signs of actual use. It has been suggested that plummets without suspension means may have been sewn into leather pockets and used in that fashion.

Plummets are often found near bodies of water, adding support to the thought that they were weights for entanglement or snaring devices for waterfowl, or were at least part of such kits. However, some plummets are beautifully made of polished hardstone and obviously were never intended for hard use. Many plummets were made of hematite or iron ore, but examples of colored quartzite or even clear rock crystal are known. Some examples were even engraved.

Rock art is a general term for incised lines or painting done on a rock surface, usually quite large. Found across the country, such pictographs (picture-writing) and petroglyphs (rock incising) are more common in the Western U.S., probably because the terrain there offered more marking surfaces. A great amount of rock art has disappeared over the centuries because the paint has faded or the rock has weathered away. And sadly, recent and modern vandals have destroyed or defaced many works of rock art.

Some rock art, however, has been done on a smaller scale. Occasionally such artifacts turn up in collections or are recovered from surface-hunting ancient sites. Such prehistoric work was often done on broken artifacts for some reason. The most common examples are incised lines that create geometric or abstract forms. The rarest are outlines of recognizable bird, animal or human figures. A large number of the latter were done in late prehistory.

Spools are short cylinders of sandstone, made by the Fort Ancient and other Mississippian-era peoples. The spool ends are high, the center lowered. At times, the flat cylinder or spool ends have indentations in each center. The cylindrical portion is covered with decorations, cut into the surface. It is believed that these scarce artifacts are doubly decorative.

While they are themselves decorated, the theory is that paint was put on the rounded surface, and this was then applied to arms and legs for personal adornment. A forked stick with dowels through each arm would have made a suitable handle. In operation, the spool would have been somewhat like our own paint-rollers, laying down an endless decoration in a short time.

These are just a few of the decorative artifact forms that were once made by prehistoric Amerinds. Each served an important function in the long-ago lifeway and is treasured by the collector of today.

OHIO DISCOIDALS, top row left to right: Grey, highly polished granite, 3¼ inches in diameter. $350
Yellow-tan flint, 2⅞ inches diameter, Warren County, ex-Meuser number 2002 over 5. $550
Bottom row, left to right: Yellow-tan flint, 1½ inches, Feurt site Scioto County, ex-Meuser number 1453 over 5, engraved with arrows and tally-marks. $95
Brown quartzite, 2¼ inches, Highland County. $175
Courtesy Gerald Bernacchi collection, Indiana

DISCOIDAL, Mississippian period, left, multi-colored granite. Large at 4⅛ inches in diameter, this piece has GIRS #N16 and was pictured in the Payne collection, 1937. It is from eastern Tennessee. $400
DISCOIDAL, tan-brown quartzite, from near Rome, Ohio, Adams County. It is 3⅞ inches and ex-coll. Meuser, number 1636 over 5. An arrow-like design is incised on the top. $775
Courtesy Gerald Bernacchi collection, Indiana

BAR AMULETS, all left to right: Humped type, grey slate, Williams County, Ohio; ⅝ x 3½ inches, $400. Brown banded slate, from Indiana, 1⅛ x 2¾ inches, $275. Green banded slate, drilled and grooved on one end, Indiana, ¾ x 2¾ inches, $200. Black slate, from Indiana, size 1 x 3 inches, $250. All specimens except the extreme left are ex-coll. Warner.
Courtesy Gerald Bernacchi collection, Indiana

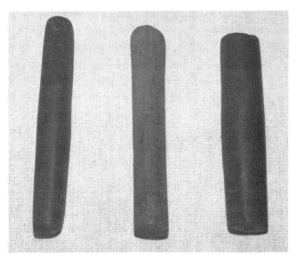

BAR AMULETS, all left to right: Black slate, ⅝ x 5⅜ inches, ex-coll. Wachtel, from Columbus, Indiana. $450
Brown slate, ¾ x 5 inches, ex-coll. Wachtel, from Drake County, OH, $350. Grey banded slate, 1 x 4¾ inches. It is from Wyandot County, OH. $350. Bar amulets are scarce artifacts, and Late Arcahic/Early Woodland.
Courtesy Gerald Bernacchi collection, Indiana

TURTLE EFFIGY, Sioux Indian, ca. 1930. It is carved from red Catlinite, with set in turquoise. The Catlinite (Minnesota pipestone) is highly polished. Size, 1½ x 2¾ x 6 inches long. $400-600
Courtesy Marguerite L. Kernaghan collection
photographers Marguerite L. & Stewart W. Kernaghan

HUMAN EFFIGY, pottery, Southcentral U.S. Size 3½ x 6½ inches. This figure, with stylized and mask-like features, is reminiscent of the long-nose god. A fine piece, in top condition. Museum quality
Courtesy private collection

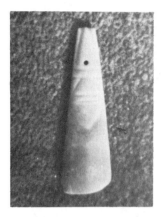

JADE PENDANT, single suspension hole, figure a stylized human (?) face. The lower portion terminates in a dulled cutting edge, which is very thin. The material is translucent green jade, and size is 1 x 3¼ inches. $350
Courtesy private collection

JADE PENDANT, highly polished translucent medium-green jade, from Costa Rica, Central America. The form is a stylized human with folded arms, and with thin adz base. Size, ⅞ x 3¼ inches. $350
Courtesy private collection

SQUASH BLOSSOM NECKLACE, made of Indian Head pennies, naja of copper, cabochon of variscite, date 1887. This is in top condition, heavy, 15 inches long and from Sanastee Trading Post, Arizona. $1000-1500
Courtesy Marguerite L. Kernaghan collection
photographers Marguerite L. & Stewart W. Kernaghan

JADE PENDANT, two small suspension holes at top, stylized face form. It is from Costa Rica, Central America, and is made of pale green jade. Size is 1 x 2¼ inches and thickness is about ¼ inch. $250
Courtesy private collection

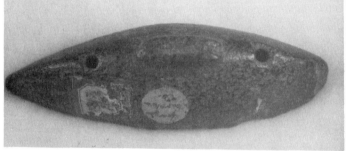

SCOOPED AND RIDGED BOATSTONE, material is a rare silver steatite. Size, 2 x 4½ inches; this piece is from Cherokee County, Georgia and ex-colls. Pohler and Payne. The artifact is nicely finished, well-drilled, bottom-scooped and top-ridged. Rare combinations. $850-1500
Courtesy Len & Janie Weidner collection, Ohio

JADE ADZ-GOD PENDANT, Costa Rica, Central America. Material is a mottled purple jade and suspension hole is beneath the head, running cross-wise. This is a fine little piece, ¾ x 3⁵⁄₁₆ inches long. $600
Courtesy private collection

CROW INDIAN BEAR FETISH, top, in pink feldspar with beads, thongs, turquoise and feathers. It is ca. 1900 and size is 2 x 5½ inches. Museum quality
CROW INDIAN SNAKE FETISH, ca. 1900, in carved horn with turquoise eyes, feathers and thongs. It is 10 inches long. Museum quality
Courtesy Marguerite L. Kernaghan collection
photographers Marguerite L. & Stewart L. Kernaghan

CEREMONIAL PESTLE OR HAND-CLUB, made of dense black basalt. Size, 4½ x 7½ inches high, from Washington state, northwest coast. Ex-coll. L.J. Marcus. The very highly developed form and excellent workstyle make this a rare and high-form artwork.
$1500-1800
Courtesy Len & Janie Weidner collection, Ohio

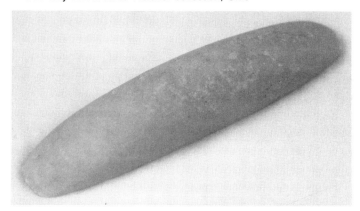

BOATSTONE, tan-cream quartzite, from Champaign County, Ohio. It is 1⁵⁄₁₆ x 5¹¹⁄₁₆ in. long and nicely polished. The base is concave and also well polished. This is a nicely formed and worked piece in a scarce material. $350-600
Private collection, Ohio

SHAMAN'S RATTLE, from Long Island on the Tennessee River, Roane County, TN. It is Dallas culture, a late phase of the Mississippian in East Tennessee. It is AD 1450-1650-plus. Material is a finely crushed shell-tempered pottery. A face is on the handle top and Dallas 3-line design on the body, which contains tiny river pebbles in the hollow space. Size, 1¾ x 1¾ x 4½ inches. $500-750
Courtesy Blake Gahagan, TN

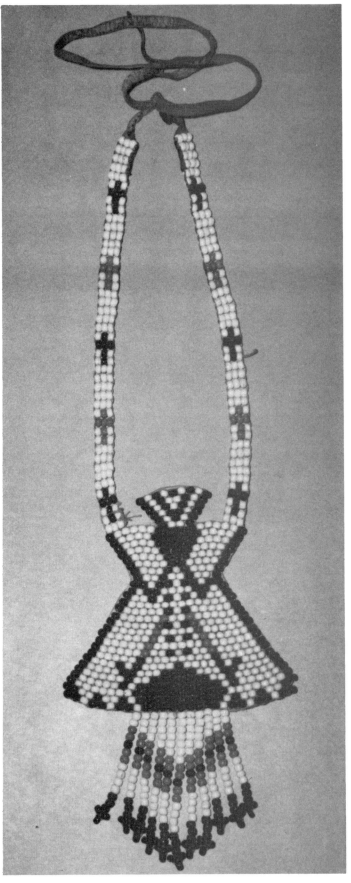

SIOUX PONY-BEAD NECKLACE, in form resembling the Flathead teepee pendant. It is mounted on leather with glue and is ca. 1920. Size, 4⅔ x 15½ inches. This was collected on Pine Ridge Reservation, South Dakota. A bright and attractive piece. $300-400
Courtesy Marguerite L. Kernaghan collection
photographers Marguerite L. & Stewart L. Kernaghan

SOUTHCENTRAL U.S. DECORATIVE POTTERY. Top, wood duck effigy, $300. Left, turtle form, $150; right, deer, $150. Bottom row, left, bird effigy, $200; right, wood duck, $125. Lower center column, top, bird effigy pipe, $100; middle, sun form, $50; bottom, turkey effigy, $35.   Courtesy Wilfred Dick collection, Mississippi

DOG EFFIGY VESSEL, state of Nayarit, Mexico. This region is noted for large, hollow effigy pottery of many kinds, including human. This is a fine piece, with reddish-tan color. $400
Courtesy Wilfred Dick collection, Mississippi

KWAKUITL MASK, Northwest Coast, with movable mouth made of wood and brass. Size 7½ x 8½ x 14 inches, this fine piece was made by Coyot. $800
Courtesy Marguerite L. Kernaghan collection
photographers Marguerite L. & Stewart L. Kernaghan

100

FALSE FACE MASK, Protruding Tongue, made by Ti'nyun'givus, Seneca Tribe, Turtle Clan. This piece is 6¼ x 11 inches and hair is 30 in. long. This is a copy of an old mask and is not ritually blessed. $500-750
Courtesy Marguerite L. Kernaghan collection
photographers Marguerite L. & Stewart L. Kernaghan

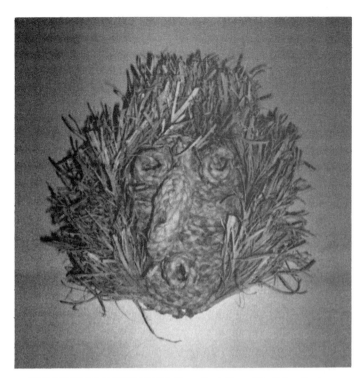

"GAJESA" IROQUOIS MASK, Corn Husk Face, Medicine Society. Full adult size, 10 x 11 inches, made by Hiya'sa TA ("He refuses everyone") of the Mohawk Tribe, Turtle Clan, Central New York state. This is a copy of an old mask but has not been blessed in ritual. $300-500
Courtesy Marguerite L. Kernaghan collection
photographers Marguerite L. & Stewart L. Kernaghan

HIDE AND FUR MASK, Eskimo, 9 x 14 inches. An attractive and carefully made piece, it is from Anavatuk Pass, Alaska and ca. 1970. It is in perfect condition. $275
Courtesy Marguerite L. Kernaghan collection
photographers Marguerite L. & Stewart L. Kernaghan

FALSE FACE MASK, Broken Nose, Iroquois, made by Sin'has ("Tall Forest"), Cayuga Tribe, Wolf Clan. Size 7 x 11 inches, hair 30 in. long. This is a copy of an old mask and is not ritually blessed. $500-750
Courtesy Marguerite L. Kernaghan collection
photographers Marguerite L. & Stewart L. Kernaghan

CHIPPEWA HAIR ROACH, with porcupine hair and leather head-
band. There are painted decorations on the band in red and blue.
Band is 18 inches and height with hair 11 inches. This is a nice
Eastern Woodlands piece. $225-350
Courtesy Marguerite L. Kernaghan collection
photographers Marguerite L. & Stewart L. Kernaghan

EFFIGY PESTLE, dense black basalt, 3½ x 6½ inches. From
Washington state, Northwest Coast, this is ex-colls. C.C. Smith and
Bunch, pictured in *Who's Who*. This is a rare effigy form with triple-
ridge top, extremely well-made and very graceful. $1200
Courtesy Len & Janie Weidner collection, Ohio

SQUASH BLOSSOM NECKLACE, silver, made of Liberty Head
dimes, pieces of abalone at tie and naja of silver. It is 13¾ inches
high, old and in top condition. From Teec Nos Pos trading post,
Navajo reservation. $1100-1500
Courtesy Marguerite L. Kernaghan collection
photographers Marguerite L. & Stewart L. Kernaghan

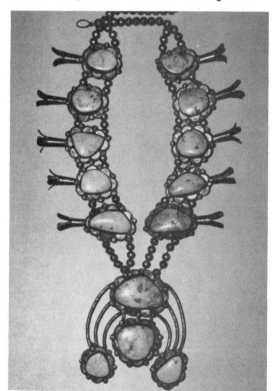

OLD PAWN NECKLACE, Navajo man's in squash blossom motif.
Done in silver and Morenci turquoise, it is well-designed and well-
made. Very heavy, it measures 4 x 17 inches at the naja. $1500-2000
Courtesy Marguerite L. Kernaghan collection
photographers Marguerite L. & Stewart L. Kernaghan

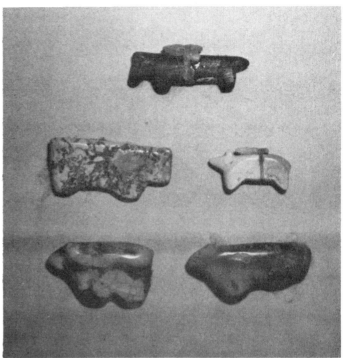

ZUNI FETISHES. Top, agate with arrow on back, ½ x 1½ inches. 2nd row, l., turquoise with arrow on back, ½ x 1 inch. Bot. row l., turquoise, 1 x 1½ inches. Bot. r., turquoise, ¾ x 1¾ inches. All pieces are well-made and highly polished.   Each, $95-200
Courtesy Marguerite L. Kernaghan collection
photographers Marguerite L. & Stewart L. Kernaghan

SILVER NECKLACE, half dollars 1900 & 1907, two Liberty quarters 1925 & 1926, Liberty Head nickel 1910, Indian head nickel with date worn, two Liberty head dimes 1912 & 1896. Naja is silver, the cabochon of turquoise. Necklace is 13½ inches high.
$800-1300

Courtesy Marguerite L. Kernaghan collection
photographers Marguerite L. & Stewart L. Kernaghan

EFFIGY POTTERY FORMS. Top left, male effigy, from Jalisco, Mexico, fine condition, $400. Top center, female effigy, from Mexico, $30. Top right, humpbacked female pot, Southcentral U.S., $385.
Courtesy Wilfred Dick collection, Mississippi

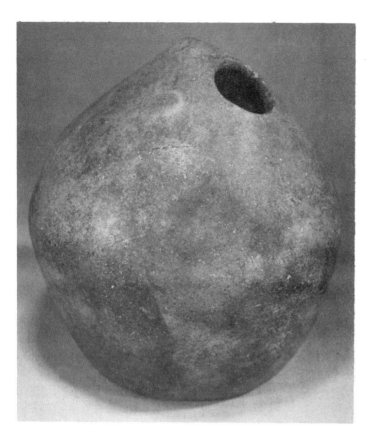

EFFIGY SEED JAR in the form of a large human female breast. It is Caddo culture and ca. AD 1200-1400 and from Clark County, Arkansas. This fine vessel is in perfect condition and measures 8 in. high, 7 in. wide. $800-900
Courtesy private collection of Sam and Nancy Johnson, Murfreesboro, Arkansas

EFFIGY BOWL, double-headed bear form relating to the ceremonial Bear Cult. Type is Hempstead Engraved and vessel is from Ka-Do-Ha Village, Pike County, Arkansas. It is ca. AD 1200-1400. Bear heads are also rattles in this rare specimen. Size, 3 in. high, 6 in. wide. $400-500
Courtesy private collection of Sam and Nancy Johnson Murfreesboro, Arkansas

DUCK EFFIGY BOWL, Mississippian period and AD 1200-1400. It is from Mississippi County, Arkansas and has fine detail. In perfect condition, the buff-colored piece is 5 inches high, 6 inches wide. $600-800
Courtesy private collection of Sam and Nancy Johnson, Murfreesboro, Arkansas

CAT-SERPENT BOWL, Mississippian, Southern Cult style. It is ca. AD 1400-1450 and is from Cross County, Arkansas. There is some restoration to the tail section; note the finely shaped head. This pottery piece is 4 in. high and 6¾ in. wide. $800-1200
Courtesy private collection of Sam and Nancy Johnson, Murfreesboro, Arkansas

CERAMIC FIGURINES, Mexico or Central America. Top center, clockwise: Small clay face; clay face; clay torso; clay face; bead or spindle-whorl weight; miniature pot. Scale, doll or torso figurine, 1½ x 3 inches. Values for such pieces range from $3 to $15 each
Courtesy Jon and Bonnie Mau collection, Wisconsin

DECORATED PITCHER, Tularose black-on-white, Anasazi culture. It is circa AD 1100-1250 and measures 4 x 5 inches. The handle is in the form of a dog's head. From Catron County, New Mexico. $350
Courtesy Lee Fisher collection, Pennsylvania
Anthany Lang, photographer

DECORATED WATER BOTTLE, Neeley's Ferry Plain, with human faces on the sides. Mississippian period, Southern U.S., and ca. AD 1000. Size, 5½ x 7½ inches. This is a well-formed vessel. $375
Courtesy Lee Fisher collection, Pennsylvania
Anthany Lang, photographer

DECORATED BOWL, Mississippian (late prehistoric) in the form of a wood duck effigy. This is a well-executed piece, and from the Southern U.S. It has slight restoration and is 6 x 9 inches $275
Courtesy Lee Fisher collection, Pennsylvania
Anthany Lang, photographer

POTTERY JAR, Hodges Engraved Caddo, from Clark County, Arkansas. Shown in the frame are points which were found inside the jar. The center point is a Howard type, 1⅝ in. long. The others are Alba types.   Pottery jar, $400
Courtesy private collection   Point group, $350

ORNAMENTAL POTTERY. Both pieces are red and white painted greyware and are from Pemiscot County, Missouri. Left, head-effigy with child-like features. $1500-1750
Right, breast-effigy, rare form. $750-1000
Courtesy Blake Gahagan, Tennessee

Chapter 20
THE TOURIST TRADE

Many an old Indian piece stuck away in a drawer or in the attic or on a shelf was indeed made by American Indians, but not for their own use. Such pieces were often made simply for sale, as an item of commerce.

When the bison disappeared from the Plains, when the fur trade slowly faded, when other ways of earning a livelihood no longer were satisfactory, many Indian artisans developed new markets. After the upheaval of the Civil War ended, and the Inter-continental railroads made travel faster, easier and less expensive, a new breed of traveler developed.

These were people who moved about to see and experience new places, and went on traveling vacations or tours to do so. These tourists gradually became an important source of income to the Indians, who only had to stay in one place and make useful or decorative items to sell. This commerce of course exists to the present day, often with Indian trading posts and catalogs and dealers and auctions as intermediaries.

It should be noted that for many years prior to the tourist trade era as such, Indians had been creating objects for sale or trade to European-settled homesteads and villages. This trade might consist of baskets, smoke-or brain-tanned leathers, moccasins, necklaces or carved dolls.

Making items for the tourist trade was strongly underway by the late 1870's and 1880's, so there now has been more than a century of decorative and ornamental artifacts that have accumulated. At times the wares (pottery) are similar to what the Indians themselves used, while others (replicas of Plains shields) were largely made to resemble the older items, but were not made in the same way or with the same materials. It is simply a human tendency to put more care into an item one uses and keeps than one that will be sold.

This said, it is recognized that the Indian craftsperson eventually dealt with two broad classes of tourist-customer. One was the general public, with a tendency to buy anything that ''looked Indian'', which might be called the curio approach. Another class was the collector (or a dealer representing the collector or museum), often a person with both the money and the knowledge to acquire better pieces. This was the connoisseur approach.

In the late 1800's, there was a curio cabinet in nearly every middle-class home, and none could be complete without an Indian item or two. As decor, a pot or basket might be set at strategic locations, or a rug laid or a blanket hung. While partly to truly showcase the piece as good Indian art, the other purpose was to suggest a certain inter-cultural and well-traveled sophistication on the part of the owner.

Indian craftspeople turned out a nearly full range of Indian-made goods for a cash income. Included in all this were beaded necklaces and pendants, sashes and belts. Basketry figures (non-traditional) of humans and animals were made, also a number of miniature forms. Basketry cradles were made, both full-size and doll-size. Innovations were Indian baskets that were fully beaded on the exterior, with designs and fully beaded glass bottles and jugs. Much work of this sort was done in the 1900 - 1940's period.

Pottery began to be marketed early, but there was a late resurgence with high-quality ceramic ware in the 1920's and 1930's. Traditional forms and decorations were again used; this has been a strong and growing market.

As with weavings, early traders helped create a successful blend of style and form. Style, using pleasing designs in complementary colors; form, in thicker, stronger weaves, and in larger sizes for use as rugs. Tourists had little use for wearing blankets except as sofa (davenport) covers or wall-hangings. Instead, rugs were needed and rugs were made. This, too, is still a very widespread endeavor for Indian weavers.

Jewelry, especially silver, served several purposes. Indian jewelry was generally heavy as it also served as a store of wealth, a wearable bank account. Good, heavy pieces could be pawned with the trader and the process was the equivalent of security for a loan. Silver jewelry made strictly for sale was often lighter in weight. This brings to mind the much earlier practice of trade silver items to the Indians, when lighter weights meant larger or more ornaments for the same amount of silver.

Also for sale were well-embellished artifact types no longer in use, such as wrist bow-guards. Keeping up with tourist needs, items never originally made for Indian use were turned out. These included in the 1920's and 1930's, ashtrays, watchfobs, compacts and cigarette cases. Very much trade in tourist-type artifacts took place in the West due to the large influx of visitors.

In the Great Lakes region, especially around Niagara Falls with its huge volume of sightseers, a specialized beadwork form developed. The items were small sewing baskets and pin-cushions, the last made in a great array of sizes and styles. This output lasted from the early 1900's well into the 1940's.

Pin-cushions were made of trade cloth stuffed with sweetgrass and beaded designs were sewn on one side. If the buyer wasn't that much into sewing, most cushions were thoughtfully provided with a hanging strap so the cushion could be hung for decoration. One late example was dated, in beadwork, 1938. These creations ranged from small and simple to large and ornate. Many of these cushions survive as family heirlooms and some can be seen in the shops of antique dealers.

Canada, with many United States citizens heading north to hunt and fish, also had native craftspeople willing to satisfy the desire for Indian-made goods. These included many different kinds of birchbark containers, plain and decorated. Items as diverse as duck decoys, fishing lures, napkin rings and toy canoes were made.

In the Northwest, argillite (a dark metamorphic stone between slate and shale, but without cleavage layers) was carved into numerous fanciful forms. These included totemic poles, human and animal figures and pipes. Wood was carved into masks and dippers and rattles. Pine-needle baskets were made in the Southeast and Florida, pipes in the Carolina mountains and masks and baskets came from the Northeast.

Elsewhere, Indian items for sale to tourists included: Pottery figurines that were doll-size or smaller, with cloth Indian-style or European clothing; horsehair hatbands; pine-bark carvings; beaded gauntlets and moccasins; cloth dolls with sewn-in features; wooden toys of many kinds; figures depicting Indians and the Indian lifeway in almost any material; buckskin covered and beaded cradles in all sizes and much more.

Many of the tourist trade items were decorative, ornamental or both. In fact, this would be a good area for a collector to specialize in – Indian goods within the past century. In some way, this field has been an overlooked category.

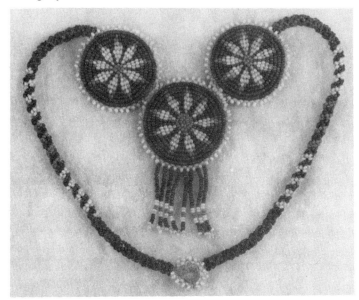

NECKLACE, recent Indian manufacture, with designs done in white, orange and blue seed beads on white-tanned deerskin. Medallions are 1¾ inches across. $170
Private collection

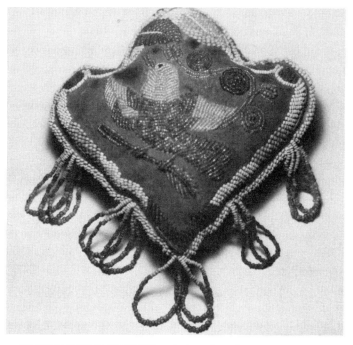

GREAT LAKES BEADWORK tourist item from the early 1900's, this New York state collected piece is 2½ x 7½ x 7½ inches. Done in colored seed beads the design represents a singing bird on an arrow-branch. Near-mint condition on yellow-brown velvet. $150
Private collection

BEADED NAPKIN RINGS done on birchbark with floral and butter-fly motifs. Each is 2¹/₁₆ in. long. Such tourist items were widely made.
Private collection   Each, $7-10

TOURIST BEADWORK, this shoe is unusual in that both seed beads and cylindrical beads were used. Typical of early 1900's Indian work in the Great Lakes region, it is 3¼ x 3¼ inches. The background is red velvet. $25
Private collection

NIAGARA FALLS BEADWORK, this pin-cushion is unusual for sim-ple styling, sparce decoration and the date only. Done on red velvet, size is 2 x 5¼ x 5½ inches. $50
Private collection

107

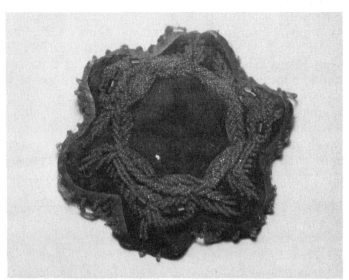

GREAT LAKES BEADWORK, this six-pointed pin-cushion wreath-design item is typical for the early 1900's. Ornamentation is in frosted beads on purple corduroy; size, 5 inches in diameter. $50
Private collection

LOOM AND WEAVER, American Southwest, a fairly scarce tourist item. Base is wood covered with thin hide, while figure has cloth clothing and seed-bead belt and necklace. Cradleboard and baby are to the right; loom frame is wood, woven rug is wool. Size 5 x 8 x 11½ in. high. $125
Private collection

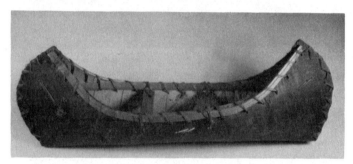

INDIAN MADE CANOE, birchbark with several porcupine-quill decorations on each side. Size is 2¹⁵⁄₁₆ x 3½ x 11 inches long. One end is marked ''Windsor, Canada.'' $30
Private collection

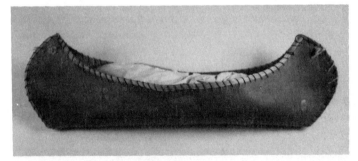

INDIAN MADE CANOE, birchbark and long a favorite tourist item, marked ''Frankford, Mich.'' Size is 2⅜ x 2¹⁵⁄₁₆ x 10 in. long $25
Private Collection

TIPI SCENE, Great Lakes area, unusually complete tourist item. It has the tipi, canoe and paddles, firewood, cradle-board inside and a black bear in profile on the side, made of felt. Basal dimensions, 5¼ x 7½ inches. $65
Private collection

NAPKIN RING Indian-made tourist item, Great Lakes region. It is decorated with porcupine quills in three areas, done on birchbark with a sweetgrass border. Size, 1¾ inches long. $6
Private collection

108

Chapter 21
DECORATIVE AND ORNAMENTAL FACTS

Ingalik Indians of southwestern Alaska had various animal-ceremony masks. Male masks might have protrusions beside the chin, while female masks might have nose-suspended beads and marks indicating chin tattoos. Masks had different names and decorations, and were carefully carved from wood. (Helm, *Handbook Of North American Indians*, Vol. 6, 1981, p 391)

Interesting artifacts were recovered some years ago from historic Pawnee sites in Nebraska, especially the Hill Site (abandoned ca. 1810). These were tablets or slabs with deeply incised marks, the rock being limestone, shale and possibly Catlinite. The slabs may have been molds, as one design when rounded was the same shape as heavy finger rings found that had three parallel ribs. Other indentations in the molds would have manufactured some objects such as belt buckles and buttons. (Wedel, *An Introduction To Pawnee Archeology*, 1936, pp 78-79, 90)

Large and ornate bone combs were typical of the Vine Valley Aspect of the Point Peninsula Focus, once existing from Virginia to New York and into Canada. Examples have teeth about half the length of the comb, and some combs were over a foot long. Tops were of varied shapes, straight, excurvate, incurvate and very deeply "V"-shaped. Teeth numbered from 4 to 8 for each specimen. Most combs had the tops decorated with incised lines and some of the work was very well-done and intricate. Combs have been found on many sites of this period. (Ritchie, *The Pre-Iroquoian Occupations Of New York State*, 1944, pp 184-185)

While traveling, some historic Indian groups in the Great Lakes region carried arrows in a special bag to keep them from the weather. One such example, ca. 1850, is made of a whole beaver skin. The legs and tail are layered with cloth and beaver skin with silk, and the five areas also have beadwork designs. (Trigger, *Handbook Of North American Indians*, Vol. 15, 1978, p 781)

Some of the finest bone hairpins ever recovered came from near Menard Landing, Arkansas. A mound was explored which was in the form of a cut-off cone. It was 34.5 feet high and had a diameter of 167 feet. A *cache* of slightly curved hairpins was found, seven of them complete and two with broken tips. The head ends were decorated with three to six thin grooves or were expanded and notched on the sides. Only one hairpin was plain or without incised markings. Lengths of the pieces ranged from 7⅝ to 8⅝ inches. (Moore, *Certain Mounds Of Arkansas and Mississippi*, 1908, pp 486-490, Fig. 2)

The Snyders Site and Klunk Mound No. 7, both Illinois, produced two distinct plummet forms. The Snyders Grooved plummet is long and tear-drop shaped, with a thin groove around the pointed top. Gilcrease Grooved plummets from the Klunk Mound, have various shapes but tend to be shorter and broader. Also, the groove extends around a flattened top. Opinion is mixed as to the actual purpose or use of plummets, and suggestions include personal adornment. (Farnsworth & Emerson, *Early Woodland Archeology*, 1986, pp 336-338, 342)

An unusual figurine carved from yellow fluorite was found during excavations of the Angel Mound Site, Indiana in 1940. The object was that of an adult male, sitting, with an ear-to-ear extension that may represent a headdress. It is thought the material originally came from Illinois or Kentucky where natural deposits are known. (Black, *Angel Site*, Vol. I, 1967, pp 248-251)

Mirrors may have been used in the prehistoric Southwest according to findings at and near Snaketown, Pinal County, Arizona. A stone disc, after various preparatory steps, had one face fitted with a mosaic of thin sheets of iron pyrites, which were then polished. There are two mirror types, one with mosaic to the edge, and one with mosaic to an edge-border. (Gladwin, et. al., *Excavations At Snaketown*, 1975, pp 130-134, Plates 59, 60, 62)

Decorating stone or rocks by incising (marking with a sharp instrument) was begun in North America sometime before 6000 BC. Such markings may be simple or elaborate, and may have been ceremonial or merely decorative. (D'Azevedo, *Handbook Of North American Indians*, Vol. 11, 1986, p 230)

Some of the most unusual mound findings were the pottery figurines recovered from the Turner Mounds, Hamilton County, Ohio. Though badly broken (perhaps ceremonially "killed") the objects (somewhat similar to the Knight figurines from Illinois) represent men and women from the Hopewell lifeway. There is a variety of positions and the clay was very well molded before firing. The objects are important because the Turner Figurines give details of clothing (women, wraparound skirts; men, abbreviated breechcloth), hairstyles and ornamentation. (Willoughly, *The Turner Groups Of Earthworks*, 1975, pp 71-75)

Southwestern historic Indians often wore woven or leather headbands to provide some decoration and to add to the appearance of hair. Horsehair was sometimes included to enhance fullness and length. One headband, woven on a horizontal loom, was done in four colors of cotton. (Ortiz, *Handbook Of North American Indians*, Vol. 10, 1983, p 158)

Ball-headed clubs were a favorite fighting tool in the Eastern Woodlands during proto-historic times. Made of hardwood, most had a handgrip, a graceful downward-curving handle and terminated in a heavy rounded striking area. Examples might be decorated with shell, carvings of many kinds, or be painted. (Hothem, various sources)

The bull-roarer – so-called because the noise was similar to the bellow of a bull – was widely used in North America. It was a long, flattened piece of wood with a hole in one end, to which a thong or cord was attached. This was swung in a circle around the user or twirled around one hand, creating a vibrating sound that carried a great distance. Intended for ceremonial and social use, the bull-roarer was usually decorated with paint in a number of designs. Bull-roarers were also known as "thunder-sticks". (Ortiz, *Handbook Of North American Indians*, , Vol. 10, 1983, p 139)

Pestles or seed-pounding tools were made of both wood and stone, but few of the former have survived. Occasionally pestles were decorated and/or extremely long. Some of the best pestles came from the Northwest Coastal groups. One example is 24 inches high with a bear's head top, while another, with snake effigy on the side, is 29 inches high. Both were collected by Ernest Cowles, the state of Washington. (Russell, *Indian Artifacts*, 1962, p 77)

Decorated gaming or gambling tokens and markers were widely used in North America, even in prehistoric times. Such objects included painted and incised stones, bits of shell and antler, or nutshells. Bone gambling rods and sticks were of many shapes and sizes. Wood was even more common and the pieces were often painted with identifying marks. Pottery sherds and bits of bone were also used. (Hothem, various sources)

The excavations by Squier and Davis in 1846 of Mound No. 8, Mound City, Ross County, Ohio, located the greatest single compact trove of Hopewell effigy platform pipes ever found. Nearly 200 pipes of all kinds, mainly in Ohio pipestone from the Lower Scioto Valley, were present, many in damaged condition. Birds, animals, fish and reptiles were depicted in natural poses, i.e., heron with fish or hawk with bird. Hopewell craftspeople were unequaled in their effigy pipe forms. (Hothem, *Treasures Of The Mound Builders*, 1989, pp 108-109)

The Archaic Lamoka Phase of New York state made heavy use of antler ornaments. Such use included pendant forms and long, flattened objects with notches on the edges. Interestingly, a number of these antler ornaments were once painted; traces of red pigment have been found on at least three examples. (Ritchie, *The Archaeology Of New York State*, 1980, p 68)

While some Indian basketry in certain regions was made entirely from a few major plant materials – such as sweetgrass, pine needles or yucca fiber – California groups had a very wide range of natural plants to choose from. These included splints from hardwood trees (white oak), shrubs (elderberry), rushes (tule), ferns (brake) and grasses (squaw). For the region mentioned, at least 35 different basketry materials were employed at one time or another. (Heizer, *Handbook Of North American Indians*, Vol. 8, 1978, p 632)

Painted stone artifacts from the Southwest are very rare, but one example is a mortar from Pueblo Bonito, New Mexico. It is 5 inches in diameter and 8½ inches high. The zigzag designs are in red, green and brown. and may have been taken from cotton weavings. The mortar decorations are similar to that on some pottery vessels. (Douglas & D'Harnoncourt, *Indian Art Of The United States*, 1941, pp 20-21)

The Kipp Island Phase of the Northeastern U.S. Woodland period is noted for higly unusual and decorative combs. These were made from moose antlers and some are very large, up to 15 inches long and 5 inches wide. The tops are decorated with incised triangles of many kinds. (Ritchie, *The Archaeology of New York State*, 1980, p 250)

At the McCollum Site, Ontario, Canada, a very unusual *cache* of copper artifacts was found in 1955 on a sloping beach above a lake inlet. Many Old Copper Culture artifacts were picked up, some of them ornaments. These included 13 copper discs, round to oval, 12 with one hole near one side, one with 2 holes. These were possibly pendants. Two pairs – one set large, one small – of copper bracelets were found, with an embossed surface. Three copper beads were also recovered. Old Copper decorative objects are quite rare. (Griffin, *Lake Superior Copper And The Indians*, 1961, pp 91-94, Plate XIX)

Basket-making has a long prehistory in North America. Perhaps one of the earliest known examples is from Fishbone Cave, Nevada and dates to 9300 BC – 11,300 years ago. It was a section of a flexible bag or a pouch. Another basketry object dates to 7590 BC, from another Nevada site. Such very early basketry forms, involving coiling, twining or plaiting, include mats, bags or pouches, bowls, burden baskets, plaques and trays. (D'Azevedo, *Handbook Of North American Indians*, , Vol. 11, 1986, pp 197-199)

Among the greatest wood-carvers in North America, at least in terms of objects that have survived until the present, were the Tlinget (or Tlinkit) Indians of southeastern Alaska. Much of the best work was done in early historic times, and included carefully made and elaborately carved chests, boxes, rattles and masks. They steamed and bent wood to make one-board sided containers and the exteriors were carved in conventionalized designs. Motifs ranged from naturalistic to highly abstract. (Douglas & D'Harnoncourt, *Indian Art Of The United States*, 1941, pp 178-179, 182-183)

A class of artifacts found in the Midwest and from both Adena and Hopewell times is the cone. They mav be abbreviated forms of *Atl-atl* stones, miniature mound representations or something else entirely. Of the 12 specimens found in West Virginia's Cresap Mound (Adena), 7 were made of hematite, 1 of barite (crystalline mineral of barium sulfate), 1 of calcium carbonate, and 2 of siltstone. (Dragoo, *Mounds For The Dead*, 1963, p 79)

Pre-Columbian artisans of Central and South America were masters at ornamental metal-working and employed half a dozen sophisticated techniques beyond cold-pounding into shape. Metals worked included gold and silver, copper and platinum. In addition, an alloy was created – called tumbaga – that combined gold and copper, or, gold, silver and copper. Objects made included miniature human groups, nose ornaments, pendants, chest pectorals, mantle pins, breastplates, head-bands, necklaces, ceremonial *Atl-atls*, headdress elements, earstuds, earrings, nose plugs and lip ornaments. (Kelemen, *Art Of The Americas*, 1969, pp 149-157)

Boatstones – so-called because turned upside down some do resemble tapered-end watercraft – are probably a highly developed form of *Atl-atl* weights. Some very rare effigy examples have been found in Hopewell mounds in Ohio and Michigan. The open base-center and hollowed interior may have contained quartz pebbles for ceremonial rattles and the pebbles have been found with non-effigy forms in copper. Creatures depicted include birds of various types, owls(?), tadpole(?), cicada in pupae form, beetle, deer-head and a mythical four-horned monster-like effigy. Hardstone, antler, calcite, serpentine and red slate were among the material used for the objects described. (Willoughby, *Annual Report Of The Smithsonian Institution / 1916*, p 498, Plate 11)

Some artifacts served a double life through salvage in prehistoric times. When decorated pottery broke, the sherds or pieces might be "remade" into decorations, mainly buttons and pendants. Examples from Arizona ranged in shape from oval to rectangular to pear-shaped. Most were drilled near an edge with one hole, while a few had two. As they were made from redware potsherds, most were red on one side and black on the other. Such pendants are sometimes associated with beads in necklaces and bracelets. (Roberts, *Archaeological Remains In The Whitewater District / Eastern Arizona*, 1940, p 110 Plate 31)

Catlinite or red Minnesota pipestone was used for more than pipes. George Catlin (1796-1872), the famous painter, first called major attention to this quarry site in 1836. (It should be noted that a very similar material, probably at times mis-identified as Catlinite, came from quarries in Barron County, Wisconsin.) While the main use of Catlinite was indeed for pipes of many kinds, beads, pendants and small slabs that were incised with birds or animals were also made. (Hothem, various sources)

One of the many well-decorated items made by the Anasazi of the Southwest (ca. AD 1000) was the well-known Mesa Verde mug. These are quite modern-looking, somewhat like small unspouted pitchers with a large curved, closed handle on the side. Many were painted with black designs on a white ground, the patterns derived from earlier basketry-work. (Snow, *The Archaeology Of North America*, 1980, pp 146, 148)

While it is little-known, some Indian groups of historic times learned to make glass ornamental objects. Discarded glass or trade bottles were melted at high heat and poured into native-made molds. Usually the artifacts were beads, necklace elements, ear-drops or pendants. Occasionally glass was mixed to form decorative patterns. Among such innovators were the Arikara of Missouri, in the period ca. AD 1800-1830. (Wedel, *Prehistoric Man On The Great Plains*, 1978, Plate XV)

At times, decorative objects were made in unusual ways. Parts of the trigger-guard mechanism of early flintlocks have been drilled for suspension and this was often done with coins. Thimbles became decorative tinklers. At times, glass beads were set in clay to form unusual pottery. Even earlier in the Southwest, shell fishhook blanks from the California coast became earrings for Arizona Indians. (Hothem, various sources)

Among the more interesting artifacts made by Eastern Midwest Mound Builders (Hopewell) were ear ornaments of goldstone. This is a brown micaceous material and was found in Ohio's Hopewell Mound Group. The ornaments are in the form of hollow discs, with an indented rim. Many are so perfectly round that there is a strong possibility that a primitive but workable lathe was used for turning, shaping and polishing them. A perfectly round polished disc of fossilized ivory came from an Indiana mound, as well as some shell beads "... altogether too symmetrical to have been made by any other known process." (Willoughby, *Annual Report Of The Smithsonian Institution / 1916*, p 499, Plate 12)

In the 1903 excavation of Ohio's Edwin Harness Mound, Ross County, thousands of artifacts were found, including a string of 2100 pearl beads. Of more interest in terms of decorative objects were a number of imitation pearl beads. These were round, fired clay balls covered with flecks of mica. The Hopewell Indians were masters at improvising imitation materials and artifacts when the originals were either in short supply, or at least had been selected as worthy of being copied. (Hothem, *Treasures Of The Mound Builders*, 1989, p 75)

Pictorially painted buffalo (bison) and elk hides from the Great Plains can be a form of writing, in that the images tell a story. Such work was usually done by men and might be in two forms. One was the "count," in which years were depicted by significant symbols and was an historic record. Another was a pictorial rendering in some detail of a single occurrence, such as a bison hunt or battle. Surviving examples in good condition are rare. (Douglas & D'Harnoncourt, *Indian Art Of The United States*, 1941, pp 36-37)

Very decorative dog blankets were used by the Kutchins of the Sub-Arctic. One example is made of black velvet, edged with wool fringes in various colors, plus a set of bells down the center which divides sections of seed beads, and cotton braid. Such fine blankets were used with sled dogs on special occasions. (Helm, *Handbook Of North American Indians*, Vol. 6, 1981, p 391)

In the Eastern Midwest, the most skilled workers in copper and mica were the Hopewell Indians of Middle Woodland times. Their metal-work has never been equalled and most such artifacts served as ornaments. While the scarce and elaborate pieces - antlered headdresses of copper, the breastplates and intricate earspools - may have been reserved for ranking people and important events, copper has worked into more common forms. These included beads, a few pendants and *Atl-atl* weights or emblems and large numbers of sheet-copper cutouts. These were in the form of rounded or angular symbols, birds, humans, animals and fish. Mica and sheet copper forms were sometimes similar and were probably fastened to clothing. Some silver and meteoric iron was also worked. (Martin, Quimby & Collier, *Indians Before Columbus*, 1949, pp 271-276)

The Hohokam Indians at the prehistoric site of Snaketown in Arizona made many beautifully decorated stone containers. There were many shapes and sizes, and simpler forms had series of lines incised and grooved on the exteriors. Effigy vessels were also made of stone and figures represented the horned toad, birds, bear, tortoise, coiled rattlesnakes (many designs), frogs, lizards, mountain sheep and humans. (Gladwin, et al., *Excavations At Snaketown*, 1975, Plates 57-76)

The Late Archaic Glacial Kame culture used copper beads for decorations. These have been found in a number of deep burial sites, though some are unaccountably shallow. Often the beads are in graduated sizes, small to large; they were made by cold-pounding raw copper strips into a circular ball, with the hollow center serving as the string-hole. Some copper beads were tubular. Typical of such artifacts was a necklace found at the Isle La Motte Site, in Vermont. It had 15 beads ½ to ⅝ inches long, and had been strung on a cord of bast fiber. (Ritchie, *The Archaeology Of New York State*, 1980, pp 133-134)

The Red Ochre people (Late Archaic / Early Woodland) of the eastern Midwest and elsewhere had a range of ornamental artifacts. These included round and tubular copper beads, shell beads and beads made from fossils. Large, round shell pendants were made, as were elongated examples. Unusual ornaments (Corwin Mound, Pike County, Ohio) included a bar amulet (*Atl-atl* handle?), a galena (lead ore) 2-hole gorget or weight, and a hardstone bust-type birdstone. (Hothem, various sources)

The creative ability of North American Indians can be seen all across America in the form of marks on rocks. There are two forms. **Petroglyphs** are artworks pecked or abraded onto the rock surface, exposing a different colored and contrasting sub-surface. **Pictographs** are mainly done with paints (though the outline may be incised in some cases), and are found largely in sites (rock shelters, under overhangs) with some protection against weathering. Some incising or scratching was done in the Great Plains. While much such rock art has disappeared or faded, a surprising amount remains. Most work was done in areas with large, projecting natural stone surfaces, and there are many more sites in the Western U.S. than in the Eastern section. Forms include naturalistic, stylized and abstract. (Grant, *Rock Art Of The American Indians*, 1967, pp 16-20)

Broken steatite vessels in the Late Archaic of New York served several further purposes. Beads were made from the pieces, so also a crescentic ornament with two holes. Heavy rectangular ''gorgets'' (*Atl-atl* weights) were also made, these typically having 2, 4 or 6 drilled holes. Such weights, with more than the customary 2 holes, are unusual (Ritchie, *The Archaeology Of New York State*, 1980, p 159)

Some of the most careful and detailed artwork ever created was done by Eskimo crafters on walrus-tusk ivory. Lines were incised with a sharp-tipped graving tool and lamp-black or soot was used for outline and shading darker areas. Most work was pictorial, with miniature scenes of hunting, fishing, travelling and home life. Some work is direct and simplistic, lifeway snapshots, while other examples are both intricate and sophisticated. (Miles, *Indian & Eskimo Artifacts Of North America*, 1963, pp 184-185)

The Cree Indians of the Sub-Arctic used ceremonial straps to carry or drag game back to camp. One example of red-dyed plaited caribou hide over 100 inches long has decorative tassels of wool suspended from strips of seed beads. Bear, beaver and waterfowl might be transported in this fashion, (Helm, *Handbook Of North American Indians*, Vol. 6, 1981, p 202)

One of the oldest decorated objects known from the Americas is a 6-inch piece of pelvic bone from a mastodon, found in Mexico in 1959. Incised upon it are figures like camels, mastodons and tapirs, and other animals, long extinct. The bone is believed to be about 30,000 years old. (Editors, *The American Heritage Book Of Indians*, 1961, p 28)

Ear-ornaments of various kinds were used by many different Indian groups. Some California tribes had pierced ears and men wore decorative rods in them. One pair, over 7 inches long, is made of wood with incised and stained spirals. Another is made of bird bones about 5 inches long, and has paint-filled lines. (Heizer, *Handbook Of North American Indians*, Vol. 8, 1978, pp 293, 376)

Probably the greatest trove of large, well-made varied-form flint artifacts ever recovered in North America was the Duck River Cache, from Humphreys County, Tennessee. It came from the farm of Banks Links, near Painted Rock, in December of 1894. Made of layer Dover chert (plus some implements of Fort Payne chert), there were 46 flaked artifacts and two statues of limestone. One was female, 24 inches high and the other, a male was 30 inches high. The large chipped objects included discs, human profiles, maces, swords, turtle-like effigies and barbed, arrow-like forms. Most objects were in pairs of two similar forms. The longest sword-like blade was 1¾ x 28 inches long. These are Mississippian (late prehistoric) artifacts and undoubtedly were ceremonial-ornamental in purpose. (Peacock, *Duck River Cache*, 1984, pp iii-16)

The Middle Woodland Hopewell Indians in the Eastern Midwest became highly accomplished at covering or coating objects with very thin, beaten metal. The materials were mainly native copper and silver (in several instances, gold), either imported from the Great Lakes region or found in the glacial drift. (Thin deposits of silver were sometimes found with copper.) The sheets were pounded ultra-thin, and foil-like, used to cover wooden handles, silver-over-copper earspools, buttons, beads and the like. Many such pieces were found in the Hopewell Mound Group, Ross County, Ohio. (Hothem, *Treasures Of The Mound Builders*, 1989, various pages)

An unusual decorative work done by the Cree Indians of Canada, was design on birchbark done by biting. A piece of bark was folded in a number of ways and was then bitten between the teeth, designs clearly incised in the bark. Very detailed and complex scenes could be made by one experienced in the art. (Helm, *Handbook Of North American Indians,* Vol. 6, 1981, p 268)

Paint palattes are found in several North American Indian cultures, but some of the best were made by the Hohokam in Arizona's valleys of the Salt and Gila rivers. These palattes, themselves decorative objects, are rectangular, thin and carved from stone. The back is plain, while the front has a carved and decorated border, raised from the flat interior or actual pigment surface. There is a possibility that the artifact style was imported from Mexico. Some palattes have small animal figurines carved on the front border or frame, or projecting from the smaller sides of the pallattes. (Jennings, *Prehistory Of North America,* 1968, pp 262-263)

California has long been well-known for the so-called "charmstones," elongated artifacts often with a small hole at one end. Sometimes resembling plummets, the Windmiller culture (beginning ca. 2500 BC) was noted for fine examples made of stones like alabaster, diorite and serpentine. Some examples still have traces of asphaltum and cordmarks near the suspension holes. Charmstones were made in a very wide range of shapes and sizes. (Heizer, *Handbook Of North American Indians,* Vol. 8, 1978, pp 332-333)

One does not think of scraping as a way to decorate objects, but this indeed was done in the Northern Woodlands region. The material was birchbark, which was first made into boxes or containers. Then, the white outer bark was cut along outlines and the interior sections scraped away, exposing the brown underlying surface. Very intricate patterns could be made in this fashion. Among the groups skilled in the process were the Montagnals and Cree. (Douglass & D'Harnoncourt, *Indian Art Of The United States,* 1941, pp 154, 158)

Some of the more unusual decorative artifacts were made by the Ozark Bluff-Dweller people of Arkansas and Missouri. They had some seed and shell beads, and an occasional shell pendant. The Bluff-Dwellers were one of the few prehistoric Amerind groups known to have made ornamental fans from feathers, which were fastened together with quill-strips or fiber thongs. (Martin, Quimby & Collier, *Indians Before Columbus,* 1949, p 341)

Collectors in the 48 contiguous states tend to think of certain classes of scarce decorative artifacts as being exclusive to the United States, while many are in fact of North American distribution. For example, Canada's (the world's second largest country in terms of area) province of Ontario (north of the Great Lakes region) has a number of slate and hardstone artifacts that are also found south of the Great Lakes and elsewhere. These decorative artifacts include: Stone elbow and elbow flared-rim pipes, effigy pipes, pendants, birdstones, ceremonial picks, knobbed lunate bannerstones, pick bannerstones of many forms, bar amulets of several forms, expanded-center and grooved-center elongated-bar weights, hollowed-base boatstones, and non-hollowed boatstones. *Annual Archaeological Report / The Legislative Assembly of Ontario,* 1912, pp 16-35)

In the Lake Erie region, the early historic Iroquois Indians placed much emphasis on tools and weapons as opposed to purely decorative objects. They did, however, decorate pipes and pottery vessels and had some rather plain shell and bone beads and shell pendants. (Vietzen, *Indians Of The Lake Erie Basin,* 1965, p 299)

The practice of permanently marking designs on the face and/or body of early Indians was probably rather common in certain regions and times. There is no direct proof of such very personal decoration, tattooing, but there are indirect hints that this was done. In the Okvik culture of Northern Alaska are found ivory figurines with tattooed faces. The Adena people of the Eastern Midwest had small stone plaques or tablets with raised designs engraved on one side. The reverse usually has several deep grooves. It is suspected the designs were painted and applied to the skin and sharpened bone splinters were used as tattooing needles. The plaques are so few that this was probably only done on special ceremonial occasions. (Hothem, various sources)

Some interesting beads were excavated from the Lewiston Mound, Niagara County, New York state. This was a Middle Woodland earthwork with Hopewellian traits. Found were both small and large beads of sheet copper and a button-cover of sheet silver with edges that were perforated. (Ritchie, *The Archaeology Of New York State,* 1980, p 218)

One of the great decorative substances in all North America is called ocher or ochre. It was so widely used it is probabaly the origin of the old-fashioned term "Redskin". The human body and artifacts were painted with ochre, and in powdered form it was used in many kinds of ceremonies and rituals. It has been found in almost all cultural periods, including the Late Paleo. Ochre is generally considered to be powdered hematite, natural iron ore in black-red to yellow to brick-red, but the story is not always so simple. The natural iron ore limonite (yellow-brown to black) was also widely used. There is evidence that to get a bright and uniform ochre color, the material (especially hematite) was heated or roasted. Application might be in loose, powdered form or as the pigment in paint, itself probably based on rendered animal fat. And ochre itself, from whatever source, can be colored yellow, brown, all shades of red, orange and yellow-orange. Red Ochre in fact can be color-adjusted by the degree of heat applied. In general, the greater the heat the brighter the color, at least up to a point. Still another substance used for red pigment is cinnabar, a heavy reddish mercuric sulfide, also called vermillion. (Hothem, various sources)

An unusual human head pendant was found in a Kentucky mound prior to 1929. About an inch high, it was flattened on the back and a transverse hole through the headdress or top-knot indicated wear for personal use. The material was a translucent light blue to purplish stone, thought to be amethyst. (*The Williams Site*, University of Kentucky, Vol. 1. No. 1, 1929, p 13 and Fig. 17)

Two rare, well-polished bone gorgets or *Atl-atl* attachments were found in a Kentucky mound prior to 1936. Both were of the two-hole type. They measured, respectively, 1.6 x 7.5 inches, and, 1.5 x 8 inches. Counter-balances for the throwing stick of this material are most unusual, and few have survived until today. (*The Chilton Site*, University of Kentucky, Vol. III No. 5, 1937, pp 200-201)

Five Adena (Early Woodland) semi-keeled gorgets or *Atl-atl* symbols (weights) were removed from the Hartman Mound, Kentucky, sometime between 1940 and 1943. Artifact materials were: 2, hematite; 2, limestone, 1 slate. Lengths ranged from 3 to 3.5 inches, widths from $1\frac{5}{8}$ to $1\frac{7}{8}$ inches and thicknesses from $\frac{5}{8}$ to ¾ inches. Only the slate artifact is known to have been drilled from both faces. Semi-keeled gorgets are not a common Adena type and are usually found sparingly. (*The Crigler Mounds / The Hartman Mound*, University of Kentucky, Vol. V No. 6, 1943, pp 544-545)

Chapter 22
FAKE ARTIFACTS

Fake or well-made copies of American Indian artifacts of decorative and ornamental classes are a real problem today. The problem is hardly new, since spurious examples have been around since the late 1800's. As a matter of history, the U.S.-based International Society of Archaeologists in 1909 – in addition to the regular slate of officers – had a special position. This was a person known as the "Fraud Detector." Members could send suspect pieces to this Kentucky gentleman, who would then pass judgment.

Many amateur and professional associations today have committees or highly informed individuals skilled at spotting bad pieces. Most dealers and advanced collectors, at least for their areas of familiarity, have a working knowledge of what is good and what is bad. Some are so perceptive that they can not only point out a recent piece, but name the individual who made it. Unfortunately, some works are so faithful to type and so flawlessly executed that even experts differ as to whether the piece is good or bad. Then it is labeled "questionable".

Some people today as an exercise in experimental archaeology, recreate the form of ancient artifacts to see how the Indians probably did it. Such work produces facsimiles or copies, and the purpose is personal satisfaction, for teaching aids or as representative examples of scarce (and expensive) originals. (It is in fact best to take a reproduction into a classroom if young children will be handling it.) There is nothing wrong with this, especially when the pieces are permanently marked as to true origin. However, if and when such recreations reach a marketplace, there can be confusion.

The largest problem by far is the purposeful creation of artifacts and the intentional marketing of them as old or ancient and Indian-made. The purpose is money, though there is said to be a certain pride of craftsmanship involved, and the perverse satisfaction that one possesses the ability to fool supposedly wary and knowledgeable people. Probably several hundred persons are skilled enough to get away with this on a regular basis, and many thousand spurious pieces are created each year.

Once upon a time, fake pieces could be rather easily spotted. They tended to be of certain classes and look rather fresh or new. No longer. The fakes can be anything the maker wishes to duplicate, and there are numerous techniques to "age" or patinate the material. Plus, some can even put in a few use-marks and some very minor damage for that final touch that mimics authenticity.

The ongoing problem is not so much the person that knowingly buys bad artifacts direct from the maker, because collectors quickly learn to stay clear of such collectors and dealers. It is more subtle anymore, in that the pieces can quickly be dispersed across the country by flea-market sellers, from auctions, or via mail-order. Some dealers travel widely with a fine selection of artifacts in the trunk of a car and the pieces are not always good.

The fake problem becomes even more complex when the pieces enter collections and acquire a few catalog numbers or names, and the origin no longer becomes as important as it might once have been. Collectors also tend to have a mind-set (involving a piece they own or want to own) that if there is doubt, there is not quite enough doubt. They *want* the piece to be good, and so treat and present it as good.

Such bad pieces enter the marketplace in a number of ways, but flea-markets and antique fairs are notorious for this. Other bad pieces avail themselves to collectors in antique shops and at auctions. Collectors themselves are to blame sometimes, and a number of fraudulent specimen make the rounds from one collection to another, never staying for too long, trailing a unique and unfavorable reputation.

A good question a perspective buyer should ask is, if this piece was indeed in such-and-such a collection, why isn't it still there? Why is it being sold or traded? If the answers are plausible and satisfactory – a pure financial need, or to upgrade the collection – this may not be significant.

But sometimes it not only pays to ask questions, it saves. And fakers and those who knowingly sell or trade fake pieces are becoming increasingly innovative when it comes to "discovering" them. While this technique is most often used with artifacts of flint, hardstone and slate, it can be also used with any non-perishable artifact class.

One method is to provide staged photographs of the artifact "in situ", or supposedly as it was found. Another is to "find" the artifact while surface-hunting (still legal in most states, on private property with the landowner's permission to hunt). The piece, of course, has been prepositioned by the lucky finder, who usually manages to have several people as witnesses.

Without getting into an individual class coverage of what to look out for – and perhaps giving the fakers a few tips on how to improve their wares – there are some classes where great care must be exercised simply because of the artifact type.

This is especially relevant to fairly small artifacts with relatively high values. These classes, bannerstones and birdstones and pipes, have been heavily faked for a long time. These are highly attractive to collectors who may ignore nagging doubts in search of a bargain.

As an aside, there are two views regarding faking Indian artifacts and artworks. One is that faking is not so bad in that it weeds out gullible collectors and keeps the others on their toes; it is simply part of the game, and the goal is to avoid being taken. The Author's view is that fake artifacts are both a waste of money for the buyer and an encouragement for the faker. It supports an unethical, in some places illegal, practice. Further, and very importantly, when bad pieces are accepted as good and studied for clues to ancient lifeways, misinformation can result and incorrect conclusions can be drawn. That is the real tragedy.

Several knowledgeable people assert that there are many more fake birdstones flying around than there are genuine specimen. The ratio of bad to good varies depending upon whom one listens to and has been averaged from 10 or 50 to one. The ratio is probably lower in the bannerstone family, but not by much. The old belief that modern pieces could be identified by the marks of power tools isn't that valid anymore. The initial work is power-assisted (saws, penumatic hammers, grinders, drills) but the better pieces are hand-finished, just like the Indians did it.

Gorgets and pendants have long been reproduced because of their basic simplicity. The stone or slate is worked flat, the edges are shaped and hole(s) drilled. Again, much of the primary work can be done by machine tools. Lately there has been a large number of hardstone gorgets and pendants that have appeared on the market. These were always much fewer in number than their slate counterparts, so one must wonder why they seem to be more available today. No doubt, the fact that they are often several times as valuable may be worth noting.

Copies of prehistoric shell beads are not much of a problem, but copies of shell gorgets are. Some of the elaborate Mississippian conch-shell pendants are being made in numbers, because the material is easy to work and can be readily "aged" in a number of ways. A mixture of cider (mildly acidic) and tea (for a touch of darkening or stain) works fairly well. Prehistoric copper has been faked, especially the large and valuable pieces.

There is some problem with glass beads, this in two directions. Recent glass may be presented as old glass. More common is misrepresentation of beads traded to Africa (and collected there recently) as beads traded to North American Indians. There has also been some faking of trade silver.

For Plains Indian material, problems include later items that are offered as earlier, false provenance (a major piece with spurious papers suggesting association with a famous historic person), and repairs or parts substitutions that are often professionally done and well concealed. Celluloid (early plastic-like material) may be portrayed as bone or ivory. Pipes (especially those of Catlinite and steatite, that work fairly easily) have been recreated in large numbers. The list could go on and include weavings from Mexico, pottery from Asian countries and jewelry in the "Southwest style".

Misrepresentation, or faking the origin, does occur. Bits and pieces of early iron, brass and copper, metal-detected from some pioneer homestead, have been sold as coming from an historic Indian encampment. There's nothing wrong with the items, just the information about them. Years ago, when the Author traveled in South America, some Indian arrows from the Amazon watershed were obtained. These were nice, long beauties with decorative colored thread securing the foreshafts and slender iron points. These were sold to a dealer for what they were, South American pieces of modern origin. They later appeared in the dealer's catalog as "rare Seminole arrows," at many times the price I received. This happens.

There are many ways of looking at the possibility of a fake piece, whether it is a $5 pendant, a $50 gorget, a $500 trade-silver beaver, a $5000 bannerstone or a $50,000 beaded Plains warrior's outfit.

One aspect is the piece itself, whether all factors are "go" in terms of authenticity. For top dollar, the piece should have perfect provenance, or a known and proven record of where it came from and who has had it up to the present. The perfect collector item should have a one-hundred percent pedigree behind it, not just an interesting and appealing story.

As to authenticity, the collector should know everything possible about what is being collected, and this cannot be stressed enough in terms of fakes. The collector should spend as much time and energy learning about what is being collected as searching out the artifacts themselves.

BELL-TYPE PENDANT, Adena (Early Woodland) period from Muskingum County, Ohio. Size, 3/8 x 2½ x 4¼ inches, smoothly finished and polished. This piece, though, has a problem. It is authentic and old, but was never drilled. A modern hole was put in to "complete" the artifact, this shown by the too-small hole and lack of patina on drill-hole sides. Original value, $150; modern hole cuts $50 from this. Private collection $100

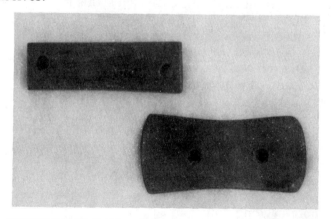

FAKE SLATE. Top left, bar-type of no precise artifact type, modern machine-polished and holes drilled of same diameter. Bottom right, a gorget form about 3 inches long. This piece is too thin for type and of a suspect miniature form. Instructional value only. Private collection.

Chapter 23
STUDY SPECIMENS

One reason – besides the pleasure of reading and pride in owning a good reference library – that good Indian artifact books are much in demand is because the photos and descriptions are both crash-course and reviews. It's truly doing things by the book. This is why (in late 1989) collectors gladly pay $200 and up for Knoblock's *Bannerstone* book, and $500 and up for Townsend's *Birdstone* book.

Indirectly, the artifacts pictured in these and other publications are not only works of prehistoric art, but study specimen for those who want to learn all they can about what they collect or would like to collect. The book owner may look to learn, and often fakers look to copy. So if an artifact turns up that closely resembles a known, good specimen and has similar provenance to it, a second look is called for. This may be a coincidence only, but perhaps not. And sometimes, to the joy of the collector, the exact piece is found that was pictured and described in some old book or journal, adding a quarter or half a century to the provenance of a good piece.

Another way to observe study specimens is to visit a museum with pieces on display, those found in early farming/ranching days, or excavated under controlled circumstances. (Some museums do have fake pieces, donated for tax purposes or a gift from heirs.) At museums, and beyond photos in books and periodicals, one at least can see the objects in three-dimensional aspect.

An even better method is to have understanding relationships and friendships with other collectors. This usually works best when both collectors are on about the same level of acquisition and expertise, give or take a few rungs on however long a ladder to the top. A beginning collector cannot expect to invite him – or herself into the home of an advanced collector in order to fondle prize specimens. There is a whole school of protocol regarding whether, or when, pieces can even be seen, touched or especially, picked up.

Simply show *at least* the same respect to someone else's pieces that you would want shown your own. This means placing artifacts back in cases, and cases back on shelves, walls, or wherever, if this is what the owner wishes. If in doubt, ask. It is all just courtesy and common sense. The fine advantage to all this is seeing the variety of artifacts that come from your geographic region, beyond those you are already familiar with. It is also instructive to see collections from neighboring states, for the long-ago trade routes meant a certain amount of material and artifact exchanges.

In the classes of hardstone and slate artifacts, less-than-perfect and even broken specimen can be very worthwhile. The main importance is that they are almost always old and authentic. Take, for example, half a slate bannerstone, broken – as so many are – along the central drill-hole. The breakage pattern itself, if old, may indicate something about the use. If the break is recent (agricultural equipment) the interior material will tell much about authentic patina on the surface of the piece. This will be educational in terms of appearance (exterior layering or color) for that material in that area. It is how a genuine piece ages.

Drill-holes of the same piece mentioned deserve close examination, for pendants and gorgets were usually perforated with flint-tipped drills and for some forms this was done in certain ways. For bannerstones, solid wooden wands or hollow-cane drills were used, rarely flint-tipped drills. Typical marks will be left on the drill-hole sides, and some types (knobbed crescents, double-lunates) may have more drill-hole wear than other classes. Geniculates have reamed-out holes, somewhat oblong and reamer marks should be present to some degree.

Check different areas of the surface to note the finishing touches of a genuine artifact – a magnifying glass can help. Different people recommend different powers ranging from 3X to 20X. Use a power that suits you and lets you see what you are looking for. This means the presence and extent of polish, manufacturing marks below the polish level and use marks, if any, over or in the polish itself. These are tiny things, but once seen they will be remembered. What you want to see is exactly how the Indian artisan let the work out into the world.

At auction, don't be afraid to bid-in the box of odds and ends that most collectors ignore. At least you will know your material is good and you will learn a lot for not much cash outlay. Field-finds should go into boxes marked as to sites; this is also the way to find missing sections and eventually assemble a complete artifact.

Study specimens can be anything of true American Indian origin, no matter how large or small, how old or valuable. This includes pottery sherds, and texture, decorations, thickness, tempering agent and hardness should be noted. Rim sections are especially good, as they give an idea of the top configuration and vessel size.

The same with basketry; materials, tightness of weaving, colors, sizes, all are important. The aim here is not so much to identify fake basketry (not much has been made, too skill-demanding and time-consuming) as to learn about regional Indian styles. Basketry has, however, been made in older styles and set outside to fade and weather a bit in the sun and rain.

Whatever class of ornamental artifacts one cares to collect, study specimens are collectible for educational value alone. Here, you are your own best teacher and student.

STUDY PIECES, all field-finds from Ohio. Top, left to right: Tapered gorget or pendant and rectangular gorget. Bottom, left to right: An expanded-center gorget and a bi-concave gorget both from the Adena lifeway. Size of top right piece, 1 x 1½ inches. These are interesting because they show prehistoric breakage patterns, some of which may have been purposefully done.
Private collection

STUDY PIECE, about 45% of a single-notched winged bannerstone, from early in the Archaic period. Part of the central hole break area is ground down, indicating this artifact was broken in prehistoric times. From Ohio, size is 3 x 3⅛ inches. Intact, this specimen would be worth $2000-$3000; as-is, a good example of authentic prehistoric decorative work.
Private collection

STUDY PIECES, both Ohio. Left, the remainder of a large gorget. Right, a probable bar weight from Delaware County. Both were extensively damaged in prehistoric times and neither piece was salvaged. Size of right specimen is ⅝ x 1⅝ x 1⅞ inches. It is instructive to see the forms and manufacture techniques on such genuine pieces.
Private collection

STUDY PIECES, both Ohio. Left, half a notched ovate bannerstone, probably broken by farming equipment. Right, portion of a knobbed crescent, also called a knobbed lunate bannerstone. Both forms, if whole, would be extremely rare. Left specimen is 2¼ x 3¾ inches. Close examination of such pieces shows how authentic decorative artifacts were made.
Private collection

SALVAGED BANNERSTONE. This 2-inch section of a rare geniculate banner in banded slate had a small protruding section near the original oblong central hole. This was grooved so that the remaining section could be suspended as a pendant. Unusual. $25
Private collection, Ohio

118

Chapter 24
VALUE FACTORS

It is difficult to draw up lists of value factors in a broad and diverse field such as ornamental and decorative Indian artifacts. Some factors (like condition) are valid for all categories, while others (such as unbroken attachment holes in birdstone bottoms) are specific to that class. However, here are some main points to consider when contemplating an acquisition in an area covered by this book.

Atl-atl stones should be of a quality material that took, and has, a good polish. Size is relevant to the type; elongated stones benefit from clean, well-done lines when seen from both the sides and top. Incising of any sort is usually a plus. The presence of grooving or notching adds to value if either are artistically formed, placed, and in harmony with the rest of the piece.

Effigies should be the appropriate length for size; sometimes, the tail section was broken in prehistoric times, and the tail area reworked to make a complete but shorter piece. The salvage factor should be kept in mind. Effigies are generally valued higher when the material (usually banded slate for the slate types) has attractive banding and high polish. Features on effigies such as mouth or eyes are positive factors even when, as if often the case, they are not too carefully done.

Birdstones are more common (or, less rare) in slate, and here, too, the quality of the slate – color and/or banding patterns – is important. Red slate is generally more scarce than solid-colored grey, black or green slate. However, the presence of features – eyes, nostrils, mouth, one or all of them – usually indicates an animal-type birdstone, not the long and elegant types. Certain type-indicators, such as pop-eyes or fan-tail, should be bold and well-formed for the type.

Hardstones birds should be of quality material, and usually this is one of the spotted porphyry stones. Here, too, the eyes and tail are important, this for the compact types. Elongated bar-type birdstones made of hardstone are very rare. For all birds, and for the two kinds of drilling – "L"-shaped and perforated-ridge – values are enhanced if the material between the holes is not broken out. And as with other prehistoric slate and hardstone artifacts, the absence of plow marks and disc-strikes is certainly a positive factor in terms of unmarred finish and increased value.

Hardstone banners in a number of cases have unfinished holes. This is especially present in the very hard quartzite banners, where the hole has been started from one or both ends but was never completed. Banners with incomplete holes are generally not as valuable as those with complete and well-centered holes. Size, workstyle, material and polish are all value factors. Some of the finest grades of material, such as rare colored quartzites, are near-gem quality and are highly translucent.

Slate bannerstones have value factors in common with their hardstone counterparts, though the size range here is larger. Holes of course should be complete for highest values, and many more slate banners in fact have end-to-end or completed drilling because of the softer material. Strong, contrasting banding is important for banners made of this material, especially when this accents the hole region to center attention and add to the symmetry or overall physical and visual balance of the piece. Good polish is important.

Gorgets should have similar ends and the holes, however many, should be equidistant from the ends. A few rare hardstone types of ultrahard materials may also have incomplete drilling. Banded slate gorgets benefit from bold lines and high polish which brings out the color and color contrasts. The fairly common presence of tally-marks is a plus because it is added prehistoric work and decoration. The occasional incising of these pieces adds artwork to artwork, and is usually more highly valued than plain examples. Gorgets with convex obverses and flat or concave reverses are usually valued more because of purposeful differences in faces and added detailing to the overall piece. Here, some collectors value extra-thin gorgets higher than those of normal or usual thickness, because this adds to a certain delicacy of artistry. Symmetry also is an important plus factor.

Pendants should also be completely drilled and rare forms are often more highly valued due to the complexity of the design or added work or both. Materials are important, and the more compact and dense the material usually the higher the polish such a piece takes. As with many artifact types, larger specimens are generally valued more than smaller artifacts.

Beads should be in good to fine condition. The historic beads of shell are often deteriorated to some extent. Matched-size and graduated-size strands are the more highly prized, and the more beads the better. Glass beads should be in as nearly the condition as when made as possible, and without chips or cracks. Generally speaking, the earlier the trade beads the more scarce they tend to be.

Beadwork and quillwork are valued as to size and complexity of the beaded area(s), and the size and condition of the object that was beaded or quilled. Due to rarity, an all-quilled or beaded-quilled piece will bring more than all-beaded work, other factors being equal. Condition is very important, and the fewer the damaged quills or missing beads, the better.

Plains Indian works are valued partly by size and material, with decorated clothing or a baby-carrier being worth more than smaller *parfleche* containers, for example. The earlier pieces are more scarce, especially quilled and quilled/beaded clothing. Decorative horse-related and weaponry of all kinds are much in demand also, and any ceremonial or festive regalia.

Antler, bone, ivory, shell and wooden artifacts (condition is very important here, for these organic materials) are valued as to culture that made them, size and amount of decoration present. Again, earlier pieces tend to be more scarce and valuable, at least if well-made. In any of these materials, effigies or small figurines of animals and people tend to be the most sought-after by collectors.

Pipes have long been favored collectibles, and top condition is very important. Stone pipes are generally more highly valued than pottery pipes and those made of the various fine-grained pipestones are more valued than those made of lower-grade stone materials. Pipes from earlier cultures are quite scarce, adding a rarity factor. Effigy pipes, and those decorated with carvings or inlays are generally worth more than plainer examples. And a Plains Indian pipe with the original (or at least matching and very old) pipe-stem makes a complete and very desirable set, again if in top condition.

Beyond a few tips for each category, as given, there are some broad observations that can be made. There are usually exceptions to generalities, but still that is part of what makes collecting decorative and ornamental Indian artifacts such a fascinating field.

The cost of living is reflected in the cost of collecting. Prices tend to be higher on both the East (especially northeast) Coast and West Coast (especially central and southern). In short, prices tend to be higher for everything, and it is all a sort of geographic inflation. To a certain extent, larger cities have higher prices than do smaller towns for similar items.

Artifacts within the geographic area where they were once made tend to be more in demand for collectors from that region, due to familiarity and established collecting habits and patterns. Bargains can occasionally be had when a totally out-of-area piece is available, because prospective buyers either do not collect such pieces, or feel unsure about either the true quality or price or both. So a collector with broad knowledge can sometimes obtain superior decorative pieces at well below the usual prices.

The business establishment itself can have a strong bearing on price, and itself can be a value factor. Usually larger stores with more personnel and upkeep simply need to obtain higher prices for what they sell, though volume can be a mitigating factor. Smaller stores with fewer sales can be involved in similar high prices, so it really depends on the individual store and how it operates.

Antique shops and shows can be good places to at least see American Indian goods. However, only a small percentage of antique dealers truly know the quality of any given piece. Prices may be unusually high or low for various reasons. Some dealers feel that if an artifact of any kind is American Indian, it is worth a lot of money. Others simply don't know or care, and the value can wander across the spectrum.

It is difficult to generalize about auctions because there are so many different kinds. A simplification is that if a sale has quality pieces and is well advertised, many collectors will attend and the prices will average at about the going rate or higher. The presence of a number of fakes in any one auction tends to pull down the value of authentic pieces that are present, simple guilt by association. However, in such cases, extremely knowledgeable collectors may still pay high prices for individual artifacts they know to be good. If a large number of pieces are fake and only a few genuine, the good pieces may go at lower prices because many collectors may not attend the auction.

Again, in general, specialized Indian artifact auctions with good notification lists tend to draw collectors of all kinds. Bidding for choice, authentic pieces may thus run higher than average due to these circumstances and unusually intense bidding competition. It is of course every collector's dream to spot that one superb artifact or artwork overlooked or unrecognized by all the others and obtain it. Sheer chance is not a value factor, but upon occasion luck plays a role – and plays it well.

Chapter 25
ARTIFACTS AS ART

Very briefly described, artifacts are objects made by North American Indians, and as that term is used here, usually in the prehistoric (before AD 1650) timeframe. Art (good art, that is) is something so extremely well made that it elicits responses of admiration and enjoyment. This is true in both the viewing and/or touching, or for collectors, the whole pleasure of ownership.

This is the key aspect, the soul if you will, of collecting. The owner is not necessarily anxious to gather in artifacts to be greedy or have the most or the best. Ownership offers one hundred percent satisfaction, in that the artifacts can be viewed and studied and the artistic qualities experienced at any time. In many ways and for many people, ownership is the ultimate appreciation of artifacts as art because hard-earned money (concentrated time and effort) has been exchanged for things of great and long-lasting beauty. This enhances comprehension and understanding of an ancient world.

Philosophy aside, not all North American Indian art is good in the sense that it is artistically fine. Most in fact is, of course, which is why there is so much interest and activity in the field. The generally high level of artistic accomplishment is so consistent that to find or view a piece that is of lesser quality or just plain bad comes as a surprise in the first case, a shock in the second. This is especially true for the decorative and/or ornamental objects, to which more attention and time were often devoted.

Indian art has a number of characteristics that separate the field from mass-produced, machine-made objects no matter how well these are or were made. Natural materials were or are used, whether these were stone, leather, clay, slate, feathers, whatever. And, the best of the example materials was selected and then treated in known and proven ways to produce a superior object. Leather-working, for instance, included a choice of animal skins to be tanned, sizes, thickness and a half dozen methods to process the leather into the final product.

Technique is an integral part of Indian artifacts and helps set the things made apart from most others. Pottery was (and is, or should be) totally made by hand, without the use of a potter's wheel. Looms for weaving are hand-powered. Handwork, with total control of all manufacturing phases, is the hallmark of good Indian art. It is certainly very old-fashioned, but then it is supposed to be.

Form or class is another indicator of true Indian art. Some – pottery, weaving, beads – are common throughout the world in early societies. Other artifacts – birdstones, bannerstone, gorgets – are more nearly special in type and style for the forms in North America. For many types of artifacts, there was no counterpart elsewhere, and this culture exclusivity is part of the allure of Amerind artifacts.

Style is very much part of good Indian art. This is the peculiar and particular way the forms were treated. Style is what makes, for instance, pottery a good indicator of when it was made in certain prehistoric times and locations. Even today, an expert can look at a recent piece of Southwestern pottery and give the pueblo where made, approximately when, and sometimes the pottery-making family or even the individual potter that made it.

Design goes along with style, and can be the final, decorative touches that complete a piece. Again with pottery, a fine example of ornamental work, this would be the kind of paint or other decoration applied and how it is applied. Design can be the pattern of beadwork or quillwork, or even the incising on an ancient slate artifact.

North American Indian artifacts have these very general characteristics that relate to the artistry of the final piece. The materials used are natural, or at least are for traditional pieces made in the old ways. Native styles and designs were used, and all the touches large and small were put on that make such work recognizable as Amerind even to the untrained eye.

Finally, there is the matter of time. While some utilitarian artifacts (points, blades) could be completed in less than an hour, many of the decorative artifacts required amounts of time that are almost incomprehensible today. To make a good pottery piece requires many hours, a fine piece, dozens. Many of the prehistoric ornaments (birdstones, gorgets) required dozens to hundreds of hours of work. A fine large weaving today or a quartzite banner of 4000 years ago account for the expenditure of many hundred hours to complete. Basket-weaving, beading and many other activities were extremely time-consuming.

In the final analysis, good American Indian art is weighed and judged by collectors who pay for artifacts in money, but in doing so pay the highest respect. The collector decides intellectually on the merits of the piece, which translates to the emotional aspect, or how much he or she is willing to pay to acquire it.

However, to those either uncaring or untutored as to what American Indian art is all about, it seems strange (even a little wierd) to see someone pay large sums for small objects. Here, accurate information is crucial because sometimes minor details make major differences in value.

Here is an example using five possible scenarios or examples. The bannerstone is a rare bottle form, made of a classic material, rose quartzite. One is a preform, only roughed out and undrilled. One is a damaged artifact. One is a broken piece, half a banner. One is a recent copy – though well done, it is a fake. And one is a fine, old, genuine banner with a long, unquestionable pedigree. It is instructive to examine each in turn.

The preform will have a certain value to a collector of banners because it shows some of the first steps in making the type. The value will vary but will not be high because it is only in the early stages of completion. It is good work, but unfinished.

Damaged, the banner value will be lessened to the degree that the damage detracts from the integrity of the whole. Very minor damages may detract very little. Major damage, as in the case of the next specimen which is broken in half along the drill-hole, means that someone might acquire the piece but for only a small sum. Some collectors value half a banner because, knowing the form, it can be fairly accurately restored.

The fake piece is worth nothing to a serious collector, though some are acquired at up to a hundred dollars or so for study examples. As in many other collecting fields, it is helpful to know the bad in order to know the good. Collectors mainly resent fakes because of the blatant effort to fool them and take their money. Also, a fake piece can be so well done that even experts can't decide for certain, which makes for uncomfortable feelings of indecision and suspicion.

Finally, there is the good and authentic old bannerstone, which can easily bring from three to eight thousand dollars. To stay on the subject, let's say the fake banner and the good banner are nearly identical in shape, size, etc. The essential question is, why is the first practically worthless, the second worth many thousand dollars, when perhaps the average non-collector might not even be able to see any or much difference? All collectors know part of the answer, in that a fake is merely a copy and not the original.

The fake is a counterfeit copy of a good piece, and has no "life" of its own, no pedigree, no authenticity, no great age, no Indian touch or use, no high value. The honest, old piece, on the other hand, has all this and much more.

Why spend, say, $5000, for something that many people would see as just a pretty rock? How do a few ounces of non-precious material get to be so attractive that people will fly halfway across the country for a chance to buy it? What's involved here, what makes the banner (and it could be almost any other top-of-the-line artifact or artwork) so attractive, so valuable?

This is the artifact as art key, somewhat of an answer to almost a mystery. Granted, some high values result from fiercely competitive bidding, supply-demand, but this means a number of people think quite highly of whatever the artifact is. In the case of the beautiful banner, one buys the art aspect of the high-quality piece, the attractiveness, but there is something more.

Provenance ("papers," "pedigree," the true story of the bannerstone since it was found) adds to the value. The fact that it was made and used by prehistoric Indians adds to value. The knowledge that it is truly old adds to value. All these, plus the desire of the collector to acquire a really fine and rare piece, make up the final monetary figure.

There is an important thing that can only be called sharing. This is a feeling that the person is touching something that was touched by a hand from the past. Some of the same thoughts of appreciation must be similar, of admiration for good work lovingly done, of a superb object made as well as it could be made.

And there is a final thing that is rarely discussed and cannot be measured, but which has an enormous impact. That is the element of mystery, even awe, that forms (for want of a better term) almost an aura that surrounds the piece. You can see this in some collectors who have tremendous respect that approaches reverence when in the presence of a high-art artifact. In a sense, it is a deep failure to understand the true story of the piece that creates a mental distance that places the artifact on a sort of psychic pedestal where it can never really be reached. In a sense, it is a respect for the unknown and the can-never-be-known. This is a large part of an artifact as art, fully appreciated but never fully known or understood.

There is more, such as admiring creations of people long-gone, beautiful things to remember them by, true works of art that survived them and will survive us. There is even a sort of beginning but no end involved, an eternity, though all this is rarely verbalized or even recognized. A truly fine piece can command the ultimate respect from some very experienced collectors. It leaves them with plenty of feelings but no words.

In most cases, the artifacts are all that remain of a people much like us. They saw the shadows creep across the land and the stars wheel across the sky, and now they are no more. Their works alone are left to us, gifts from the past to our present, gifts from us to the future.

RECTANGULAR BARRELED WINGED BANNERSTONE, made of olive-green nephrite jade. It is 2¾ x 3⁹⁄₁₆ in. long, from Cass Township, Richland County, Ohio. It is ex-coll. C.R. Palmer. The workstyle, color, form and symmetry make this banner one of the finest of the type ever found. Outstanding in every respect. Private collection, Ohio $2800-5000

HOOKED SADDLE-FACE FLUTED-BASE BANNER, (Reverse), black and tan porphyry. Adams County, Illinois, 2⅞ x 3⅜ in. long, ex-coll. C.R. Palmer. The reverse is also very finely made with a narrow groove that parallels the central hole. See accompanying photo for the obverse face. $4500-6200
Private collection, Ohio

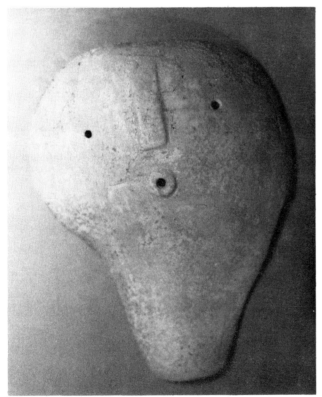

HUMAN FACE GORGET, marine shell from an island in the Tennessee River, Marion County, Tennessee. This is a large and fine piece, 5¾ x 7¼ in. high. This item is Mississippian in origin.
$1500

Courtesy James E. Maus collection, North Carolina

HOOKED SADDLE-FACE FLUTED-BASE BANNER, (Obverse), in black and tan porphyry. It is 2⅞ x 3⅜ in. long, from Adams County, Illinois. Ex-coll. C.R. Palmer. This is a very highly developed type, beautifully worked, exquisite in all respects, and a very rare piece. See accompanying photo for the reverse face. $4500-6200
Private collection, Ohio

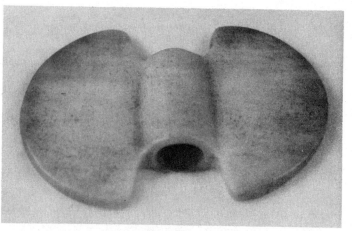

NOTCHED OVATE WINGED (BUTTERFLY) BANNER, made of translucent cream and rose-colored ferruginous quartzite. Size 2¾ x 4 inches wide, it is from Allen County, Ohio. Highly advanced form and top workstyle make this a very rare piece, and is the finest of the type ever found in the state.　　$3100-5000
Private collection, Ohio

HOURGLASS LENS-SHAPED BANNERSTONE, made of quartz-jasper conglomerate hardstone. It is 2½ x 3 in. long, from Montgomery County, Ohio. This artifact is very well-made, with fine lines and graceful contours. This, added to pleasing colors, creates a solid, upper-level piece.　　$1750-2250
Private collection, Ohio

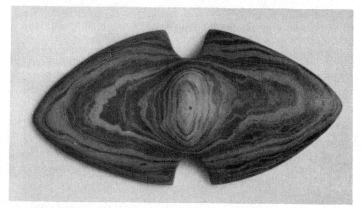

ELLIPTICAL WINGED BANNERSTONE, glacial banded slate. It is from Cessna Twp., Hardin County, Ohio and is ex-coll. Dr. Gordon Meuser. Size, 2¹⁵⁄₁₆ x 6 inches. Note how the ancient worker made use of concentric banding to emphasize the center of the artifact. This was Dr. Meuser's favorite winged slate banner, deservedly so.　　$4500-5500

Private collection, Ohio

ROCK-CRYSTAL FLUTED D-TYPE TUBE BANNER, made of clear quartz crystal. At 1¹¹⁄₁₆ x 2¹⁵⁄₁₆ in. long, it is from Hardin County, Ohio. This is a finely made rare bannerstone form made from an equally rare gem-quality material. Outstanding specimen.　　$3200-4500
Private collection, Ohio

TRIANGULAR PANELED BANNERSTONE, material a black and yellow-cream granite. From St. Charles County, Missouri, it was formerly in the Camp Museum, W. Memphis. This fine piece is very thin in cross-section, and luckily survived the years intact. A top artifact, beautiful work-style, fine lines.　　$3000-3500
Courtesy Len & Janie Weidner collection, Ohio

124

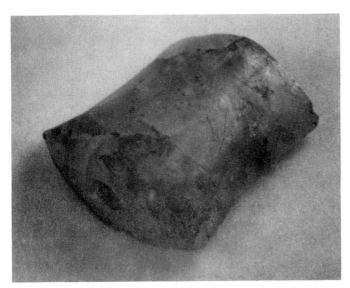

HOURGLASS BANNERSTONE, transparent to opaque fluorspar with purple tinges. From Sullivan Co., IL, size is 2⅞ x 3 inches. Ex-colls. Dr. Bunch (1940's), Wachtel, Kley and Davidson and in WW #I. Only two other examples are known to exist in this material. A very fine example of prehistoric art and a very rare artifact. $7500-10,000
Courtesy Len & Janie Weidner collection, Ohio

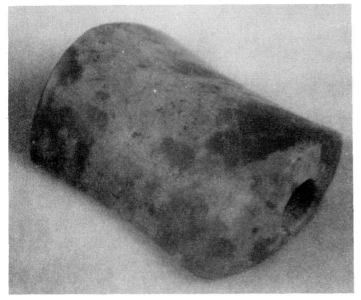

SADDLE-FACE BANNERSTONE, quartzite in shades of mint-green, blue and grey. Size 2¼ x 2⅞ inches, it is ex-colls. Hansen, Goodrich, Roman and Shenk. From Posey County, Indiana, this piece is finely finished, in top condition and in a rare material. $3500
Courtesy Len & Janie Weidner collection, Ohio

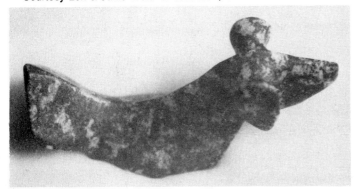

POPEYED BIRDSTONE, material is a black and cream speckled granite and size is 1⅝ x 3⅝ inches long. It was found east of Battle Creek, Michigan along the Kalamazoo River in 1947. A very highly developed specimen, it is one of the finest of the type ever found.
Private collection, Ohio $4500-5800

NEGATIVE-PAINTED BOTTLE, an uncommon decorative method or technique. The design is made when the areas to be emphasized are outlined with a material that melts or evaporates so that the color on them does not fix. A fine piece, from southern Missouri and 6 x 8½ inches. $3000
Courtesy Dr. Gary Meek collection, Arkansas

HALEY BOTTLE large size, from Hot Springs County, Arkansas. It is Caddo culture, beautifully decorated and polished. Note the graceful lines to this vessel. Size 6½ x 10 inches. $2500
Courtesy Dr. Gary Meek collection, Arkansas

HUMAN EFFIGY FACE, cedar wood, 2¼ in. high x 1½ in. wide. This piece has shell-inlaid eyes and was once covered with sheet copper. It is late prehistoric and a beautiful work of art. Southcentral U.S.   Museum quality
Private collection

125

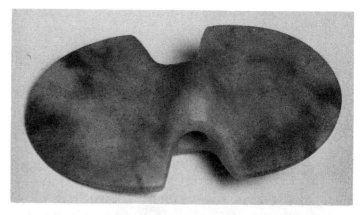

CLASSIC C BUTTERFLY-TYPE BANNERSTONE from Missouri. It was found four miles north of Fletcher, Jefferson County, in 1941. Size is 67 x 122 mm, and material is a pink and red ferruginous quartz with excellent patina. Ex-colls. Gustafson (IA) and Callaway (LA). This piece is both beautiful and quite rare. $4000 plus
Photo courtesy Chris Callaway, Louisiana

EFFIGY PENDANT made of Catlinite (red pipestone from Minnesota) and found in Holt County, Missouri. It is ¼ in. thick, excurvate toward the face portion and a little larger than a quarter. This is an attractive, well-made image. $200
Photo courtesy Mike George, Missouri

BIRDSTONES. Left, 30 x 80 mm, material dark green porphyry with tan to cream phenocrysts. Drilled front and rear, it is ex-colls. Gustafson (IA) and Callaway (LA). $6000 plus
Right, 28 x 78 mm, material a spotted black and white hardstone. Drilled both front and rear, excellent patination. Ex-colls. Pohler (LA) and Callaway (LA). $6000 plus
Photo courtesy Chris Callaway, Louisiana

CLASS C SADDLE-FACE BANNERSTONE, from Greene County, Illinois. Size is 60 x 93 mm and material is a dark green porphyry hardstone with cream phenocrysts. Ex-colls. Freudenburg (IA) and Callaway (LA). This type (Knoblock, p. 161) is mainly distributed in the states of IL, IN, KY, MO and TN. This is a top, well-developed form. $1500-2000
Photo courtesy Chris Callaway, Louisiana

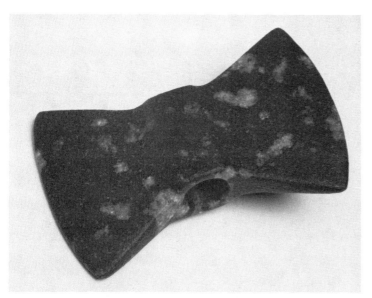

CLASS C WISCONSIN WINGED BANNERSTONE, from Marion County, Missouri. It is 65 x 95 mm and material is a dark green porphyry with spots of light green feldspar. A very well-made and attractive piece, it is ex-colls. Gustafson (IA) and Callaway (LA).
$1500-2000

Photo courtesy Chris Callaway, Louisiana

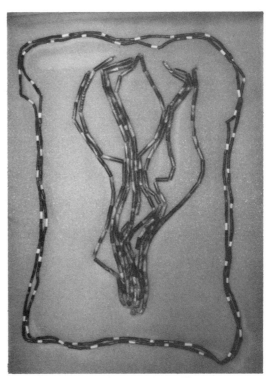

WAMPUM, two strings, 48 in. long, nine strings 11 in. long. Extra-fine example made from the quahaung (Venue mercenaria) native to the NE Coastal waters. Excavated in 1906 in Old Town, Maine. Such pieces in high quality with good age are quite rare. Museum quality
Courtesy Marguerite L. Kernaghan collection;
photographers Marguerite L. & Stewart W. Kernaghan

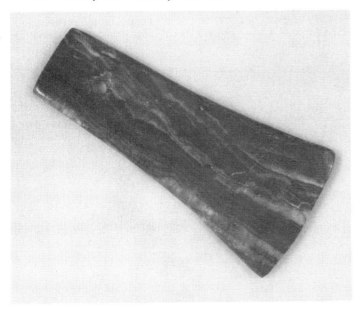

BELL-SHAPED ADENA PENDANT made of a rare material, multi-colored petrified wood. Found in Ashland County, Ohio, in 1931, it is ex-coll. Arthur George Smith. Size, 2⅛ x 4½ inches high. This is a strikingly beautiful artifact, made from gem-like material and artistically shaped. Fine piece. $1500-2500
Private collection, Ohio

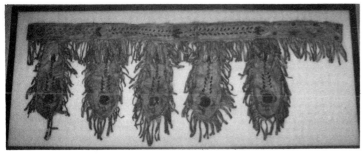

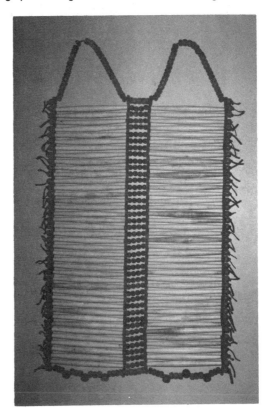

OJIBWA DANCE BELT, five beaded flaps ca. 1900. Size is 14 x 44 inches and leather is hard and fragile. It is decorated with seed bead designs and fringes. Unusual piece. $600-1000
Courtesy Marguerite L. Kernaghan collection;
photographers Marguerite L. & Stewart W. Kernaghan

SIOUX BREASTPLATE all trade beads which were dug and restrung. From South Dakota, makeup is hairpipes, red and blue frosted round-ed tube beads, round brass fluted beads and small bells. Size 11½ x 19 inches. $700-1300
Courtesy Marguerite L. Kernaghan collection;
photographers Marguerite L. & Stewart W. Kernaghan

POTTERY VESSEL the design a very rare 4-Mile Bird. The artistic design on this peice is extremely fine, and overall condition is superb. The vessel is ca. AD 1200-1400, and is from Arizona. Size, 8 inches in diameter. Many museums do not have pottery of this quality.
$2000-3000
Courtesy private collection of Sam and Nancy Johnson
Murfreesboro, Arkansas

NEZ PERCE BAG, woven design with trade beads on hide-strip fringes. Size, 6¼ x 10 inches. Of twined construction, this is a fine old piece from the Herron & Mullen collection. $600-1000
Courtesy Marguerite L. Kernaghan collection;
photographers Marguerite L. & Stewart W. Kernaghan

CEREMONIAL MAUL, Pacific Northwest, a rare piece. Size is 3⅝ x 10 inches and weight is 6¾ pounds. Made of a dark green porphyry material, it is highly polished overall and has no use-signs or damage. The bird-head has bulging eyes, a beak and a crest.
Museum quality
Photo courtesy Harold Grubenhoff collection, Washington

128

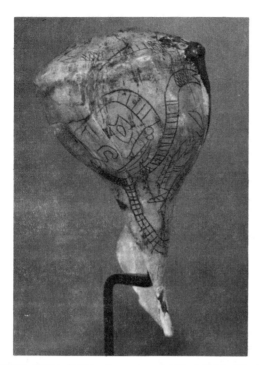

ENGRAVED SHELL CUP for the ceremonial Black Drink. (The Black Drink contained yaupon or cassina holly, and was used as a stimulant or in purifying rituals.) The design is of human heads and rattlesnakes. A very fine and rare piece, it is ca. AD 800-1200 and from the Spiro Mounds, LeFlore County, Oklahoma. It is 9 inches high.

$4000-6000

Courtesy private collection of Sam and Nancy Johnson, Murfreesboro, Arkansas

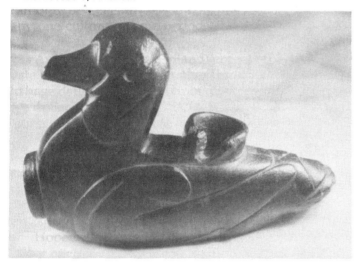

DUCK-EFFIGY GREAT PIPE. Dark steatite, approximately 7 x 11 inches. Len Weidner: "Purchased in 1968 by Mrs. Betty Markey from an older widow lady in Johnstown, PA. This older lady had an uncle who (as she stated) collected that "dirty old Indian stuff". About the turn of the century he later moved in with her. When he died all of his belongings were left in the attic and upon the widow's moving back to Philadelphia all was to be sold. Mrs. Markey said the attic was packed completely full of relics, beaded shirts, spears, war-clubs, etc., which she did not collect but when she spied the above pipe on the floor she asked what it was. Neither knew, but thought it might be a Chinese opium pipe. It was purchased for $20. The rest of the attic contents were hauled to the dump or given to the Salvation Army. Mrs. Markey used the pipe as a doorstop for the next 20 years. Fortunately it sat on carpet. Historic tag lists provenance as being from Tennessee. The intrinsic value of this authentic piece cannot be truly stated, but it would certainly be high."

Courtesy Len & Janie Weidner collection, Ohio

POTTERY VESSEL, Southwestern prehistoric, with designs of red and black on a white ground. It is 10 inches high and has a concave base. It was formerly in the Judge Claude Stone collection, Peoria, Illinois. Two side views are shown.   Museum quality
Courtesy Guy Brother's collection, Pinckneyville, Illinois

CEREMONIAL-GRADE BLADES top to bottom: Etley type from Troy, MO. $1000-1200
Ramey blade, 10 in. long from Green County, IL, found in 1936. $2000
Very colorful (black, cream and amber) Graham Cave-like blade from Missouri. $650
Courtesy Larry G. Merriam collection, Oklahoma

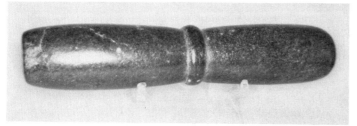

SHAMAN'S MEDICINE TUBE BICONICAL PIPE, found in Jefferson Co., TN, July 1974, by Fayne Morgan. It is 12½ in. long and one of the longest of this prehistoric pipe type. Center ring has a zigzag design carved around it, and on the pipe's side is an engraving resembling a turkey-track. GIRS auth. #J3. Only two of these pipes are longer than this example, and both have restoration; this example is perfect-condition. $25,000
Courtesy John Baldwin collection, Michigan

EAGLE EFFIGY GREAT PIPE, black steatite, 10¾ in. long. Found prior to 1900 in Washington County, TN, it is Woodland time period, possibly Hopewell. This specimen has bird of prey talons on its carved feet. Found by R.W. Bronson, collected by Edward Payne. GIRS authentication #L1. Pictured Payne collection book, 1937, p 109. This is said to be the finest of all great pipes, having all the features – classic head, tail, wings, feet, bowl or stem. Most others have only 2 or 3 of these features. $75,000
Courtesy John Baldwin collection, Michigan

CLASS B RECTANGULAR BARREL BANNERSTONE size 38 x 113 mm. Material is a brown hardstone with a quartzite vein running the entire length. The central perforation is complete. The piece is from Illinois and ex-colls Freeudenburg (IA) and Dyson (LA). This type (Knoblock, p. 165) is found mainly in Illinois and portions of surrounding states. Piece is from Illinois, county unknown. $1000-1200
Photo courtesy Chris Callaway collection, Louisiana

SPRIO MOUND HAFTED COPPER AXE found at the Great Temple Mound, LeFlore County, OK in 1935. The axe-head is 9½ in. high, the wooden handle is 16 in. long. It has GIRS authentifaction #N17. JB: "There are only two of these in private hands; the other is a blade only with a small piece of wood attached. This is one of only 30 found in the Mound, and the others are in the Heye Foundation."
Museum quality
Courtesy John Baldwin collection, Michigan

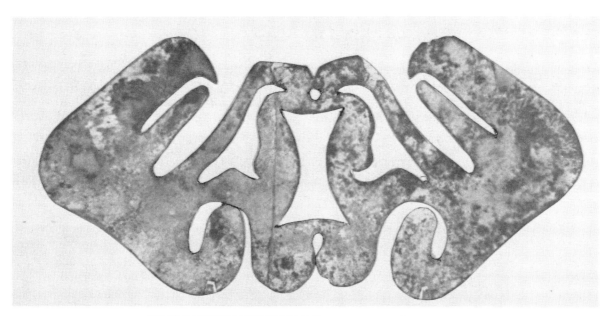

DOUBLE-HEADED COPPER EAGLE, a rare gorget or breastplate. Hopewell in origin, it was excavated from a small mound in Franklin County, Ohio, by a construction crew. (A shopping center is now on the site.) It is 10¼ inches long by 4 inches high. The eye areas are hollowed out and probably once had shell inlays in them. The copper used was probably carried in from Michigan. JB: "There are only a very few of these in private hands." Museum quality
Courtesy John Baldwin collection, Michigan

CEDARLAND CEREMONIAL CACHE, exceptional artifacts found in a shell-ring site, Hancock County, Mississippi. Left, bottle banner, rose quartz, 39 x 40 mm, found 11-21-88. Right, bottle banner in rose quartz, 39 x 30 mm, found same date. Top center, butterfly banner in rose quartz, 82 x 130 mm found 12-3-88. These are all highest quality, including the bottom polished jasper pendant or point. Ca. 2500 BC - AD 900. Group, $22,500 plus
Courtesy Chris Callaway collection, Louisiana

Chapter 26
ACQUISITION SUGGESTIONS

The best suggestion that could be made to a beginning collector is this: Don't spend the first five hundred dollars or so on artifacts. Buy books. These can be general books on the prehistory of the region where the collector lives, or more specialized books that concentrate on the artifacts. While beginners are likely to say that they are interested in artifacts, not books, the simple fact is that good books are one of the best ways to learn about good artifacts.

Such books do not necessarily need to be new or in-print titles. Often helpful books were written years ago, and are collector items in themselves. The spin-off knowledge isn't just for the sake of information, for it is no coincidence that many of the top collectors have extensive personal libraries. There do not seem to be educational courses or classes where one can learn about American Indian artifact collecting, so good books take the place. And, they are available and helpful anytime.

The collector should not ignore learning from other, more advanced collectors. There is a certain amount of competition for artifacts in each region, and sometimes this rivalry carries over so that it can be a barrier for some collectors. However, many strong and lasting friendships do begin, and they are both pleasurable and educational. Most collectors, if approached with courtesy, are glad to answer questions and share information. Artifacts help create a bond that is beneficial to all.

Many states have amateur archeological societies with meetings and newsletters or journals. These groups are extremely helpful to collectors of all kinds, and most of the information will pertain to the prehistory and early history of the area within which the collector lives. Dues are typically $15-25 a year, a small investment for a large return. Even if artifact collecting is not the primary interest of some state societies, there is still an enormous amount to be learned about the ancient lifeways of any U.S. Region.

Another good way to learn more about the prehistory of a state, region or particular site is to visit some of the many fine U.S. museums. Often, well-done displays and dioramas portray life of long ago, and a number of museums have fine artifact collections. This is an enjoyable way to learn, plus some museums have shops where books and pamphlets can be obtained. Take advantage of these facilities.

Many collectors buy, sell or trade to enhance their collections of decorative or ornamental artifacts. If this is done wisely and well, the collection is upgraded. In order to be successful in buying, the collector should know the quality of the pieces and general value figures. The same factors operate when selling and trading.

The problem of fake artifacts (and pieces with undisclosed restoration or repairs) is a growing one, and one of growing concern.

As to authenticity, the collector should know everything possible about what is being collected – the geographic range of the artifact type, the usual material(s), size, shape, workstyle, known variations and so forth. Rarely do fakers get everything right on a modern piece. The more a person knows, the more likely good artifacts will be obtained and bad ones avoided. One gets this information, this experience, in many ways and these include seeing and studying both good and bad artifacts.

A fine way to learn is to attend auctions, especially those that specialize in Indian artifacts. Not only will many experienced collectors be present who generally will answer a few questions, but the bidding itself is instructive.

If a piece that normally would bring $1000 goes for $125, you need not assume that all the collectors interested were half asleep. About 95% of the time, this is because (and assuming the piece had no breakage, restoration, etc.) many of the prospective bidders had an opinion as to whether the piece was good. In the case of a valuable artifact bringing perhaps a tenth of that worth, the concensus is that the piece was bad or at least highly questionable.

Also, watch who bids, the advanced collectors and dealers who have top assemblages of fine material. They did not put these solid collections together by making numerous and serious errors in judgment. Sometimes even better than learning by doing, there is learning by watching whose who indeed know what they are doing.

Another aspect goes beyond the piece itself. In non-auction situations, this is the place, the setting, the circumstances, the situation, the environment. On the proverbial scale of one to ten, here's a one. Everything at the flea-market dealer's table is obviously fake, except the piece you are looking at. Your chances of getting one good artifact out of all the mass of hundreds of bad pieces is not only about a one, but a minus one. The association is terrible, the origin of the piece obvious.

Scene two. A private museum closes down forever, and an auction is held. Most items were collected 75 and more years ago, and most items have numbers and detailed acquisition dates and information for each number. Your chances are much higher here, perhaps seven or eight. Also in this category would be completely and carefully assembled old-time collections, though a fake or two might well have crept in along the way. A true ten can be assigned only to all pieces personally found, and these on sites that are not near the residence of any other artifact collector. It has happened that collectors have thrown away bad pieces.

Basic to identifying and avoiding fakes is experience and knowledge. Investments in good books, trips to visit other collectors, auctions, museums – all these will help. After all, the goal is not simply to recognize fakes, because this is somewhat on the negative side. The goal is also to recognize good, authentic and original North American

Indian artifacts, the things to be collected.

Eventually, as the collector progresses, genuine artifacts will be available from a number of sources. Keeping an open mind is very important. All collectors know of people who have disregarded the wisdom of experienced collectors and dealers, and have spent large sums of money on bad pieces. They simply felt they knew better, or more, than anyone else and would not listen to sound advice. Attending a dispersal sale of such a collection, one wonders why so much money was wasted over the years, and on obvious fakes at that. In all, these are tragic investments.

Collectors should also be aware that no matter how attractive the price and piece, especially when either or both are too attractive, the absence of a good provenance or pedigree is cause for concern. A good story isn't enough to make a bad artifact good. Remember that if the artifact is truly as good as it is proclaimed to be, it doesn't have to be, and will not be, sold at a huge discount. The top value of such a piece is illusionary, because it is based on what an authentic piece would bring.

If a collector is so inclined, it is good to specialize in some one or two areas of American Indian artifacts. This way, a familiarity and solid body of information can be built round a relatively small collecting field. This means fewer mistakes will be made and better pieces will be acquired.

In general, it is wise to obtain the best-grade artifacts one can afford. Again, this means knowing enough about what is being collected to know the differences between good, better and best. Such qualitative terms are based on average examples, and average infers common or mediocre examples. These will always be valuable to some extent, but never as in-demand as the higher grades which are much less common. Most collectors prefer quality over quantity if given the choice, and the best of both worlds is a large collection of fine pieces.

A collector should thoroughly know what is being collected. The plain fact is (as in most things) that those who know what they are doing are most successful at collecting. Collectors should not be afraid to reach outside their world of knowledge to get informed and experienced opinions. All this is just common sense, but it is surprising how often basics like these are ignored, and some truly awful decisions made.

Of all the hundreds of different things one can collect today, the field of American Indian artifacts has it all: Beauty, quality, scarcity and in most cases age. It is no wonder that each year thousands of people become collectors of ancient Amerind artifacts and artworks. One of the many positive aspects is that the pieces that have survived to the present will be in good hands and protected. Both the artifacts and the information they contain will be invaluable for the future.

And a final note...

Often, letters and phone calls request information in two areas. One is publications that are mainly collector-oriented, but with much additional information. Here are two that are recommended; write for subscription details.

Indian-Artifact Magazine
Rt. 1 - Box 240
Turbotville, PA 17772

Prehistoric Antiquities
P. O. Box 88
Sunbury, OH 43074

Also, many people want to know about various kinds of frames to display artifacts. Recommended:

Indian River Display Case Co.
13796 Robins Road
Westerville, OH 43081